DEMOCRATIC PROFESSIONALISM

DEMOCRATIC PROFESSIONALISM

CITIZEN PARTICIPATION AND THE RECONSTRUCTION OF PROFESSIONAL ETHICS, IDENTITY, AND PRACTICE

ALBERT W. DZUR

The Pennsylvania State University Press
University Park, Pennsylvania

Library of Congress Cataloging-in-Publication Data

Dzur, Albert W.
Democratic professionalism : citizen participation
and the reconstruction of professional ethics,
identity, and practice / Albert W. Dzur.
p.   cm.
Includes bibliographical references and index.
ISBN 978-0-271-03332-7 (cloth : alk. paper)
1. Social advocacy—United States.
2. Professional employees—United States—Political activity.
3. Professional ethics—United States.
4. Political participation—Moral and ethical aspects—United States.
I. Title.

HV95.D98 2008
362.973—dc22
2007031903

The Pennsylvania State University Press is a
member of the
Association of American University Presses.

It is the policy of
The Pennsylvania State University Press
to use acid-free paper.
This book is printed on Natures Natural,
containing 50% post-consumer waste, and meets
the minimum requirements of American National Standard for
Information Sciences—Permanence of Paper for Printed Library Material,
ANSI Z39.48–1992.

CONTENTS

Acknowledgments   vi

Introduction:
The Ethics and Politics of Professions   1

1
The Missing Agents of Contemporary Democratic Thought   13

2
Beyond Self-Interest:
The Apolitical Picture of Professionals   43

3
Professionals versus Democracy:
The Radical Critique of Technocrats, Disabling Experts,
and Task Monopolists   79

4
Task Sharing for Democracy:
Themes from Political Theory   105

5
Public Journalism   135

6
Restorative Justice   173

7
Bioethics   207

8
Context and Consequences:
The Duties of Democratic Professionals   245

Conclusion:
The University's Role in the Democratization
of Professional Ethics   267

Index   275

ACKNOWLEDGMENTS

I was fortunate to begin and end this work in residence at intellectually stimulating interdisciplinary environments. The program in Social Theory at the University of Kentucky allowed me a postdoctoral year to set the course to explore democratic professionalism, and the Institute for the Study of Culture and Society at Bowling Green State University provided an unencumbered semester to bring this project to harbor. I am also grateful to the Social Philosophy and Policy Center at Bowling Green for its support of my research.

An earlier version of Chapter 4 appeared in *The Good Society*. Parts of Chapter 5 were published in *Polity*. Parts of Chapter 6 draw on collaborative research conducted with Susan M. Olson and published in the *Journal of Social Philosophy* and the *Utah Law Review*. An earlier version of Chapter 7 was published in the *Journal of Health Politics, Policy and Law*.

I want to thank Richard Dagger and Alan Wertheimer for their excellent comments on the entire draft manuscript. Ellen Frankel Paul was invaluable in honing the book's prospectus. Sandy Thatcher, Kevin Mattson, and an anonymous reviewer offered a number of fine suggestions and fostered a constructive review process.

I will take this opportunity to thank three teachers, Stephen Leonard, Michael Lienesch, and Craig Calhoun, who each in their own way pressed on me the importance of studying living political and ethical thought in the context of concrete institutions and real social movements.

Above all, I am grateful to Rekha Mirchandani for her care, thought, and attention to what really matters; her always immanent criticisms have strengthened this entire book.

INTRODUCTION:
THE ETHICS AND POLITICS OF PROFESSIONS

Democratic Professionalism in Action

Three snapshots.

As Adele Haber lay in a hospital bed staring at the ceiling, down the hall a team of doctors and ethicists were discussing whether she should live or die. The team, at Montefiore Medical Center in the Bronx, is part of a program . . . that aims to resolve medical conflicts at the end of life.

In the waiting room of the pulmonary care unit, where a small window air-conditioner struggled against the heat, members of the medical staff gathered that Tuesday afternoon to discuss Mrs. Haber's case. The team included ethicists and staff members working with the patient. Ms. Dubler [the director of bioethics at Montefiore] led the meeting with a blend of warmth and briskness, drawing out each participant in search for consensus.[1]

On a sunny Saturday . . . citizens streamed into an auditorium on the University of Pennsylvania campus, wending their way around television trucks and a maze of wires. Inside, seated on a stage, were the five candidates for the Democratic nomination for mayor of Philadelphia.

The questioners this night would not be the usual blow-dried television anchors and print journalists in scruffy shoes. They would be citizens, clutching index cards in their hands. On each card was written a question that represented the fruit of four months of public deliberation involving over six hundred citizens and reaching into every corner of a city that is famed as a mosaic of neighborhoods. Citizen

---

1. John Schwartz, "A Team Effort to Resolve Family Bedside Conflicts," *New York Times,* July 4, 2005, B1.

Voices was one newspaper's [the *Philadelphia Inquirer*] attempt to engage a cross section of a diverse city in a yearlong civic conversation.[2]

Police caught Craig Langsdorf urinating behind a trash bin last July in downtown Minneapolis. He'd been out drinking with friends, was walking to his car and, well, he had to go.

For his offense, Langsdorf could have pleaded guilty, paid a fine and gone on his way with a petty crime on his record. Instead, he chose to face upset neighbors, take responsibility for his actions and clean urine off the loading dock of his downtown workplace.

Over two years, this sort of justice has been used . . . under a program of the Central City Neighborhoods Partnership, a coalition of neighborhood groups in Minneapolis.[3]

All across the country, similar efforts by reform-minded professionals are bridging gaps between the lay public and key social institutions traditionally dominated by professionals—hospitals and clinics, newspapers and broadcast studios, courtrooms and corrections facilities.

Why have doctors, nurses, and hospital and clinic administrators carved out an institutional place for laypeople incompetent to treat but well equipped to discuss ethical problems related to patient care and institutional standards? Why have these bearers of considerable power over human lives chosen to share some of that power not just sporadically but daily as a feature of organizational life?

Why have journalists, editors, and newspaper owners conducted public forums designed to foster conversations about social security, welfare reform, economic policy, and other current topics? Why have they pressed one another to include the voices of laypeople prominently in their stories, voices unaffiliated with the world of state and national capitals, not officials, not business representatives, not political operatives, not academics well versed in the public policy concern of the week?

Why have judges, defense attorneys, prosecutors, and corrections administrators sought out citizen boards to hear some kinds of criminal offenses? Why

2. Michelle Charles, Harris Sokoloff, and Chris Satullo, "Electoral Deliberation and Public Journalism," in *The Deliberative Democracy Handbook,* ed. John Gastil and Peter Levine (San Francisco: Jossey-Bass, 2005), 59–60.

3. James Walsh, "Restorative Justice Program in Minneapolis Showing Results," *Minneapolis Star Tribune,* February 16, 2000, 1B.

have they decided to share some of their authority and include members of the lay public in discharging some of the responsibility of keeping the public safe and doing justice?

There is a fragmented but forceful reform movement in a number of socially and politically significant professions that deserves a good name. I call it "democratic professionalism" because bioethics, public journalism, and restorative justice reformers are drawing new attention to the democratic significance of professional domains such as hospitals and clinics, newspapers and television stations, courtrooms and corrections facilities and to the fact that these are public places in which members of the public can share authority over tasks that affect them. Far from a deprofessionalization or anti-institution movement, these reformers still value the specific, specialized knowledge of the seasoned journalist and editor, well-studied and practiced physician, and well-trained and experienced judge and attorney. As they try to be more democratic and help laypeople gain useful civic skills, they also seek to transform ossified conceptions of professionalism, but they are in no way antiprofessional.

The questions stated above are political, ethical, and practical questions about the status of contemporary professionalism. Accordingly, this book tells the theoretically rich story of democratic professionalism from three related perspectives. From the perspective of political science and political theory, the democratic professionals in journalism, criminal justice, medicine, and elsewhere are fascinating bridge agents—people who can mediate between complex institutions and members of the lay public who lack hands-on knowledge of these institutions and the political issues related to them. Though professions, professionals, and ideals of professionalism are not presently studied by political scientists and political theorists, for reasons I will suggest shortly, they ought to be included prominently in the burgeoning research on civic engagement and public deliberation.

From the perspective of those generally interested in the ethics of professions, democratic professionals suggest a new way of approaching traditional questions about the specific social responsibilities of journalists, lawyers, doctors and others—one that draws attention to the civic and democratic nature of these responsibilities. Reform-minded journalists, for example, write about the civic responsibilities of journalists to ensure greater accountability of elected officials to citizens. But they also claim a democratic responsibility to include citizens in dialogue about what, exactly, the social responsibilities of journalists are. This is an exciting shift in focus for professional ethics, I believe, that emphasizes the public justification of normative issues that are currently private and extremely academic.

From the perspective of professionals themselves, the new model of professionalism suggested by reformers is both challenging and rewarding. At a time when even traditional professions are losing ground in public opinion, democratic professionalism shows how to regain trust, respect, and perhaps even authority. By sharing in some of the experiences of the journalist, physician, judge, or prosecutor, lay citizens come to recognize the complexity of these roles and better discern what good reporting, doctoring, or judging looks like. Yet sharing tasks and authority pose difficult trade-offs for democratic professionals who now hold themselves to both professional and democratic standards of conduct. How reform-minded people in three professions have resolved and struggled with some of these role conflicts is the third story of this book.

Professionals and Modern Democracy

The role of those with specialized knowledge in modern democracy has been an unresolved issue since public intellectuals began to confront it in the Progressive Era. Most recognized the necessity for specialists in applied sciences such as engineering and applied social sciences such as economics to be engaged in policy implementation, if not policy making, in the wake of the massive economic and social changes of industrialization and urbanism. Intellectuals such as John Dewey, Herbert Croly, and Walter Lippmann had come to question the modern relevance of old-fashioned ideals of face-to-face democracy—in Dewey's words, the "local town-meeting practices and ideas" that still had a hold on the hearts of Progressives.[4] Some proposed a new ideal of professionalism grounded in natural and social science methods and the special training needed to solve complex social and economic problems but also dedicated to public well-being and responsive to public opinion. As Woodrow Wilson wrote in his early contribution to this discussion, "The ideal for us is a civil service cultured and self-sufficient enough to act with sense and vigor, and yet so intimately connected with the popular thought, by means of elections and constant public counsel, as to find arbitrariness or class spirit quite out of the question."[5] Herbert Croly

4. John Dewey, *The Public and Its Problems* (1927), reprinted in *John Dewey: The Later Works, 1925–1953*, ed. Jo Ann Boydston (Carbondale: Southern Illinois University Press, 1981–90), 2:306.
5. Woodrow Wilson, "The Study of Administration," *Political Science Quarterly* 2 (1887): 217.

and Walter Lippmann proposed that such a professionalized cadre of policy specialists and civil servants, if removed somewhat from the democratic political process and allowed to take their cues from their professional training, experience, and fellow colleagues, would be uniquely capable of solving social problems and making difficult policy choices in the best interests of the public even if the public did not immediately recognize this.[6] For Croly and Lippmann, as with Wilson before them, popular elections would ensure that these professionals and those who appointed them could be held accountable for their policy failures.

Other Progressive Era intellectuals such as John Dewey, though sympathetic to the new ideal of public-spirited professionalism, worried considerably about the gulf separating these specialists and the rank-and-file citizens purportedly served by them. If the outcomes of American democracy were determined by experts behind closed doors, then to what extent could the political processes open to laypeople, such as elections, really give voice to the collective interests of the public? The horn of the dilemma facing Dewey, however, was the obvious problem, as he was quick to point out, that the American mass public was too "scattered, mobile, and manifold" to follow policy deliberations or even to determine what its public interests were in order to voice them to policy makers. Even policy deliberation on issues that directly affect citizens, such as public transportation, admitted Dewey, could hardly be done in public by the public given "the very size, heterogeneity, and mobility of urban populations" and "the technical character of the engineering problems" involved.[7]

Dewey's contribution to this debate was to conceptualize the democratic professional, the applied social scientist, the engineer, the teacher, and the reporter who worked *with* rather than *for* the public, who *facilitated* public understanding and practical abilities rather than *led* the public. I will argue in Chapter 4 that Dewey's thoughts on professionalism help us understand the significance of current reform movements and assess their strengths and weaknesses, but that they are far from contemporary theories of professionalism and democracy.

The gap between professionalized politics in American democracy and a mass public that is only minimally participatory and only barely knowledgeable about public affairs and political institutions is perhaps even greater now than it was in the Progressive Era. As in that period, scholars and intellectuals are

6. See Herbert Croly, *The Promise of American Life* (Cambridge, Mass.: Belknap Press, 1965); and Walter Lippmann, *Public Opinion* (New York: Harcourt Brace, 1922).

7. Dewey, *The Public and Its Problems*, 137.

pressing for new conceptions of democracy that can bridge this gap. Unlike the Progressive Era, however, professions, professionals, and ideals of professionalism barely appear in contemporary discourse as key actors. In part, this is due to the negative connotations of professionalism in relation to democracy—elitism, technocracy, inequality, superior knowledge, hierarchy, meritocracy. More important as a reason for neglect, however, is a disciplinary ignorance of professions in political science. They have been taken simply as something sociologists study when they study occupations or something that philosophers study when they study the applied ethics of professions such as law and medicine. One prominent exception, discussed in Chapter 3, is the topic of technocracy— the counterdemocratic situation of professionals as high-level advisers to elites and elites in their own right that has interested some political scientists, especially those who study comparative politics.

The Neglect of the Significance of Professions to American Democracy

The professions have been neglected in political theory with negative consequences for the field in general and for the development of democratic theory in particular. To see this, we do not have to fully agree with Talcott Parsons that the professional complex is the "crucial structural development in twentieth-century society," something he believed had displaced the state and the "capitalistic organization of the economy."[8] We need only recognize, as many Progressive Era intellectuals did, the political implications of professional knowledge and practice.

The function, status, and authority of professional work have not been even minor topics in political theory. There is no doubt that political theorists have dealt with issues that overlap professional domains. Michel Foucault's treatments of disciplinary power and Jürgen Habermas's concern for instrumental rationality in the system world are two strong examples. However, political theorists have not analyzed the specificity—what Emile Durkheim would call the "moral particularism"—of professional activity in public life. They neglect to see professions as political agents separate from other powerful economic and political organizations, particularized in their functional and associational differences

---

8. Talcott Parsons, "Professions," in *International Encyclopedia of the Social Sciences,* vol. 12 (New York: Macmillan, 1968), 545.

from each other (e.g., the political agency of law is different from medicine in part because of the different functional roles and the different organizational histories of the two professions), and as mediating between self, other, and group in ways that have both harmful and beneficial consequences for democracy. Nor have political theorists taken up traditional questions of power, representation, and equality within the work setting of specific professions. Surveying the leading journal *Political Theory*, for example, one finds no explicit treatment of professions as political agents or professional environments as political contexts.

This is partly due to the successful claims of sociology and economics to the empirical dimensions of occupations and the lack of counterclaims by other disciplines. Political science claims political events, agents, and institutions as its proper jurisdiction and has not traditionally included professions and professionals under the category of political.[9] The practices of traditional professions such as law and medicine are seen as "political" by political scientists only when they interact with the state or with social movements. For example, when professions form powerful interest groups, as medicine has with the American Medical Association, the discrete state-oriented action of the interest groups draws the attention of political scientists studying health care politics. The relationship between professionals and laypeople within domains such as hospitals, courts, prisons, news organizations, and business firms is considered a sociological or economic issue. Given the dearth of empirical work on professions by political scientists, that the subfield of political theory has had limited contact with the topic is not surprising.

Just as the empirical dimensions of professional practice have been covered by other disciplines, so have the normative dimensions been largely considered the domain of philosophy. Even though professional practices are marked by relations of power and authority and raise questions of proper representation and accountability—all central concepts for political theorists—professional ethics has come to be seen as primarily the jurisdiction of philosophers rather than political theorists. In large part, this is because the attention of political theorists has followed the empirical concerns of political science and has been directed toward normative questions of state and social movement action. The great works of normative political theory of the 1970s, John Rawls's *A Theory of Justice* and

---

9. An exception that proves the rule is Sheldon Wolin's far-reaching work, *Politics and Vision* (Boston: Little, Brown, 1960). The last chapter of this influential text addresses then current social and political theories of large-scale organizations.

Ronald Dworkin's *Taking Rights Seriously*—famous for sparking widespread interest in the field of political theory—dealt with issues of justice, rights, and legitimate authority predominantly centered in the state. These works drew attention to constitutions, judicial judgment, and the justice of what Rawls called "the basic structure of society." The focal question in the massive outpouring of scholarly writing following in the wake of these foundational texts is how the liberal-democratic *state* is to treat people with equal concern.

Political theory has overlooked the ground-level politics happening all around us, often outside the executive briefings, judicial decisions, legislative debates, and electoral combats of formal politics. It has neglected the politics of newswriting, of source and story selection; the politics of quality of life assessments, of criteria for organ rationing; the politics of victim impact statements, of community service orders. These are all "micro" issues if your perspective is focused on the state and its actions, yet they have "macro" implications that have only barely been understood.

Consider two largely pessimistic surveys of the political theory field written ten years apart and published by the primary professional organization of political scientists, the American Political Science Association.[10] These widely read accounts forcefully argued that political theory had become alienated from political reality. To combat this problem, William Galston urged that "theorists should try harder to take real political controversies as their point of departure and to attend to the terms in which these debates are conducted." He continues, "Theorists too often assume that pointing to flaws, real or alleged, in the theoretical justification of a particular political system suffices as a critique of practices within that system. There should be less top-down theorizing [and] more of an effort to [judge] abstract principles in the light of concrete political realities."[11]

It should be no slight goad to political theorists that since the 1960s philosophers have been doing just what Galston had in mind. Most notably in the medical field, but also in law, business, and engineering, ethicists have confronted real-world dilemmas within the realm of professional work using a language not too far removed from the terms and contexts of professionals. In this way,

10. John Gunnell, "Political Theory: The Evolution of a Sub-Field," in *Political Science: The State of the Discipline,* ed. Ada W. Finifter (Washington, D.C.: American Political Science Association, 1983), 3–45; and William Galston, "Political Theory in the 1980s: Perplexity Amidst Diversity," in *Political Science: The State of the Discipline II,* ed. Ada W. Finifter (Washington, D.C.: American Political Science Association, 1993), 27–53.

11. Galston, "Political Theory," 40.

ethicists have been able to both actively engage in problem solving within professional domains, such as hospitals, clinics, and business firms, as well as foster rich academic research programs. This sort of applied and engaged work, according to Stephen Toulmin, has "saved the life of ethics," "has given back to ethics a seriousness and human relevance which it had seemed . . . to have lost for good."[12] It is not too much to hope that political theory might also gain from a similar ground-level focus on relevant social problems and the agents who grapple with them.

It is one thing to agree, in general, that political theorists can be more concrete and more attuned to actual politics, but why follow the specific path of applied ethicists into the domains of journalists, doctors, and lawyers—the newsrooms, editorial conferences, clinical sessions, hospital ethics committee work, courtroom discourse? The answer is that one can, of course, do more applied political theory without ever thinking about professions. Yet some topics within political theory require this focus on these seemingly micro domains. More generally, too, professional practices raise issues of power and authority relevant to democratic citizenship that have been left largely untreated by philosophers of the professions.

As we will see in Chapter 1, contemporary political theory has taken what some call a "deliberative turn." Many scholars believe that features of contemporary politics, such as declining citizen participation, are signs of deep alienation from collective decision making. As citizens have become bystanders to collective decisions, they have become distanced from one another and have lost opportunities for advancing public goods. The distance between citizens reduces awareness of others' lives and lessens engagement in the social practices that would allow citizens to learn how others different from them in class, region, race, and gender are affected by collective decisions. The solution for many scholars is public deliberation in which collective decisions are more closely tied to public forums marked by equality, active participation, and reasonableness.

Missing from contemporary scholarship on public deliberation is attention to questions of agency and context: who, what, when, and how in the terms of traditional political science. So far, students of public deliberation have largely ignored a crucial dimension of the intermediary realm between individual and state in which professions that possess the power to distract, encourage, limit,

---

12. Stephen Toulmin, "How Medicine Saved the Life of Ethics," *Perspectives in Biology and Medicine* 25 (1982): 748.

and inform democratic deliberation exist. Moreover, some of the most aggressive current efforts at fostering public deliberation are located in just this intermediary realm.

A closer relation between political theory and professions would also contribute to the body of work on professional ethics. Indeed, it would allow professional ethics to catch up with the developments such as those illustrated by our initial snapshots of increased lay participation in professional decisions and activities. Reform-minded professionals show a growing awareness of how the institutions and practices they so strongly influence—the hospitals and clinics, the newspapers and news stations, the court rooms and correctional facilities—can either exclude or engage lay members of the public and can either play a disempowering or empowering function in American democracy.

Rightly understood, professionalism has a civic dimension. The theory of democratic professionalism presented in this book holds that a number of key professions have civic roles to play in contemporary democracy and that such civic roles both strengthen the legitimacy of professional authority and render that authority more transparent and more vulnerable to public influence. Once it is understood that professionals can help mobilize and inform citizen participation inside and outside spheres of professional authority, many of the negative, counter-democratic connotations of professionalism fall away. Indeed, rightly understood, democratic professionals are some of the best candidates today for bolstering the deliberative democracy urged by contemporary commentators. This is not to ask professionals to substitute political for occupational duties but rather to become aware of, as well as enlarge and enrich, the already existing connections between professional and democratic practice.

Plan of the Book

Chapter 1 introduces the core concept of public deliberation and the idea of "middle democracy," the ground-level network of lay participation outside the formal politics of American democracy that has gone understudied. The next three chapters build the foundation for a theory of democratic professionalism by showing why professions are key players in middle democracy and are viable candidates for facilitating public deliberation. Chapter 2 examines the special social responsibility that professions such as law, medicine, and academics have traditionally held themselves accountable for promoting. This responsibility is articulated in the once dominant and still influential "social trustee" model of professionalism. Then, Chapter 3 draws out the political characteristics of this social responsibility by taking up salient criticisms of social trustee conceptions of professional and expert authority. These criticisms form a second, "radical critique" model for understanding professionalism and its connection to democracy. In Chapter 4, I build on both social trustee and radical critique models to construct what I consider a superior account of the relationship between professionals and democracy, the model of democratic professionalism that will be useful in considering real-world cases of reform efforts urging professionals to foster public deliberation and civic involvement, each in their own ways. The cases of public journalism, restorative justice, and the bioethics movement considered in Chapters 5, 6, and 7, respectively, give a face to the theory of democratic professionalism and flesh out its motivations and orienting values. These cases also raise issues that are likely to be continuously contentious for democratic professionalism in theory and practice. Chapter 8 builds key insights drawn from the cases into the theory while addressing a number of major practical and normative questions relevant for scholars and practitioners alike. In the Conclusion, I suggest how current well-meaning efforts to revise ethics pedagogy in professional schools and training seminars can be modified to foster greater awareness of the democratic consequences of professional practices.

1

THE MISSING AGENTS OF
CONTEMPORARY DEMOCRATIC THOUGHT

This book shares a number of assumptions with contemporary political theory about the prospects of enhancing American democracy even in the face of depressing general trends in political behavior among elites and ordinary citizens. In particular, it favors institutions and practices, both political and social, that encourage, respect, and heed citizen participation and deliberation. Citizen participation and deliberation are at the center of contemporary political theory, where advocates of what has come to be called deliberative democracy make strong claims about the value of face-to-face, public deliberation. Indeed, there is surprising agreement across normally divisive intellectual fault lines on what, ideally, deliberative democracy would entail. Deliberative democrats have failed, however, to satisfactorily indicate just how participation and deliberation can emerge under the unpromising conditions we face. Though it is only one piece of a larger puzzle, the role of professionals is critical. In fact, in professional domains we currently see some of the most important experiments in public deliberation.

This chapter seeks to do three things. First, it establishes a political concept on which we will rely throughout the book: public deliberation. This means exploring the justifications for a more deliberative democracy. Second, it fixes our attention on questions of motivation and leadership: how, exactly, is public deliberation to emerge in American political culture, which to most accounts is only nominally participatory and deliberative? It examines the limited answers posed in the political theory literature, then proposes the role of professionals as a viable alternative. Finally, it argues for seriously considering the intermediary realm between state institutions and individual political choices and actions—the realm of "middle democracy," where citizen competencies are honed in the everyday work of collective, local, ordinary, practical decision making.

A Theory of Deliberative Democracy

Although public discussion and debate have long been recognized as character-istic features of democracy, the concept of deliberation moved to the forefront of democratic theory in the 1990s. As John Dryzek, a leading contributor to this movement, notes: "The final decade of the second millennium saw the theory of democracy take a strong deliberative turn. . . . The deliberative turn represents a renewed concern with the authenticity of democracy: the degree to which dem-ocratic control is substantive rather than symbolic, and engaged by competent citizens."[1] Though the current focus on deliberation is not an innovation but a revival of ideas prominent in ancient Greek political thought and in canonical modern Western thinkers such as Edmund Burke, John Stuart Mill, and John Dewey, the term "deliberative democracy" was rarely used prior to 1990.[2]

What is deliberative democracy? As James Bohman, another proponent, writes: "Deliberative democracy, broadly defined, is thus any one of a family of views according to which the public deliberation of free and equal citizens is the core of legitimate political decision making and self-government."[3] Most dem-ocratic theories agree that democratic legitimacy is based on the equal consid-eration of interests by institutions of collective choice. And most agree that individuals themselves, rather than experts or guardians, are the best judges of their interests.[4] Deliberative theories are distinctive because they hold that norms of reasonable public dialogue are necessary for a democratic procedure to equally

---

1. John S. Dryzek, *Deliberative Democracy and Beyond* (New York: Oxford University Press, 2000), 1.

2. For example, see Dryzek, *Deliberative Democracy and Beyond;* Jon Elster, "Deliberation and Con-stitution Making," in *Deliberative Democracy,* ed. Elster (New York: Cambridge University Press, 1998), 97–122; James Bohman, "The Coming of Age of Deliberative Democracy," *Journal of Political Philos-ophy* 6, no. 4 (1998): 400–425; and James Bohman and William Rehg, "Introduction," in *Deliberative Democracy: Essays on Reason and Politics,* ed. Bohman and Rehg (Cambridge, Mass.: MIT Press, 1997), ix–xxx. All cite Joseph Bessette as the inventor of the term "deliberative democracy." See Bessette, "Deliberative Democracy: The Majority Principle in Republican Government," in *How Democratic Is the Constitution?* ed. Robert A. Goldwin and William A. Schambra (Washington, D.C.: American Enterprise Institute, 1980), 102–16. Most also acknowledge Bernard Manin and Joshua Cohen as key figures who gave impetus to the term. See Manin, "On Legitimacy and Political Deliberation," *Polit-ical Theory* 15, no. 3 (1987): 338–68; and Cohen, "Deliberation and Democratic Legitimacy," in *The Good Polity,* ed. Alan P. Hamlin and Philip Pettit (Oxford: Blackwell, 1989), 17–34. The widespread appeal of the term is indicated by the fact that in the 1990s the most prominent liberal theorist, John Rawls, and critical theorist, Jürgen Habermas, both identified themselves as deliberative democrats. See Rawls, *Political Liberalism* (New York: Columbia University Press, 1993), 374; and Habermas, *Between Facts and Norms* (Cambridge, Mass.: MIT Press, 1996), 287–328.

3. Bohman, "Coming of Age," 401.

4. Robert A. Dahl, *Democracy and Its Critics* (New Haven: Yale University Press, 1989), 65–79.

consider interests rather than merely register the most popular private preferences. Deliberative democrats see interests as emerging from reasonable public
dialogue after individual preferences have been subjected to an informative and
analytical debate where counterarguments are aired. In nondeliberative institutions and practices, such as those found in pluralist and participatory democratic
theory, those who lose have only the minimally considerate explanation that
they were less politically powerful, less skillful at bargaining, or less numerous.
Those who lose in a deliberative procedure ideally have had their interests considered and have been offered acceptable reasons for why a policy they opposed
was chosen.

Two features of Bohman's definition deserve additional comment. First, deliberative democracy has no definitive "theory." Deliberative democratic theory is
the work of many writers who share a general perspective but do not always
agree on a number of particular issues, some of which are fairly fundamental,
as we will see. Second, Bohman's definition rightly places public deliberation at
the center of deliberative democratic theory. Within the study of politics, the
term "deliberation" has been applied to a broad range of activities, including
an individual's private contemplation of political issues, everyday political talk
among family and friends, and the ongoing public conversations about politics
carried on between average citizens and their leaders largely through the media.
Most of the normative studies of democratic deliberation use the term in a much
narrower sense in which deliberation refers to a face-to-face discussion about
politics carried on in a public forum between participants for whom the outcome matters. When deliberative democrats speak of public deliberation, they
typically mean a public, face-to-face conversation between equal participants
constrained only by the norms of rational discourse.

Norms of Deliberation

Proponents of deliberative democracy hold two types of norms as critical to supporting real as opposed to merely symbolic public deliberation. Agent-level norms
apply to individuals and constrain their nondeliberative actions within political
forums. System-level norms apply to the forums themselves and seek to protect
them from the influence of nondeliberative forces seeking entrance from outside.

The most important agent-level norms to be met by participants in public
dialogue are rationality, respect, and integrity. The norm of rationality requires

participants to justify their positions with reasons and evidence. Rational participants are motivated by what Jürgen Habermas calls the "forceless force" of the better argument.[5] They seek to persuade others over to their point of view only by articulating arguments and mustering evidence, and never through threats, coercion, or inducements other than the best argument. Rationality also implies that participants ought not advance arguments or make decisions based on rationally inarticulable preferences, no matter how deeply held.

The second norm, respect, means deliberators are expected to put arguments in terms others could possibly accept and to be willing to be persuaded by, or at least give a serious hearing to, the arguments of others. Respect leads deliberators to apply what Amy Gutmann and Dennis Thompson call the "economy of moral disagreement" and put forward arguments that are least antagonistic to the positions of others.[6]

The norm of integrity constrains participants to make arguments they themselves hold to be true or choice worthy, to accept the consequences and implications of their arguments, and to apply them to their own case. Integrity leads deliberators to be sincere and consistent in their arguments and actions. As with the norms of rationality and respect, integrity is more than a call to be logical, precise, and informed. Rather, all these agent-level norms are best seen as expressing a general moral commitment—to frame it in Kantian terms, to treat others as ends in themselves rather than as means to one's own end.

Agent-level norms are no mere moral bonuses, such that following them is nice but not required. They are necessary for political deliberation to be more than the pursuit of self-interest, for it to reflect the moral status of each citizen as free and equal. Deliberators unconstrained by such norms under conditions of disagreement are showing that they do not "take each other seriously as moral agents." Their failure to follow such norms usually means deliberators are pursuing "nonmoral" means of settling disputes: bargaining, deals, and perhaps even violence.[7]

The system-level norms of equality and accessibility are also nonoptional; though, in contrast to the agent-level norms that bear on individuals, system-level norms must be met by society itself to foster reasonable public dialogue.

5. Jürgen Habermas, "Hannah Arendt's Communications Concept of Power," *Social Research* 44 (1977): 3–24.

6. Amy Gutmann and Dennis F. Thompson, *Democracy and Disagreement* (Cambridge, Mass.: Belknap Press, 1996), 84–85.

7. Amy Gutmann and Dennis F. Thompson, *Why Deliberative Democracy?* (Princeton: Princeton University Press, 2004), 80.

The norm of equality can be seen as both a procedural and substantive commitment. All deliberative democrats favor procedural political equality, which dictates equal weighting of each citizen's vote and equal standing to raise issues and set agendas in a public forum.[8] Many are also concerned with structural constraints on the force of the better argument, such as social and economic inequalities, believing that deliberative democratic procedures have the substantive expectation that collective decisions be protected from economic or social forces outside the public forum. For reason-based arguments to hold sway, the practical ability of deliberators to influence others and to utilize institutional powers must not be muted or amplified by threats or rewards offered by those privileged by their socioeconomic status.[9]

The norm of accessibility is also conceptualized in procedural and substantive terms. As with equality, all deliberative democrats favor procedural guarantees on accessibility, even though some balk, for different reasons, at including too many substantive guarantees of accessibility.[10] Procedurally, accessibility means that all citizens affected by a decision should be allowed a hearing and that public forums be open and well publicized so that participation is a real option for people. More substantively, accessibility calls for public education that equips would-be deliberators with the skills of argumentation needed to exercise public reason.[11]

Although deliberative democrats agree on these norms, they disagree on how to apply them in practice. The most significant division is between liberal deliberative democrats, such as Gutmann and Thompson, and critical deliberative democrats, such as Dryzek, Habermas, and Seyla Benhabib, on the specification of agent-level norms. Liberals argue that more substantive and restrictive norms of discussion are needed for a collective decision to be legitimate, while critical theorists argue for more open and wide-ranging debate with minimal restrictions on content and procedure.

Related disagreements concern where authentic democratic discourse is to take place and who is to participate in it. Liberals favor discourse within familiar

---

8. See, for example, Seyla Benhabib, "Deliberative Rationality and Models of Democratic Legitimacy," *Constellations* I, no. I (1994): 26–52; and Cohen, "Deliberation and Democratic Legitimacy," 21–23.

9. James S. Fishkin, *Democracy and Deliberation: New Directions for Democratic Reform* (New Haven: Yale University Press, 1991), 33.

10. James Bohman, "Deliberative Democracy and Effective Social Freedom: Capabilities, Resources, and Opportunities," in *Deliberative Democracy*, ed. Bohman and Rehg, 321–48.

11. John S. Dryzek, *Discursive Democracy* (New York: Cambridge University Press, 1990), 41–43.

constitutional structures (i.e., within the state) to protect individual rights and to produce durable decisions. Critical theorists, concerned that citizen deliberators may defer too readily to state authority and official expertise and worried that critical or nonconventional perspectives could be co-opted or quieted by authorities, favor deliberation that occurs in the "public sphere" outside the state; although, this location raises issues of how discourse in the public sphere can influence actual public policy. As for who deliberates, liberals assert that a limited group—either legislators or a randomly selected group of citizens—can deliberate and make recommendations or policy that would count as representative of more widespread public deliberation. Critical theorists, on the other hand, are wary of restricting access and argue that open and widespread participation produces more democratic results.

Why Deliberate?

The ideal of public deliberation has become enormously attractive to democratic theorists, scholars interested in public opinion and citizen participation, and practitioners seeking new solutions to policy problems. Three aspects are particularly important for understanding the appeal of public deliberation: legitimacy, practicality, and diagnostic relevance.

Legitimacy

The most common justification for public deliberation is legitimacy—that is, a democracy that embraces a process of decision making characterized by extensive rational discussion among citizens as to what decisions ought to be made is more legitimate than a democracy with minimal opportunity for citizen deliberation. But legitimacy, though rightly understood by contemporary theorists as the belief that laws deserve to be obeyed, is a complex concept because there are different ways to conceptualize why laws deserve to be obeyed. Three distinct arguments connect public deliberation to legitimacy.

First, a more deliberative process is more legitimate because it allows value-laden questions to be taken seriously in political decision making. In contrast to more economically oriented visions of democracy, deliberative democracy begins from the premise that politics is about values, not just interests. Gutmann and Thompson argue that the chief reason for deliberation is the need for participants in collective decisions to take into consideration values held by others.[12] The prevalence, importance, and pluralistic nature of moral discourse about the subjects of collective decisions call for something more than the vote counting, interest-group bargaining, and cost-benefit analysis of contemporary politics. To those who lose in a morally charged political debate, merely offering the reason "the votes were against you" is insufficient.

With matters of ethical consequence, participants accept an outcome emerging from debate if they believe all relevant value positions were taken seriously. Thus, write Gutmann and Thompson, "in the face of scarcity, deliberation can help those who do not get what they want or even what they need come to accept the legitimacy of a collective decision."[13] In a political decision about defunding organ transplants, for example, because of the serious—indeed mortal—consequences to potential recipients, more is owed to them than the bare assurance that "the votes were against you." For losers to accept ethically consequential losses, they must believe their needs and their reasons were seriously considered and that they were reasonably outweighed by similarly grave needs and similarly powerful reasons.

Deliberation also fosters legitimacy when it allows citizens to express their value conflicts and allows them to address these conflicts without necessarily removing them. Under conditions of value pluralism, no overarching theory of social justice can guide policy making. Therefore, normative legitimacy must depend on procedural norms that guarantee inclusive, equal, rational, respectful, honest, sincere, and consistent debate yet do not stack the deck in favor of one or another "comprehensive moral viewpoint."[14] "Agreements in societies living with value-pluralism," writes Benhabib, "are to be sought for not at the level of substantive beliefs but at the level of procedures, processes, and practices for attaining and revising beliefs. Proceduralism is a rational answer to persisting value conflicts at the substantive level."[15] Deliberative democrats ask only that citizens agree on the norms of procedure, not on substantive theories of justice.

Because of its content and process, then, value-sensitive deliberation clarifies ethical commitments. "Clarify" is perhaps too passive a word since public deliberation aims to both filter and provoke reason-giving about the values we

---

12. Gutmann and Thompson, *Democracy and Disagreement,* 18.

13. Amy Gutmann and Dennis F. Thompson, "Deliberating About Bioethics," *Hastings Center Report* 27, no. 3 (1997): 39.

14. Rawls, *Political Liberalism,* 243.

15. Benhabib, "Deliberative Rationality," 34.

hold or should hold. Sometimes issues of justice, for example, do not emerge in political debate because of entrenched beliefs and attitudes on the part of both majority and minority groups. Decision making that simply accepts these beliefs and attitudes without subjecting them to the expectations of public defense can perpetuate historical injustices. Our preferences adapt to our circumstances, tragically so when a person accustomed to being an excluded minority with diminished civic status does not protest that condition because he sees other possibilities as unobtainable.[16] He has "freedom" to participate in politics or not, freedom to advocate his interests, but his freedoms have been structured by a history of marginalization and neglect. In his famous "Letter from the Bir-mingham City Jail" in 1963, Martin Luther King wrote of this as the "force of complacency" that affected those "who, as a result of long years of oppression, have been so completely drained of self-respect and a sense of 'somebodiness' that they have adjusted to segregation." Such entrenchment can also affect those with civic status when they hold selfish and prejudicial views even though these could not be defended in public deliberation open to those bearing the brunt of these views. Entrenched preferences are more likely to be unearthed and ex-posed in deliberative procedures than under conditions where preferences are simply tallied up. Deliberation in public cultures marked by a history of social injustice should provoke and make participants more aware of that history and thus clarify for them their fundamental interests in being treated as equals and in treating others as equals.

A third way public deliberation connects with legitimacy is when it allows a public interest different from and superior to the aggregation of individual inter-ests to emerge. The idea that there are public interests and goods that can only be discovered through the process of public deliberation draws its strength from civic republican arguments that hold a conception of the res publica—or common thing—that is distinct from the aggregation of private interests.[17] This idea also connects to the critical theorists' aim of making contemporary democracy more authentic—more reflective of rationally considered interests rather than brute

16. Jon Elster, *Sour Grapes* (Cambridge: Cambridge University Press, 1983); and Cass R. Sunstein, "Democracy and Shifting Preferences," in *The Idea of Democracy,* ed. David Copp, Jean Hampton, and John E. Roemer (New York: Cambridge University Press, 1993), 196–243.

17. Jane Mansbridge is a chief proponent of this view, but it is also held by those who come to deliberative democracy from civic republican leanings, such as Cass Sunstein. See Mansbridge, *Beyond Adversary Democracy* (New York: Basic Books, 1980), 26–28, and "A Deliberative Theory of Interest Representation," in *The Politics of Interests: Interest Groups Transformed,* ed. Mark P. Petracca (Boulder, Colo.: Westview Press, 1992), 36–37. See also Sunstein, "Democracy and Shifting Preferences," 197.

preferences too strongly influenced by conventional cultural attitudes toward politics, society, and economy. From the vantage point of the public interest perspective, public deliberation is a way of defeating the tendencies of symbolic and merely conventional politics.[18]

How would public deliberation lead to different and superior articulation of public interests? Deliberative democrats point to gaps between what people prefer and what their interests are, gaps created by unreflective but settled opinions, by a lack of information about factual matters or about how others will act. Scarcity of information about the facts allows mistaken preferences to persist, and scarcity of information about how others will choose prompts constrained or merely strategic preferences. In each of these cases, deliberation can clarify and provoke the realization of public practical interests.

Information provided in a debate can show our preferences to be mistaken: inaccurate, incoherent, or incomplete. An inaccurate preference is one held only because existing evidence that would produce a different preference is not known. David Miller gives a good example of an inaccurate preference:

> To use the energy policy example, someone might judge energy sources entirely on the basis of environmental soundness and begin with the rank order coal, gas, oil, nuclear power. However, in the course of debate strong evidence is produced about the atmospheric effects of coal-burning power stations which decisively pushes coal below gas and oil from an environmental point of view.[19]

Incoherent preferences are incompatible with each other, such as a desire for universal health care and for a sharp decrease in taxes. Incomplete preferences reflect our initial indifference to issues that deliberation would reveal to be quite important to us. Bernard Manin describes incomplete preferences as follows: "Participants may not be able to see just how their interests are affected by one choice or another unless they are involved in discussion. For example, they may be indifferent to a given policy proposal until they realize that it does in fact affect them."[20] These mistaken choices result from gaps between our current preferences and our considered interests that can be bridged through deliberation.

18. Dryzek, *Discursive Democracy,* 87–89, and *Deliberative Democracy and Beyond,* 8.
19. David Miller, "Deliberative Democracy and Social Choice," in *Prospects for Democracy: North, South, East, West,* ed. David Held (Stanford: Stanford University Press, 1993), 82.
20. Manin, "On Legitimacy and Political Deliberation," 350.

We make constrained or strategic choices when we must restrict our choices out of fear of victimization. In the classic prisoners' dilemma game, for example, the best result from the point of view of X is if she confesses and Y does not, while the worst result is if Y confesses and X does not. From the collective point of view of both X and Y together, the best result is if neither confesses. The collective point of view is hindered, however, by lack of discussion between prisoners and lack of trust.[21] Insofar as deliberative procedures reveal a degree of common interest and are able to reduce risk of defection from support of that common interest—defections that victimize those stuck supporting it— they can produce an outcome that is better from the collective point of view.[22] The ongoing character of deliberative proceedings fosters motivational constraints on defectors such as shame and loss of integrity.[23] As in the case of mistaken preferences, dialogue constituted by the norms of rationality, respect, and accountability produces an outcome that is preferable according to the self-interests of each party. If the case of mistaken preferences shows how we can clarify our individual interests through dialogue, the case of strategic choices shows how collective interests in public goods can be clarified. Of course, there is no guarantee of such benefits of cooperation, but such benefits are more likely to be gained under deliberative than nondeliberative procedures.

Practicality

Public deliberation, though an ideal, is more practical than other like-minded approaches in democratic theory because its central ideas do not clash significantly with modern beliefs about the relationship between citizen and state and could be put into practice in ways that would not require utopian changes.

In his famous 1819 speech on ancient and modern conceptions of liberty, Benjamin Constant starkly contrasted two models of political life. His first model was sketched from reflections on the Spartan and Athenian city–states and the Roman republic. Liberty for these ancients "consisted in exercising collectively, but directly, several parts of the complete sovereignty; in deliberating, in the public square, over war and peace; in forming alliances with foreign governments;

21. For a good discussion of the prisoners' dilemma, see Edna Ullmann-Margalit, *The Emergence of Norms* (Oxford: Clarendon Press, 1977), 18–21.

22. Jane J. Mansbridge, "Motivating Deliberation in Congress," in *Constitutionalism in America*, vol. 2, ed. Sarah Baumgartner Thurow (New York: University Press of America, 1988), 62.

23. Miller, "Deliberative Democracy and Social Choice," 82–84.

in voting laws, in pronouncing judgments; in examining the accounts, the acts, the stewardship of the magistrates; in calling them to appear in front of the assembled people, in accusing, condemning or absolving them."[24]

Though the ancients put a premium on such political or collective freedom, they discounted private or individual freedom. Indeed, wrote Constant, the ancients "admitted as compatible with this collective freedom the complete subjection of the individual to the authority of the community. . . . All private actions were submitted to a severe surveillance. No importance was given to individual independence, neither in relation to opinions, nor to labour, nor, above all, to religion."[25] Ancient liberty meant collective self-determination, something requiring merely fluid boundaries between citizen and citizen, and citizen and state. Government was direct, participatory, and demanding.

Modern French, English, and Americans, by contrast, privilege private or individual freedoms over political or collective freedoms. Moderns understand "liberty," wrote Constant, as

> the right to be subjected only to the laws, and to be neither arrested, detained, put to death or maltreated in any way by the arbitrary will of one or more individuals. It is the right of everyone to express their opinion, choose a profession and practice it, to dispose of property, and even to abuse it; to come and go without permission, and without having to account for their motives or undertakings. It is everyone's right to associate with other individuals, either to discuss their interests, or to profess the religion which they and their associates prefer, or even simply to occupy their days or hours in a way which is most compatible with their inclinations or whims.[26]

Moderns have political rights, of course, such as the "right to exercise some influence on the administration of the government, either by electing all or particular officials, or through representations, petitions, demands to which the authorities are more or less compelled to pay heed." Yet the modern individual

24. Benjamin Constant, "The Liberty of the Ancients Compared with that of the Moderns" (1819), in *Political Writings,* ed. and trans. Biancamaria Fontana (Cambridge: Cambridge University Press, 1988), 311.

25. Constant, "The Liberty of the Ancients," 311.

26. Constant, "The Liberty of the Ancients," 310–11.

is politically sovereign "only in appearance. . . . His sovereignty is restricted and almost always suspended. If, at fixed and rare intervals, in which he is again surrounded by precautions and obstacles, he exercises this sovereignty, it is always only to renounce it."[27]

Constant believed a nostalgic return to ancient democracy impossible and undesirable, but he also thought modern government—because it did not expect much from citizens—fostered a civic inattentiveness among the general public that made modern politics vulnerable to authoritarian leaders. Constant worried that moderns, "absorbed in the enjoyment of our private independence, and in the pursuit of our particular interests," would "surrender our right to share in political power too easily. . . . The holders of authority are only too anxious to encourage us to do so. They are so ready to spare us all sort of troubles, except those of obeying and paying!"[28] Constant's essay sought to both deromanticize ancient liberty as well as agitate modern complacency. He hoped his contemporaries would reform their institutions with both kinds of liberty in mind.

Public deliberation is an ideal that combines both modern and ancient liberty. Most advocates share Constant's belief that ancient liberty is an ideal that should be resurrected, albeit modified to protect basic individual rights. Their attempt to combine ancient with modern distinguishes advocates of public deliberation from other democratic theorists.

On one flank are liberal and pluralist democratic theories, contemporary versions of Constant's modern model. These contemporary defenders of modern liberty favor representative democracy involving adversary procedures and constitutional frameworks protecting individual rights, and they assume preexisting preferences that can be aggregated and negotiated. Defenders of modern liberty include a disparate group of contemporary theorists such as William Riker and other social choice theorists, Robert Dahl and other pluralists, and John Rawls and other liberal constitutionalists.[29] These theorists share as many differences as similarities, but they are all committed to the picture of modern liberty presented by Constant, though they support it for different reasons and would resist ancient liberty in different ways.

27. Constant, "The Liberty of the Ancients," 311, 312.

28. Constant, "The Liberty of the Ancients," 326.

29. William H. Riker, *Liberalism Against Populism* (San Francisco: Freeman, 1982); Robert A. Dahl, *A Preface to Democratic Theory* (Chicago: University of Chicago Press, 1956); and John Rawls, *A Theory of Justice* (Cambridge, Mass.: Harvard University Press, 1971).

On the other flank are communitarian, republican, and participatory democratic theorists who propose contemporary versions of ancient liberty. These theorists advocate direct democracy with strong norms of participation, favor nonadversarial procedures directed toward consensus or general will formation, support a more limited role for constitutional protections, and assume that political preferences are to be developed collectively in face-to-face settings. Defenders of ancient liberty include another disparate group of contemporary theorists such as Benjamin Barber, Carole Pateman and other participatory democrats, Frank Michelman and other neorepublicans, and Michael Sandel and other communitarians.[30]

In contrast to their contemporaries, deliberative democrats support both direct and representative democracy, though they would insist on no mandatory norm of participation. They seek to make good on the promise of more meaningful and legitimate political decision making but, particularly in contrast with participatory democrats and communitarians, do not advocate wholesale modification of established representative political institutions or expect extraordinary levels of commitment to politics from citizens.

The ideal of public deliberation is more practical than other contemporary democratic theories in two senses. First, among other aficionados of ancient liberty, deliberative democrats are less susceptible to the criticism of utopianism.[31] They do not call on contemporary Americans to relinquish dearly held individual rights or abandon representative institutions. Yet they have higher expectations for the amount and kind of civic activity for both citizens and their representatives than contemporary defenders of modern liberty. Second, the ideal of face-to-face public discussion that is at the heart of deliberative democracy offers numerous possibilities for implementation. Although theorists in the deliberative camp debate over the best place to locate public deliberation, nearly all agree that deliberation can fruitfully take place in a variety of settings to address a variety of public issues.

30. See Benjamin Barber, *Strong Democracy: Participatory Politics for a New Age* (Berkeley and Los Angeles: University of California Press, 2004); Carole Pateman, *Participation and Democratic Theory* (Cambridge: Cambridge University Press, 1970); Frank Michelman, "Forward: Traces of Self-Government," *Harvard Law Review* 100 (1986): 4–67, and "Law's Republic," *Yale Law Journal* 97 (1988): 1493–537; and Michael J. Sandel, *Liberalism and the Limits of Justice* (New York: Cambridge University Press, 1982).

31. Emily Hauptmann, "Can Less Be More? Leftist Deliberative Democrats' Critique of Participatory Democracy," *Polity* 33, no. 3 (2001): 397–421.

Diagnostic Relevance: The Vicious Circle of Ignorance, Complexity, and Distrust

At a very basic level, the ideal of public deliberation is appealing because it points out quite specifically what is missing from American democracy. Official pronouncements, legislative debate, and the chatter of pundits too frequently lack the give-and-take of reasons, often evidence disrespect of opposing or non-conventional positions, and show inconsistency and insincerity. If the norms of deliberation described earlier seem abstract, this may very well be because they are too often missing from public life.

Since the widely noticed campaign book *The Selling of the President, 1968* drew attention to the problem, techniques of advertising have become even more central both to campaigns and to the practice of governing.[32] The vanishing difference between selling something, whether it is a soft drink or a policy position, and deliberating with others is exemplified by the "word labs" of political professionals like Frank Luntz.[33] In these focus groups of up to two dozen citizens, Luntz runs videotape of politicians and officials explaining their policy positions. He tracks the positive and negative reactions of each member of the group to keywords spoken on the videotape. Each has a small electronic device with a dial they can twist to positive or negative as they watch the videotape. In the control room, Luntz carefully marks the language that has registered positively. Reporting back to his clients, Luntz draws up a list of words to use and words to avoid. This sort of instrumental, nondialogical communication is replicated in official communication with the public.

The shallowness of official discourse is often reinforced by norms and tendencies in the news media. Indeed, given tacit assumptions that politics is about the holding and gaining of power, shallowness is frequently praised by journalists who use terms such as "sticking to the message," "message discipline," and the like. Correcting earlier positions and maintaining an open mind in the official domain are seen as weaknesses in this Darwinian world. Objectivity, a core norm for journalists and an admittedly difficult standard for anyone to achieve, has in practice come to mean printing or airing pro and con sides of a story, often consisting of the official side and the opposition. This adversary journalism reproduces the image of politics as a struggle for power and oversimplifies policy problems, which may have one good answer, many good answers, or no good answers at all.

32. Joe McGinniss, *The Selling of the President, 1968* (New York: Trident Press, 1969).
33. Nicholas Lemann, "The Word Lab," *New Yorker,* October 17, 2000, 100–117.

Casting our gaze away from official discourse, public participation in politics and public opinion about government reflect depressing levels of disengagement and ignorance about institutions and policy.

Perhaps there never was a golden age of the citizen in the United States. Our history certainly is marked by formal and informal barriers to civic information and meaningful participation. Yet barriers such as the formal electoral restrictions that excluded all but white males and the less formal but no less effective racist restrictions of the Jim Crow South have fallen. Socioeconomic trends conducive to participation, such as literacy and standard of living, rose during the twentieth century. Still, we have not seen a concomitant rise in participation. Compared with other English-speaking countries with similar political cultures, such as Australia, New Zealand, Canada, and England, the average turnout for American elections in the last quarter of the twentieth century lagged by rates of 21 percent to 44 percent.[34]

Even more depressing than low participation rates is our high tolerance for public ignorance. Surveys of American public opinion reveal remarkable ignorance of government institutions, current elected officials, and the policy problems facing the country. Michael Delli Carpini and Scott Keeter examined a half century of public opinion polling on knowledge of political institutions, politicians, general political topics, and domestic and foreign policy and found that only "13 percent of the more than 2,000 questions examined could be answered correctly by 75 percent or more of those asked, and only 41 percent could be answered correctly by more than half the public." The questions did not tap trivial knowledge or information of quickly passing relevance. "Many of the facts known by relatively small percentages of the public," write Delli Carpini and Keeter, "seem critical to understanding—let alone effectively acting in—the political world: fundamental rules of the game; classic civil liberties; key concepts of political economy; the names of key political representatives; many important policy positions of presidential candidates or the political parties; basic social indicators and significant public policies."[35]

Among the many disturbing examples of public ignorance, 49 percent of Americans think the president has the power to suspend the Constitution and

34. Mark Franklin, "Electoral Participation," in *Comparing Democracies,* ed. Lawrence Le Duc, Richard Niemi, and Pippa Norris (Thousand Oaks, Calif.: Sage, 1996), 218.
35. Michael X. Delli Carpini and Scott Keeter, *What Americans Know About Politics and Why It Matters* (New Haven: Yale University Press, 1996), 102.

60 percent think he can appoint judges without Senate approval.[36] Though the U.S. Constitution is only a few pages long—shorter than most modern constitutions—and is ordinarily included in civics textbooks from junior high school on, only 35 percent of Americans can identify a right protected by the First Amendment, while a bare 20 percent can identify two rights and 9 percent can identify three rights protected by it.[37] Two of the most prominent Supreme Court decisions in modern politics, the *Miranda v. Arizona* and *Roe v. Wade* decisions, could be described substantively by only 45 percent and 30 percent, respectively. These percentages are low, considering the frequency of fictional Miranda warnings on popular cops and robbers television programs and the prominence of abortion as a political wedge issue in recent elections.

One reason for apathy and ignorance is the complexity of government and modern social and economic problems. American federalism, with its patchwork of competing and collaborative authority, is not easy at times even for political scientists or officials themselves to comprehend. Why voting laws, for example, are set state by state leaves even experts scratching their heads. Thus, it is not surprising, as the *New York Times* reported during the controversial Senate confirmation hearings for Clarence Thomas, that many New Yorkers wrote and called their *state* senators to advise them how to vote.[38]

The problems dealt with in government are complex and difficult to master. As Walter Lippmann pointed out many years ago in works such as *The Phantom Public* and *Public Opinion,* even if citizens devoted their spare time to *one* policy issue, such as how to ensure an adequate level of health care nationwide, this surely would be insufficient to establish a coherent and practical position on what is a remarkably complex problem. Add to that one issue, for which we have inadequate time or resources to comprehend, all the other pressing domestic and foreign problems and the limits of political ideals that trumpet the value of citizen attention and participation become clear. A more realistic role for the public, argued Lippmann, was to keep an eye only on the most obvious indicators of government performance—economic health, employment, and the like—in order to reelect competent expert officials and to oust incompetents. Advice on policy problems was best seen as the ken of expert analysts and "executives"—those with some experience in a given policy domain.

Yet what Lippmann's deliberative but nondemocratic model of expert decision

36. Delli Carpini and Keeter, *What Americans Know,* 99.
37. Delli Carpini and Keeter, *What Americans Know,* 92.
38. Delli Carpini and Keeter, *What Americans Know,* 62.

making ignores is the danger that citizens removed from the expectation of public knowledge and participation become alienated from government, governors, and even one another. Such distrust has indeed grown dramatically in the last twenty-five years. The number of people who report "hardly any" confidence in the executive branch of the federal government has risen from 18 percent to 35 percent in the last three decades. The number reporting low confidence in Congress has increased even more, from 15 percent to 40 percent in the same period. Even more striking, perhaps, is the low confidence we have in one another. Respondents who report "people can be trusted" fell from 55 percent to 34 percent in the last four decades. Those who feel that "you can't be too careful in dealing with people" rose from 40 percent to 61 percent of the survey population in the same period.[39] More recent survey evidence reports that both vertical and horizontal trust trends are continuing. Younger Americans appear to have the least social trust of all the age-groups—a finding that bodes poorly for any prospect of changing these trends.[40]

Ignorance, apathy, and complexity all reaffirm the relevance of the public deliberation ideal: a more substantive, reflective, and critical form of politics removed from mere vote counting. However, distrust points to the need for widespread citizen participation in such a process—expert deliberation can never substitute for ground-level engagement. Expert deliberation, even if done in public, does nothing to repair distrust between governors and governed. The public without deliberation is ignorant, inactive, and vulnerable to manipulation, while deliberation without the public—even if it were truly "expert"—is undermined by conditions of distrust.

Putting Public Deliberation into Practice

If the norms of deliberation are justified by the need for legitimacy under current conditions, how could they be put into practice? The practical and ethical aims of public deliberation appear to require porous and educative discursive practices. The more people participate, the more information and reasons they bring into a public forum and the more they learn from others. The better they

39. Robert Wuthnow, "The Role of Trust in Civic Renewal," in *Civil Society, Democracy, and Civic Renewal,* ed. Robert K. Fullinwider (Lanham, Md.: Rowman and Littlefield, 1998), 209–10.

40. Robert D. Putnam, *Bowling Alone: The Collapse and Revival of American Community* (New York: Touchstone, 2000), 139–42.

are prepared to present and hear arguments, the better able they are to make collective choices. But most theorists of deliberative democracy consider wide-scale deliberation impractical because of mechanical difficulties, the complexity of contemporary public issues, and the time constraints on average citizens. The most empirically developed models of public deliberation are representative rather than direct and are not broadly participatory.

Representative Deliberation

Representative models are designed to consider all relevant interests affected by a collective decision through a select subgroup of citizens who deliberate for the public at large. This subgroup is representative of a "deliberative majority" of the public if its members only differ from the public in the time and deliberative resources—such as pertinent information and analysis—they have available for decision making, not in basic interests. Their policy debate and ultimate choices will roughly represent what the public at large would have done under similar circumstances with similar resources.[41] Two of the most carefully and empirically articulated representative models are the "incrementalist" model of Joseph Bessette and Jane Mansbridge, among others, and the "deliberative poll" model of James Fishkin.

The incrementalist model calls for strengthening the deliberative norms of our current legislative institutions, which entails developing incentives and sanctions for legislators to deliberate over the merits of public policy, to represent considered interests rather than unreflective preferences, and to seek an economy of moral disagreement at the least and common ground on public purposes at best. For example, traditional institutional folkways and status systems have rewarded congressional freshmen for picking issue specializations—and developing trustworthy expertise in them—that require hard work, even if it is not on a topic the media find interesting, and protect members from unreflective constituent pressure.[42] All these can be shored up and built upon. The voting

41. Joseph M. Bessette, *The Mild Voice of Reason: Deliberative Democracy and American National Government* (Chicago: University of Chicago Press, 1994), 36.

42. Mansbridge, "Motivating Deliberation in Congress," 62, 81–84. In more recent writings, Mansbridge rejects the idea that democratic deliberation must happen in any one particular ideal forum—whether formal or informal, state or public sphere, representative or direct. She argues that the norms of deliberative democratic theorists should be used, in modified form, to assess the full range of political talk that she calls a "deliberative system." See Jane Mansbridge, "Everyday Talk in the Deliberative System," in *Deliberative Politics,* ed. Stephen Macedo (New York: Oxford University Press, 1999), 211.

booth serves as an accountability check on this process, the way the public at large makes sure their representatives share their interests and are truly serving them.

The deliberative poll model establishes a separate forum outside government composed of a statistically representative cross-section of the national electorate brought together to discuss specific policy issues. This group is immersed in "carefully balanced" information and analysis of specific issues, encouraged to discuss these issues together and with "competing experts and politicians," then, after a number of days of discussion, surveyed about their reflective opinions.[43] As with its elite counterpart in government, this subgroup would have the time and deliberative resources to adequately reason through and discuss complex issues; but, unlike the elite group, it would not be under any electoral pressures and, therefore, not susceptible to financial threats or offers. In this model, the interests of the subgroup match those of the larger public because the representatives are randomly chosen from the larger public.

Either of these models would be easier to implement than widespread deliberation, but they would also be less capable of serving the practical and ethical aims that make deliberative institutions preferable to those that are only minimally deliberative. Debate on the merits of a policy option is a critical factor in producing the information and analysis needed to correct mistaken preferences. An elite subgroup of representatives is electorally vulnerable to the mistaken preferences of the public at large. Elites must be able to persuade a majority outside the legislative halls that with better information they would have reached the same positions. Consider representatives from largely middle-class suburban districts who must justify their votes in favor of a universal health care plan widely but mistakenly believed to be compatible with lower income taxes. Such a situation calls for civic education efforts on the part of the legislators and civic engagement on the part of the constituents, which illustrate the need for at least a scaled-back form of widespread public deliberation. Though immune from the problem of vulnerability at one level, Fishkin's deliberative poll would suffer from it if its results are used in policy making. Whoever acts on the results must justify them in a similarly deliberative fashion to the public at large. In other

---

This conception has much in common with the Habermas-inspired "multiple public sphere" approach discussed below.

43. James S. Fishkin, *The Voice of the People: Public Opinion and Democracy* (New Haven: Yale University Press, 1995), 162.

words, either Fishkin's polls are merely academic exercises or they are vulnerable to public ignorance.

Widespread clarification and provocation of existing preferences are needed for legislators to also safely pursue more ethical policy. When they participate in deliberation, new value-laden claims can be brought forward and assessed. By representing themselves in a forum where others must hear them, a group can challenge and educate those in society who doubt the value of their interests, goals, and views or who are scarcely even aware of them. There is also a self-educative effect to participation. In the case of entrenched preferences, the role of public dialogue is to help people realize unfair treatment by comparing their experience with others. Neither of these effects is plausibly replicated in the representative model. Without widespread rather than limited clarification of practical and ethical interests, representatives are vulnerable to the unclarified and unprovoked preferences of the electorate. A better model of deliberation would somehow expand the circle of debate.

Mass Deliberation

One way of expanding the circle while remaining realistic about the time and attention Americans can devote to politics is to mark out one day every two years for the purposes of mass public deliberation. Bruce Ackerman and James Fishkin advocate just such an idea:

> Deliberation Day—a new national holiday. It will be held one week before major national elections. Registered voters will be called together in neighborhood meeting places, in small groups of 15, and larger groups of 500, to discuss the central issues raised by the campaign. Each deliberator will be paid $150 for the day's work of citizenship, on condition that he or she shows up at the polls the next week. All other work, except the most essential, will be prohibited by law.[44]

In a series of scheduled events, citizens who volunteer to attend Deliberation Day will have the opportunity to read briefing documents on what the leading candidates consider the two to four major issues of the campaign, hear how the

44. Bruce Ackerman and James S. Fishkin, "Deliberation Day," in *Debating Deliberative Democracy,* ed. James S. Fishkin and Peter Laslett, Philosophy, Politics, and Society 7 (Oxford: Blackwell, 2003), 7–30.

candidates respond to journalists' questions about these issues, discuss the candidates' positions in small groups of fifteen, and to submit questions to the candidates in a larger forum of five hundred.

Deliberation Day satisfies most of the norms central to the ideal of public deliberation. Rationality is satisfied by the information packets provided for participants and by the opportunities available for further clarification. Integrity is satisfied, on the part of politicians, by being open to questions from journalists and citizens. On the part of citizens, integrity is encouraged by small-group discussion that presses people to formulate their views for public consumption. Deliberation Day violates the system-level norm of equality since there are built-in inequalities in the process, particularly a hierarchy of political speech that places greater importance on what the political candidates say than on what anyone else says. However, the system-level norm of accessibility is satisfied by provisions that give citizens a day off and fund monetary incentives that would help get people into the forum.

Nevertheless, Deliberation Day only weakly satisfies these norms. Deliberation, after all, is for a single day and cannot cover more than four issues during that limited time. Even those four issues are unlikely to be discussed in great detail. During the one day scheduled for mass deliberation, an individual would have only a few minutes to speak in public. As for equality, conventional political operatives—candidates, their campaign workers, and other party officials—have much more impact framing the content of deliberation than rank-and-file citizens have. Though it may produce better knowledge of candidates' positions, Deliberation Day is not structured to develop citizens' knowledge more generally. Finally, this model is hampered by the artificiality of a structure imposed from outside—who organizes the event and sets the rules for briefing documents, for guiding discussion, and for other key procedural issues? This "Wizard of Oz" problem is serious because it keeps citizens in the role of spectators rather than actors.

A different approach, flowing from the recent work of Jürgen Habermas, conceives mass deliberation in a more porous and less organized way. For Habermas, "the success of deliberative politics depends not on a collectively acting citizenry but on the institutionalization of the corresponding procedures and conditions of communication, as well as on the interplay of institutionalized deliberative processes with informally constituted public opinions."[45] A vibrant

45. Habermas, *Between Facts and Norms,* 298.

dialogue is sought within and among multiple associations, social movements, neighborhood groups, and other denizens of civil society. Most important to this conception of mass deliberation is not that every citizen participate, but "that public opinion be formed on the basis of adequate information and relevant reasons and that those whose interests are involved have an equal and effective opportunity to make their own interests (and the reasons for them) known."[46]

Critical to the Habermasian approach, then, is both the proliferation and self-regulation of what I will call "multiple public spheres." Simone Chambers, for example, advocates "opening up opportunities to participate, by including excluded voices, by democratizing media access, by setting up 'town meetings' and 'deliberative public opinion polls,' by politicizing the depoliticized, by empowering the powerless, by decentralizing decision making, by funding public commissions to canvass public opinion" and more.[47]

The multiple public spheres approach raises none of the problems of artificiality encountered with Deliberation Day. Already existing patterns of deliberative activity in civil society are built on, given support, and amplified. Also attractive is the idea of deliberation as a long-term cultural commitment rather than a brief, albeit potent, event occurring once every two to four years. With a more organic and flexible approach, however, comes a loosening of substantive connections to the norms of deliberation. No overseers and no authority of last resort are proposed as facilitators—much less as guardians—of deliberative norms.

There are good reasons for avoiding specification of facilitators. For public deliberation to represent what members of the public wish it to be, it cannot be regulated from outside:

> Participants themselves must question their motives, look at the genealogy of their beliefs, ask what interests their arguments serve. Participants are the last court of appeal on whether arguments are legitimate or interlocutors are employing undue force. Participants themselves must judge whether money and power are being used as a coercive

46. Kenneth Baynes, "Deliberative Democracy and the Limits of Liberalism," in *Discourse and Democracy: Essays on Habermas's "Between Facts and Norms,"* ed. Rene von Schomberg and Kenneth Baynes (Albany: State University of New York Press, 2002), 18.

47. Simone Chambers, *Reasonable Democracy: Jürgen Habermas and the Politics of Discourse* (Ithaca: Cornell University Press, 1996), 196.

force or as a legitimate consideration in formulating a generalizable interest. . . . Participants must themselves question the background of each other's claims and bring all relevant material to light.[48]

Failure to self-regulate, maintain inclusiveness and accessibility, and evidence reasonableness, respect, and integrity means that a group's, movement's, or meeting's discussion cannot be considered truly deliberative. Therefore, it loses its forceless force, so to speak, as an agency aiming to communicate public interests to more formal legislative and administrative decision-making bodies.

The Three Weaknesses

Though I judge the Habermasian multiple public spheres approach to be the best framework we currently have for applying the norms of public deliberation to the real world of politics, it has three significant weaknesses. First, the question of what social forces and individual actors are currently available to actuate democratic deliberation looms large. A common tendency in the theoretical literature inspired by Habermas is to either ignore the question or gesture toward social movements as the primary agents pushing for greater deliberation.[49] But, spontaneous civic pressure and widespread social movements simply cannot be taken for granted. Simone Chambers admits that deliberation requires motivated citizens willing to participate and self-regulate: "If citizens do not possess this willingness, then no matter how well designed institutional arrangements are for the purposes of discourse, discourse will not take place."[50] She makes no attempt, however, at showing where and how such motivation will develop under unmotivated conditions. As we have seen, American civic culture is currently underinformed and only minimally engaged. Even strategies at jump-starting deliberation through deliberative polls, town meetings, and the like require the "social capital" in short supply today.[51]

Second, threats to deliberative norms in the contemporary political environment are strong enough to counterbalance and even outweigh existing cultural

48. Chambers, *Reasonable Democracy,* 205.
49. Dryzek, *Deliberative Democracy and Beyond,* 99–103; and Habermas, *Between Facts and Norms,* 373–74.
50. Chambers, *Reasonable Democracy,* 195.
51. Putnam, *Bowling Alone,* 31–64.

support structures for those norms. Economic inequality in America, for example, is high enough for some commentators to call this a new "gilded age" marked by the rise of "plutocracy."[52] This bodes poorly for the promotion of public deliberation free from the coercion of money. In addition, the prevalence of purely symbolic politics, the dominance of advertising techniques in political campaigns, the softening of hard news into infotainment in order to catch viewers and generate advertising revenues are heavy counterweights to public deliberation oriented toward the give-and-take of reasons. At another level, critics such as Lynn Sanders and Iris Marion Young argue that the deliberative model favors the politically powerful because they are more capable of bringing their positions into the forum discursively.[53] Further, democratic deliberation as an ideal neutralizes "the political" by forcing conformity to calm, rational dialogue. People from the margins of society (who may not speak well or calmly) and people who wish to speak up for issues that are not seen immediately as rational may be further marginalized in deliberative democracy.

The third major weakness of Habermasian conceptions of public deliberation is that they are stuck in a conventional consumer-provider pattern of citizen-government relations. Under this paradigm, government is a service provider to which citizens bring their wants, needs, and interests to be satisfied. To their credit, theorists of public deliberation have considerably enriched the role of the citizen in making collective judgments about what government will provide. Yet the idea that public deliberation might lead to public interest satisfaction done by the deliberators themselves is not a core part of the theory thus far. One point students of citizen movements stress is the importance of shifting paradigms to the idea of "public work." There, deliberation is important but leads to decisions to do things, not just deliver opinions and make requests of others.

These three weaknesses are not unique to Habermasian theory; indeed, they are endemic to the deliberative democratic approach in general. What is needed is grounded attention to the resources, spaces, and actors available for motivating and facilitating a form of public deliberation that will have both wide and deep roots in American political culture.

52. Kevin P. Phillips, *Wealth and Democracy: A Political History of the American Rich* (New York: Broadway Books, 2002), 422.

53. See Lynn M. Sanders, "Against Deliberation," *Political Theory* 25, no. 3 (1997): 347–76; Iris Marion Young, "Communication and the Other: Beyond Deliberative Democracy," in *Democracy and Difference,* ed. Seyla Benhabib (Princeton: Princeton University Press, 1996), 120–35.

Democracy as a Way of Life

Shifting Focus Away from Formal Politics and Academic Political Theory

Democracy is composed of all the features of formal politics typically studied by political scientists: parties, elections, voters, laws, policy, offices, and officials. But an important background dimension to American democracy, what John Dewey called "democracy as a way of life," is less typically studied. His view was that the democratic value of procedures and institutions of normal politics, such as elections, depends on social contexts marked by social equality, communication, collaboration, and reflection—just the kinds of norms stressed by deliberative democratic theory. "Democracy" was not the buildings, actors, and institutions of Washington, but it had to be seen as animated by—literally given life by—a "personal way of individual life" manifesting "certain attitudes, forming personal character and determining desire and purpose in all the relations of life." Remarkably, Dewey inverted the conventional perspective of political science: "Instead of thinking of our own dispositions and habits as accommodated to certain institutions we have to learn to think of the latter as expressions, projections, and extensions of habitually dominant personal attitudes."[54]

To be interested in democracy from Dewey's perspective means to be interested in many things beyond constitutions, offices, and elections. All places where the attitudes, character, and desire for public deliberation are developed are relevant to the study of democracy. As we will see in Chapter 4, Dewey himself argued that the ways schools and workplaces were organized were integral to an active and reflective citizenship in normal politics.

The multiple public spheres approach follows Dewey in valuing this domain, as do contemporary theorists Gutmann and Thompson when they write about the importance of what they call "middle democracy":

> The forums of middle democracy embrace virtually any setting in which citizens come together on a regular basis to reach collective decisions about public issues—governmental as well as nongovernmental institutions. They include not only legislative sessions, court proceedings, and administrative hearings at all levels of government

---

54. Dewey, "Creative Democracy—The Task Before Us" (1939), reprinted in *John Dewey: The Later Works, 1925–1953,* ed. Jo Ann Boydston (Carbondale: Southern Illinois University Press, 1981–90), 14:226.

but also meetings of grass roots organizations, professional associations, shareholders meetings, and citizens' committees in hospitals and other similar institutions.[55]

Middle democracy is important for a simple reason stressed long ago by Thomas Jefferson and Anti-Federalist writers in the late eighteenth century: it is the only place where most citizens will ever take part in actually steering public life. Jefferson's republican principle, "to introduce the people into every department of government as far as they are capable of exercising it," aimed to ensure accountability on both sides: officials would serve public interests more consistently if citizens were present and paying attention, and citizens with a stake in public life would make more reasonable demands on government and on fellow citizens.[56] In middle democracy, citizens can develop skills and resources as watchdogs over their democracy, to serve as "sentinels and guardians of each other," in the words of Anti-Federalist Richard Henry Lee.[57]

Methodologically, attention to democracy as a way of life means that some traditionally nonpolitical institutions, practices, and agents take on a prominence they would not usually have and that the discourse of practitioners becomes as important as the discourse of theorists of democracy. A good example of both of these methodological points is Jane Mansbridge's work in *Beyond Adversary Democracy*. She develops a conception of unitary democracy she finds in ground-level political practice but that is largely missing from political science treatments of American democracy. The unitary ideal holds that under conditions of similar interests, citizens can productively make collective decisions by consensus. Decisions are made not by weighing votes but "in the give-and-take of discussion in a face-to-face setting." Now, since the unitary ideal could quite easily be taken as a fiction of political theory, Mansbridge conducted two case analyses to establish and hone her argument—one of town meeting government in Vermont, the other of a participatory workplace she called "Helpline." These case analyses, richly informed by interviews and participant observations, established that her unitary ideal was not just a utopian theoretical construct. The cases she

55. Gutmann and Thompson, *Democracy and Disagreement*, 12–13.
56. Thomas Jefferson, letter to the Abbé Arnoux, Paris, July 1789, in *Papers of Thomas Jefferson*, ed. J. P. Boyd et al., vol. 15 (Princeton: Princeton University Press, 1958), 282.
57. Richard Henry Lee, "Letters from the Federal Farmer," in *The Anti-Federalist: Writings by the Opponents of the Constitution*, ed. Herbert J. Storing and Murray Dry (Chicago: University of Chicago Press, 1985), 59.

studied also raised unexpected issues, through an exploration of which Mansbridge deepened her understanding of the unitary form of collective decision making.

Substantively, approaching democracy as a way of life broadens our focus to include attention to the everyday public work of democratic polities. Writing about Dewey's conception of the public sphere, Axel Honneth notes that Dewey did not see it as merely a platform for discussion and debate, but as a "cooperative enterprise" that in effect makes and remakes both public and citizen.[58] Harry Boyte and Nancy Kari explain the concept of public work in more detail:

> "Public work" is work by ordinary people that builds and sustains our basic public goods and resources. . . . It solves common problems and creates common things. It may be paid or voluntary. It may be done in communities. It may be done as part of one's regular job.
>
> In the fullest sense of the term, public work takes place not only with an eye to public consequences, it also is work "in public"—work that is visible, open to inspection, whose significance is widely recognized. And it is cooperative civic work of "a public": a mix of people whose interests, backgrounds, and resources may be quite different.[59]

Boyte and Kari contrast public work with the merely deliberative politics of contemporary democratic theory in which the citizen is seen as a deliberator rather than a producer. It is useful, as they recognize, to join these two sets of ideas for an adequate account of democracy in theory and practice.

Public work adds a number of dimensions to the ideal of public deliberation. First, such deliberation should be seen as potentially present in everyday settings, not just in "government or elections or mobilization campaigns."[60] So the workplace, the hospital, the school, and other common places are all appropriate focal points for establishing deliberative norms. Second, deliberation in the context of public work raises the expectation that citizens do more than take part in public intellectual life, giving and taking ideas, but also act as "co-creators"

---

58. Axel Honneth, "Democracy as Reflexive Cooperation: John Dewey and the Theory of Democracy Today," *Political Theory* 26, no. 6 (1998): 777–79.

59. Harry Boyte and Nancy Kari, *Building America: The Democratic Promise of Public Work* (Philadelphia: Temple University Press, 1996), 16.

60. Harry Boyte, *Everyday Politics: Reconnecting Citizens and Public Life* (Philadelphia: University of Pennsylvania Press, 2004), 4.

of a public world outside the forum of public discussion. Third, and most important, public work helps citizens become part of a public sphere. People working together on common projects may very well fail to transcend their differences and form the *sensus communis* idealized by some political theorists, of course, but they will figure out how to bridge differences and will likely develop civic skills and attitudes that will further public work projects over time. Boyte rightly stresses that democratic citizenship is more than making decisions, even the best-informed and deliberative decisions, but must include making a public life together.

Professionals versus the Three Weaknesses

This book began in a moment of frustration and exhilaration seven years ago. I was fortunate to have a postdoctoral research fellowship that provided time and support to begin a new project on public deliberation. I was frustrated, however, with the abstraction of theoretical writing on the topic and its distance from the obstreperous conditions of contemporary civic life. During this period, I slowly became aware of attempts at incorporating public deliberation into everyday work practice—in the middle democracy that was all around me but rarely appeared in academic political theory. Here were motivated actors critical for the application of deliberative norms.

The appeal of deliberative norms to reform-minded city planners, policy analysts, criminal justice administrators, journalists, and other people I came to call "democratic professionals" provides part of an answer to the questions either avoided or insufficiently answered by theorists: who will spark public deliberation, where will it take place, how will the strong counterdeliberative forces in American political life be kept at bay?[61] The work of democratic professionals who seek to encourage more lay participation in their realms suggests ways of resolving the three weaknesses of even the best theories of public deliberation.

This book is about how professionals and professional domains can play and are playing a critical role in fostering public deliberation. Professionals have much

---

61. The term "democratic professional" was used by Bruce Jennings in his "Public Administration: In Search of Democratic Professionalism," in "The Public Duties of the Professions," special supplement, *Hastings Center Report* 17, no. 1 (1987): 18–20. William Sullivan, in *Work and Integrity: The Crisis and Promise of Professionalism in America* (New York: HarperCollins, 1995) and elsewhere, uses the term "civic professional." My conception of democratic professionalism owes much to the work of Jennings and Sullivan, though the features of task sharing and lay participation that I stress are either not present or not emphasized in their work.

to contribute to the two prongs of public deliberation: deliberation and participation. As people with specialized experience and knowledge, professionals can serve as information providers. More important, professionals can exemplify how to follow the substantive norms of rational debate. Even more important, professionals jealous of the integrity of decisions made in their domains will be motivated to prevent nondeliberative forces from pressing their influence.

My research into democratic professionalism has uncovered a large reservoir of commitment among many professionals to the project of promoting citizen participation and deliberation. As we will see in the following chapters, lay participation is recognized by many to be essential to doing a good job—to maintaining the good image of a profession and other seemingly self-interested features of professional life. This is not to say that democratic professionalism is an ideal or a set of values that always aligns with self-interest; it is only to register that it does not depend on the neglect of self-interest.

While democratic professionalism entails a new way of conceiving professionalism, it in no way means replacing professionalism with political activism. Throughout the book, I follow Dewey in using "democratic" as meaning forms of decision making and interaction marked by social equality, communication, collaboration, and reflection. As we will see, being more democratic in this sense does create tensions with established occupational and organizational patterns, self-images, and expectations. Nonetheless, I will argue that professional authority untethered to these democratic norms is deeply problematic for citizen, professional, and profession alike. Being democratic, as a professional, then means being explicit about the connections between these norms and professional practice and being creative about making them more manifest in those organizations and institutions in which professionals have influence—what I call "professional domains." It does not require dropping traditional occupational activities or standards in favor of a kind of political activism in formal politics.

To focus on the role of professionals in democracy is not to conceive public deliberation as a professional sport. Indeed, the theory of democratic professionalism developed in the chapters that follow holds that one way professionals can contribute to public deliberation is by refusing to dominate discussion—by stepping back and allowing laypeople the chance to take up responsibilities. Professionals can lead and facilitate public deliberation in a way that shares power and responsibility with laypeople.

2

BEYOND SELF-INTEREST:
THE APOLITICAL PICTURE OF PROFESSIONALS

[T]he meaning of their profession, both for themselves and for the public, is not that they make money but that they make health, or safety, or knowledge, or good government or good law.

—R. H. TAWNEY, *Acquisitive Society* (1920)

Defining Professions Apolitically

What about professions, professional organizations, institutions in which professionals work, and professionals themselves may make them receptive to a role as facilitators of public deliberation? What about professional authority makes such a role inevitable? In this and the next two chapters I begin to develop answers to these questions through the work of theorists who have made significant contributions to the understanding of professionals' social responsibilities and the relationship between professional work and the public culture of democracy. This theoretical work, which spans a number of disciplines, can be grouped into three broad perspectives, or what I call "models" of professionalism. The social trustee, radical critique, and democratic professional models engaged in Chapter 2, 3, and 4, respectively, are both descriptive and normative—not only do they pick out features of professional practice, organization, and self-understanding that capture what it means to be a professional, these models also seek to promote some actions, organizational patterns, and identities over others.

The democratic professional model is the least defined and currently least understood. It is a response to the inadequacies of the other two, but it also builds on some of the core features of the others. With an eye on this reconstructive goal, then, in this and the next chapter I attend to the strengths and weaknesses of two more common models of professionalism that describe and promote features of professional life that have relevance for the public culture of democracy.

This chapter begins with basic questions: how and why are professions such as law, medicine, and education, among others, different from other occupations? These questions have not typically been approached as having politically relevant answers. Indeed, if you study professions you are probably a sociologist or philosopher. How this came to be is a topic in metasociology of the professions, but the results of this scholarly division of labor have real relevance. One chief reason professions and professionals have not been seen as democratic agents is because they have been approached as fundamentally apolitical. From the political scientist's, the sociologist's, and the philosopher's points of view, professions are seen as raising questions of work and occupation, social status, industrial organization, fiduciary trust, client privacy, and other such small-bore issues of ethical practice—certainly not things for political scientists, whose sinewy hands are grease black and toughened on the machinery of government.

This is not to say that sociology and philosophy have been uncritical about professions or that there is nothing to glean from these disciplines about the possibilities and limits of a more political understanding of professions. Far from it. This chapter examines central works in the social theory of the professions to gain insight into professional action and motivation. It also shows how an apolitical conception of the professional emerged from a sociological focus on the profession as a moralizing and functional entity and the professional as a social trustee. This social trustee model of professionalism continues to affect the more critical views of contemporary sociologists and undergirds the subdiscipline of philosophy devoted to applied professional ethics. Features of the social trustee model explain why professions are not commonly seen as democratic agents relevant to the promotion of public deliberation, yet other features point to modes of professional organization, aspects of professional identity, relationships among professions, society, and the state that are indeed relevant for a democratic model of professionalism that could support such agency.

Sociologists have never agreed on a specific definition of what it is to be a profession, in part because professions are rooted in cultures and historical periods in which the structural position and central characteristics of professions vary.[1]

---

1. Eliot Freidson, *Professional Powers: A Study of the Institutionalization of Formal Knowledge* (Chicago: University of Chicago Press, 1986), 32.

Empirically, professional practices in 1950s Chicago have a different relation to higher education, the state, and clients compared with professionals in the same field in 1890s Paris. In its more evaluative moments too, the sociology of professions over the last century has moved from seeing professionalism as a functional social morality to worrying that it is a self-serving ideology. Nevertheless, it is useful to begin with the three central components of traditional sociological definitions: knowledge, self-regulation, and social responsibility.

First, professions are linked to a body of "generalized and systematic knowledge" usually through some sort of "formal technical training."[2] This knowledge—and the ability to apply it skillfully—sets professionals apart from laypeople. "Professionals *profess*," writes Everett Hughes. "They profess to know better than others the nature of certain matters, and to know better than their clients what ails them or their affairs."[3] The professional's commitment to knowledge is neither purely intellectual nor purely technical, as Talcott Parsons affirms when he refers to the "primacy to the valuation of cognitive rationality as applied to a particular field" among professions.[4]

A second characteristic of a profession is a high level of self-regulation relative to other occupations. Clearly, if a doctor knows better than a patient what possible therapies would work, then the patient is not in a position to judge the doctor's performance. A defendant who is not an attorney is unlikely to be able to judge the skillfulness of her counsel's defense. Other members of the profession are more appropriate judges of whether the services were deficient. "The client is not a true judge of the value of the service he receives," asserts Hughes. "Only the professional can say when his colleague makes a mistake."[5] Self-regulation can also be seen in the ways professional organizations determine what counts as professional training by certifying academic programs. Self-regulation is perhaps most noticeable in the licensing necessary for some professions, such as medicine and law, to practice. A license can make the difference between an incision and a stab wound, a surgery and a felony. Licensing is the paragon of self-regulation: it excludes laypeople from performing certain tasks or roles and gives fellow professionals pride of place as gatekeepers.

---

2. Bernard Barber, "Some Problems in the Sociology of Professions," *Daedalus* 92 (1963): 672; and Talcott Parsons, "Professions," in *International Encyclopedia of the Social Sciences,* vol. 12 (New York: Macmillan, 1968), 536.

3. Everett C. Hughes, "Professions," *Daedalus* 92 (1963): 656.

4. Parsons, "Professions," 536.

5. Hughes, "Professions," 656–57.

The third traditional sociological characteristic of professions is social responsibility. Frequently, this is expressed as a contrast to nonprofessional occupations that merely exchange goods or services for fees and have as their main purpose the satisfaction of customer preferences and profit. Professions, by contrast, transcend self-interested economic rationality to some extent and hold a "primary orientation to the community interest rather than to individual self-interest."[6] To be a full-fledged profession, writes Parsons, an occupation is to have "some institutional means of making sure that [its] competence will be put to socially responsible uses."[7] This feature follows logically from the first two aspects of professionalism. The larger society can rightly expect that the influential knowledge and skills of professionals serve social purposes, especially since professions are granted significant leeway in regulating their own conduct. Social responsibility does not mean, however, that professionals strictly follow conventional morality. Indeed, sometimes deviance from conventional morality is expected in professions: "A person, in his professional capacity, may be expected and required to think objectively about matters which he himself would find it painful to approach in that way when they affected him personally," Hughes points out. "A professional has a license to deviate from lay conduct in action and in very mode of thought with respect to the matter which he professes; it is an institutionalized deviation."[8]

The way this third characteristic of traditional definitions has been interpreted by the mainstream social trustee model explains why professions appear apolitical and therefore the proper subjects of disciplines other than political science. Professions are not part of the state, nor can professionals be said to govern nonprofessionals, even within professional domains. Under the social trustee model, professions are part of civil society, broadly understood, and they serve functional social purposes. Yet though apolitical, normatively speaking, the social responsibility orientation captures a motivational element that is highly relevant to democracy and civic engagement. Many people want jobs that are more than a mere paycheck, work they can identify with because it serves goods other than consumer preferences. "An authentic profession," writes William Sullivan,

6. Barber, "Some Problems in the Sociology of Professions," 672.
7. Parsons, "Professions," 536.
8. Hughes, "Professions," 656. A wonderful fictional example of professional deviance is the television series *House*, in which a disheveled, pain pill–popping physician brilliantly diagnoses seemingly untreatable cases while breaking hospital rules and thumbing his nose at social etiquette. His unconventionality is justified by his single-minded devotion to discovering what is ailing his patients.

"is the kind of thing one can build a life around."[9] For such people, being a professional means having a distinct social status, but it also means having a purpose, a niche, a chance to do some good for others.

Though problematic in ways to be explored in Chapter 3 below, such other-orientation and social mindedness are directly relevant to the promotion of public deliberation. Just how social responsibility is given shape, how social functions and purposes are understood, and how these orientations are incorporated into professional identity are key questions proponents of social trustee professionalism must address.

Social Trustee Professionalism

The sociological interest in the professions that emerged in the late nineteenth century was sparked by the thought that industrial development and market relations had led to dangerous levels of individualism and self-interested economic rationality, as well as to the erosion of moral attachments to society. For Emile Durkheim in France, R. H. Tawney in Britain, and others, professions stood out as a countertrend that could ameliorate and check such tendencies. As Bernard Barber notes, "The professions, by setting a pattern of more direct concern with the community interest, seemed to represent quite a different principle." "In consequence," continues Barber, "those who had the moral welfare of modern society much at heart often recommended the enlargement of the professions and the professionalization of business."[10] Professions such as the classical trinity of the clergy, law, and medicine socialized their practitioners into vocations that respected and honored intellectual achievement, skill, and concern for a larger community. In this way, ambition and talent could be guided toward socially useful tasks and away from self-interested economic rationality. As somewhat self-regulated communities of practitioners built up, in Barber's words, "a high degree of generalized and systematic knowledge," and the practical capabilities to put them to use for clients, the professions could be seen by early sociologists as bulwarks protecting critical social interests in justice, health, and education, among others, from being colonized by market forces. Professions

---

9. William Sullivan, *Work and Integrity: The Crisis and Promise of Professionalism in America* (New York: HarperCollins, 1995), 6.

10. Barber, "Some Problems in the Sociology of Professions," 670.

were social trustees—guardians and servants of those public interests within their ken.

The work of Durkheim and Tawney shaped the social trustee model that would dominate scholarly and practitioner understandings of professions from early in the twentieth century until well into the 1960s. This model emphasizes the moral particularism of professions: the differences between each other and compared to other occupations, and the different operating principles they follow compared to those dominant in the state and in the marketplace. Second, this model links these differences to the functions or social purposes professions serve. Though clearly traditionalist in spirit since this model wishes to retain values under threat from forces of commercialization, social trusteeism also husbands forms of rationality and hones skills that can have profoundly progressive effects.

Moral Particularism and Social Responsibility Among Modern-Day Guilds

Emile Durkheim's complex proto-social trustee analysis points to both macro and micro aspects of professions as socializing, or "moralizing," agents and is unabashedly prescriptive in its recommendation of reforms to professions and of professions as vehicles of large-scale social and political reform.[11] Durkheim thought modern industrialized social orders lacked adequate means for orienting individuals toward group life: "[S]ociety, weak and disturbed, lets too many persons escape too completely from its influence." The modern individual needed to "feel himself more solidary with a collective existence which precedes him in time, which survives him, and which encompasses him at all points."[12] Yet the premodern modes of accomplishing this solidarity—family, religion, or state—could no longer be counted on to reliably perform this task. The family loses its grip on the individual for forty or more hours a week, modern religion has lost considerable power over the individual in light of increased secularism and freedom of choice, and the state is "too remote from individuals, its connections

11. Durkheim's treatment of professionalism is concentrated in three closely overlapping works: (1) lectures given at Bordeaux between 1890 and 1900, translated into English by Cornelia Brookfield and published as *Professional Ethics and Civic Morals* (New York: Routledge, 1957); (2) "Practical Consequences," chapter 3 of *Suicide: A Study in Sociology,* published in French in 1897 and translated into English by John A. Spaulding and George Simpson in 1951 (Glencoe, Ill.: The Free Press); and (3) the preface to the second edition of *The Division of Labor in Society,* published in French in 1903 and translated into English by W. D. Halls in 1984 (New York: The Free Press).

12. Durkheim, *Suicide,* 373–74.

with them too superficial and irregular, to be able to penetrate the depths of their consciousness and socialize them from within."[13]

Though he sees them as inculcating general morality, Durkheim is keenly aware of the moral particularism of professional morality. "As professors, we have duties which are not those of merchants. Those of the industrialist are quite different from those of the soldier from those of the priest. . . . [T]here are as many forms of morals as there are different callings." This particularism, seemingly in tension with the demands of general morality, is a natural expression that professional ethics "govern functions not performed by everyone, that not everyone is able to have a sense of what these functions are, of what they ought to be, or of what special relations should exist between the individuals concerned with applying them."[14] Professions moralize and orient their members toward social ends, but those ends vary according to professions. Doctors serve the health and well-being needs of society, while lawyers serve justice needs. Both professions moralize their members toward social purposes, but their internal ethical codes and their approaches to resolving characteristic professional dilemmas will be quite different.

Durkheim saw professionalism as the development of occupational autonomy and solidarity that could provide normative orientation to economic and political life. He was particularly worried about the normlessness of economic competition in business: "[T]his amoral character of economic life amounts to a public danger. . . . If we follow no rule except that of a clear self-interest, in the occupations that take up nearly the whole of our time, how should we acquire the taste for any disinterestedness, or selflessness or sacrifice?"[15] He thought it preferable to correct self-interested individualism in business life by encouraging professionalism rather than through external state regulation, however. Because of the increasing specialization of economic activity, Durkheim felt the state was incapable of providing effective regulatory authority. Only those "close enough to that profession to be thoroughly cognizant of how it functions, capable of perceiving all its needs and following every fluctuation in them," namely, the "professional group" itself, would have the skill and knowledge necessary for effective regulation in a given domain.[16] Further, the bounded cooperative relations within flourishing professional groups lead spontaneously to a kind of

13. Durkheim, *Division of Labor*, liv.
14. Durkheim, *Professional Ethics*, 5, 6.
15. Durkheim, *Professional Ethics*, 12.
16. Durkheim, *Division of Labor*, xxxv.

moral socialization—or moralization—of individual members that Durkheim believed to be a more effective source of constraint than external regulation.

Flourishing professional groups have a "moral force" that restrains self-interested activity and nurtures feelings of internal, group solidarity and external, social solidarity.[17] This moralizing function is not an explicit goal of professions; it is not formulated in the informal or formal rules of professional organization. Professions have moral force simply because they are sites of collective activity marked by frequent interaction, shared interests, sentiments, affinities, and co-operative arrangements:

> [O]nce such a group is formed, a moral life evolves within it. . . . It is impossible for men to live together and be in regular contact with one another without their acquiring some feeling for the group which they constitute through having united together, without their becoming attached to it, concerning themselves with its interests and taking it into account in their behaviour. And this attachment to something that transcends the individual, this subordination of the particular to the general interest, is the very well-spring of all moral activity.[18]

> What we particularly see in the professional grouping is a moral force capable of curbing individual egoism, nurturing among workers a more invigorated feeling of their common solidarity, and preventing the law of the strongest from being applied too brutally in industrial and commercial relationships.[19]

The moral force of professional life is particularistic—stemming from subgroups in society and closely related to the specific tasks, problems, and experiences of these groups—and indeed this is why flourishing professional groups can be expected to self-regulate. Yet this particularistic moral life is an expression of the general moral life of well-integrated societies: "A group is not only a moral authority regulating the life of its members, but also a source of life *sui generis*. From it there arises a warmth that quickens or give fresh life to each individual, which makes him disposed to empathize, causing selfishness to melt away."[20]

17. Durkheim, *Division of Labor*, xxxix.
18. Durkheim, *Division of Labor*, xliii; see also Durkheim, *Professional Ethics*, 23–24.
19. Durkheim, *Division of Labor*, xxxix.
20. Durkheim, *Division of Labor*, liii; see also Durkheim, *Professional Ethics*, 25.

As group members begin to support one another, they also develop broader sympathies and responsibilities.

The subgroup morality of professions ripples outward since members carry into their relations with nonmembers the self-discipline and other-orientation developed within their group life. Durkheim thought that besides this informal linkage between profession and polity, more formal organization was possible and necessary to combat individualism. Drawing on an updated version of the medieval guild, in the political system he advocated a corporatist scheme in which occupational groups would be the primary representative units for voters. Members elect administrative councils to handle professional issues internally as well as nominate political representatives to further professional interests in government. Professions are sites of close reflection on the occupational and other interests of members and can filter internal deliberations prior to their release to general political debate and decision.[21] But, once again, we must not see these political functions of professions in an overly cognitive way. Durkheim thought professions allowed individuals to *feel* connected to the larger collective purposes of society, something the state in its size and complexity could not offer. "A nation cannot be maintained," writes Durkheim, without a range of "secondary groups" interposed between the state and the individual. "These must be close enough to the individual to attract him strongly to their activities and, in so doing, to absorb him into the mainstream of social life."[22] For Durkheim, professions were particularly well-suited for this critical intermediary role. Economic and political interests are served by membership in such groups, but also served are the needs of individuals to find larger meaning and significance in their work lives.

Durkheim helps us see generally how bounded and interactive occupational groups can be the source of moralized—other-oriented—work lives; as such, they can help spontaneously integrate and coordinate the activities of the occupation in the larger society, serving as a node of communication bringing reflective social sentiments into professional practice and extending reflective opinions of members out into social and political discourse. He does not clearly specify, however, just how work life becomes moralized by professional organizations, thus raising questions about how easily translatable subgroup morality is to social morality.

---

21. Durkheim, *Division of Labor*, liii–lvii; Durkheim, *Professional Ethics*, 36–41.
22. Durkheim, *Division of Labor*, liv; see also Durkheim, *Suicide*, 379.

Durkheim glosses over the problem that group morality may conflict with social or individual morality because he assumes a seamless connection between spheres of morality. Roman guilds, on which Durkheim drew as models of professional organization, were like families that protected their members and inculcated a sense of mutual aid and collective responsibility.[23] This small-scale development of collective responsibility for the identifiable lives of one's occupation ideally ramifies outward to foster large-scale collective responsibility for the statistical lives of society at large. Yet Durkheim ignores the possibility that occupational morality can develop in such a way as to exclude concern for the others outside as professions become merely self-protective interest groups. Durkheim's theoretical leaning toward a naturalistic functionalism may have led him to see fundamental conflicts of interest between members of groups and non-members, and unjust social relations more generally, as abnormal mutations in the division of labor.[24]

Much depends on the permeability of the particularistic moral life of occupations to the reflective sentiments of the particularistic moral lives of other occupations—an issue Durkheim neglects. Durkheim does argue that the moral particularism of groups broadens through communication: "[E]ach particular group is less inclined to see and pursue only its own interest, once it is in regular relationship with the directive center of public life. Only on this condition, indeed, could awareness of the public welfare be kept constantly alert in the individual consciousness."[25] Yet he does not develop this idea much further than these comments. To be fair, Durkheim frequently notes that he is idealizing the possible role of professions.[26] At these moments, he points to the steps current occupational organizations need to take to be suitable bulwarks against individualism, in particular to the development of sanctions—both internal to the profession and juridical—that could regulate individual behavior.[27] Yet his most general suggestion is for occupational groups to become more organized, to become more guild-like—a solution that would seem to exacerbate the problem of how to deal with others not like one's own group members.

I call Durkheim's thinking about the social responsibilities of professions "proto-social trusteeship" because, even though it is quite idealized, Durkheim's

23. Durkheim, *Professional Ethics,* 20–22; Durkheim, *Division of Labor,* xxxix–xliii.

24. Carmen J. Sirianni, "Justice and the Division of Labour: A Reconsideration of Durkheim's Division of Labour in Society," *The Sociological Review* 32 (1984): 449–70.

25. Durkheim, *Suicide,* 382.

26. Durkheim, *Suicide,* 379.

27. Durkheim, *Suicide,* 10.

corporatist account of professions as organized representatives of their members' social, political, and economic interests is considerably more political than the social trustee accounts that would follow in later sociological schools. Further, Durkheim is clearly interested in how the microethics of professional life can resolve macroethical problems in the larger society, such as the general social problem of self-interested economic behavior or the particular social problem of suicide. Yet professions would accomplish this primarily through the moralization of members, not through any political activity of corporatist units. The latter were merely ways of representing members' concerns. The primary normative roles of professions, for Durkheim, were not political. They were, first, to socialize the individual generally by connecting him to that "collective existence which precedes him in time, which survives him, and which encompasses him at all points" and, second, to socialize the individual into the particular professional responsibilities that adhered to the specific roles, tasks, and powers of that occupation. Though Durkheim's thought is complex and indeed political, this apolitical understanding of the profession's normative orientation would be more dominant in later sociological treatments.

Serving Social Purposes: Professions as Functional Role Models

Like Durkheim, R. H. Tawney, writing in 1920, held professions as role models for industrial occupations more generally. While Durkheim indicated social interaction, communication, and habits of group life as the forces orienting members of a profession toward specific professional responsibilities as well as general social norms, Tawney, by contrast, emphasizes the way functional specificity moralizes professionals. Professions, for Tawney, are occupations organized to fulfill specific social purposes, and they orient their individual members toward and help them identify with these purposes. Because the professions were already functional in this way, they could be patterned by occupations and workers not currently committed to serving functional social purposes.

For Tawney, "function," is a term already laden with evaluation. "A function," writes Tawney, "may be defined as an activity which embodies and expresses the idea of social purpose. The essence of it is that the agent does not perform it merely for personal gain or to gratify himself, but recognizes that he is responsible for its discharge to some higher authority." Though the function of industry was obvious to him—"to supply man with things which are necessary, useful or beautiful, and thus to bring life to body or spirit"—it was equally obvious that this function was not recognized in modern business practices or by dominant cultural and theoretical assumptions about economic and political practice, which "replaced the conception of purpose by that of mechanism." The dominant liberalism of Locke, Smith, and Bentham placed strong rights to property and a commitment to economic freedom at the "unquestioned center of social organization" and was blind to the idea of central social purposes performed by individuals held responsible to them by commitments to higher authority.[28]

The triumph of liberalism politically and economically had led to a contemporary social order Tawney dubbed the "acquisitive society." Rather than viewing property holding and industrial management as "functions to be judged by the success with which they contribute to a social purpose," in modern times they are "regarded as rights which stand by their own virtue."[29] Economic rights are protected while economic functions are left to "fulfill themselves." In the acquisitive society, the guiding social purpose, if it can be called such, is wealth accumulation.[30] Liberalism's triumph, however, is a Pyrrhic victory because, ultimately, what gives meaning to economic activity is its social purpose. Yet the acquisitive society has divorced purpose from activity, viewing wealth as an end in itself, not as a means to accomplishing greater purpose. Like Durkheim, Tawney recognizes this cultural development as a loosening of "moral restraints," as a disorganization and diffusion of authority that has led to "malaise."[31]

How better to redirect industrial occupations away from "unrestricted pursuit . . . of their pecuniary self-interest, within such limits as the law allows" than to suggest the model of the established professions, for which narrowly self-interested economic rationality would count as "unprofessional conduct"?[32] With Tawney, professionalism becomes a thoroughly normative ideal, as when he defines "profession" as a trade organized to perform socially useful functions, a "body of men who carry on their work in accordance with rules designed to

28. R. H. Tawney, *The Acquisitive Society* (New York: Harcourt, Brace and World, 1920), 8.

29. Tawney, *The Acquisitive Society*, 24–25.

30. Tawney, *The Acquisitive Society*, 29.

31. Tawney, *The Acquisitive Society*, 33. Thomas Haskell notes that Tawney and Durkheim, along with other like-minded intellectuals in the period 1850–1930, shared "a deep-felt revulsion against certain libertarian excesses that they thought were inherent in the culture of capitalism." They saw their "public role not in terms of release and liberation, but in terms of control and the maintenance of institutional constraints on individual choice and action." Thomas Haskell, "Professionalism versus Capitalism: R. H. Tawney, Emile Durkheim, and C. S. Peirce on the Disinterestedness of Professional Communities," in *The Authority of Experts: Studies in History and Theory*, ed. Haskell (Bloomington: Indiana University Press, 1984), 184.

32. Tawney, *The Acquisitive Society*, 93.

enforce certain standards both for the better protection of its members and for the better service of the public."[33] Whether formalized in codes of ethics or left as informal norms and expectations, this ideal of "professional honor" as part of an authentic profession is a central part of social trustee theorizing.[34] Thomas Haskell notes that for Tawney and his contemporaries sharing a similar intellectual bent, professions are "special communities that deliberately intensify competition among insiders in non-pecuniary dimensions of achievement, such as glory and reputation." Professionals "compete not for money, but for the affective currency of criticism: fame instead of disgrace; honor in place of shame; compliments, not complaints, about the technical worth of one's work." The goal is not the accumulation of wealth, but the establishment and maintenance of a good reputation—"a stock of favorable impressions of himself and his work in the minds of his peers."[35]

Also important for the development of the social trustee model is Tawney's crystallization of the idea, seen already in the moral particularism of Durkheim but less rigidly expressed by him, that professions serve particular social functions that need to be sheltered from market forces—functions that would not be adequately performed simply by economic incentives or by the natural course of self-interested economic activity. "[T]he meaning of their profession, both for themselves and for the public, is not that they make money but that they make health, or safety, or knowledge, or good government or good law." Regardless of the money offered them, certain kinds of behavior would violate their professional identity: judges may not sell their decisions, and scholars and teachers may not deceive the public even if the public wishes to be deceived. "[T]he service comes first, and their private inclinations, even the reasonable preference of life to death [in the case of the professional soldier], second."[36] Commitment to their specific social function is the driving force of professional identity, both as organizations and as individuals.

Social Trustee Professionalism in Full Bloom:
The Exchange of Responsibility for Status and Privileges

A close reader of Durkheim and a graduate student of Tawney's at the London School of Economics shortly after the publication of Tawney's *The Acquisitive*

33. Tawney, *The Acquisitive Society,* 92.
34. Tawney, *The Acquisitive Society,* 126.
35. Haskell, "Professionalism versus Capitalism," 216.
36. Tawney, *The Acquisitive Society,* 94–95.

Society, Talcott Parsons held a similar esteem for the role of professions in modern life. The major social theorist of his era and a father of contemporary sociology of the professions, Parsons made significant contributions and modifications to the social trustee model. Calling the "development and increasing strategic importance of the professions" the "most important change" in modern occupational organization, Parsons codifies but also corrects, extends, and complicates the arguments of his predecessors. Though, like them, Parsons recognizes that the commitment to social rather than self-interest marks the professions as worthy of special study and emulation, he corrects the simplistic assumptions that the managers and employees of business firms and other industrial occupations are merely motivated by self-interested ends. The differences between professions and business occupations are important, but they have to do with institutional alignments that favor social responsibility, not microlevel individual altruistic motivations. For Parsons, professions express "pattern variables" commonly found in American society, though perhaps in a more extensive or complete way than other occupations. Second, Parsons characterizes the privileges and "freedoms" of professions as a functional exchange for which society receives, in return, the technical competence it needs to achieve critical ends. Third, Parsons places the university at the center of the "professional complex" as a source of technical training and knowledge, as well as a channel through which cultural values can be communicated to individuals who will take up important social roles. By adding these dimensions to the analysis of professional social responsibility, Parsons has both made social trustee professionalism a more theoretically and empirically sophisticated model and has opened the door to and invited later sociological critiques.

Professions and professionals share the same normative orientations as many other actors in modern American society. Parsons would come to call these orientations "pattern variables" in his later work, but they initially emerged in his comparison between professionals and businesspeople. Though a staple of social criticism and even economic theorizing, the idea that businesspeople are self-interested actors misses how social this behavior actually is. Parsons points to "institutions," "institutional patterns," that are "a principal aspect of what is . . . the social structure" and these "normative patterns . . . define what are felt to be, in the given society, proper, legitimate, or expected modes of action or of social relationship."[37] These macro- and microlevel patterns define social action in modern Western countries.

37. Talcott Parsons, "The Motivation of Economic Activities," in *Essays in Sociological Theory: Pure and Applied* (Glencoe, Ill.: The Free Press, 1949), 203.

Just like professions, the business world is oriented toward rationality, specificity of function, and universalism. Rationality means, for Parsons, the loosening of the grip of traditional authority over action, while traditionalism is at the opposite pole. Paradigmatically, rationality means following standards of scientific investigation, which is what professions such as medicine do. But businesspeople are also rational in this sense since they frequently violate traditional norms in favor of norms of efficiency that lead to more profit—as Marx brilliantly captured in his claim that under capitalism "[a]ll fixed, fast frozen relations . . . are swept away. . . . All that is solid melts into air, all that is holy is profaned."[38]

Specificity of function is Parsons's term for the authority given to an occupation and the social relationships related to it that are based on the tasks it performs. Doctors have a good deal of functionally specific authority to prescribe medical treatments. This authority does not extend to domains where the technical competence of doctors is irrelevant, such as city planning. At the other end of this pattern is functionally diffuse authority, such as the authority one's brother or spouse has, which does not arise out of the specific tasks they perform, but out of kinship and affective ties. But here, too, the business world is marked by functionally specific not diffuse authority and relationships. Though it has to do with bureaucratic organization and hierarchy rather than technical competence, administrative offices in business firms have functionally specific authority. And contractual relationships between two or more business entities are functionally specific; unlike kinship ties that obligate family members diffusely— namely, whenever someone is in need—contractual ties obligate each party to only that specified in the contract.

Universalism, contrasted with particularism, means that decisions are made on the basis of reasons that are abstracted from all those characteristics of the person or situation that have nothing to do with the technical task at hand. Medical specialists trying to decide whether to add patients to their practice will consider only whether their conditions make them a good candidate for their expertise: "Whose son, husband, friend he is, is in this context irrelevant." Universalism is also prominent in contractual relationships, however, and in the

---

38. Talcott Parsons, "The Professions and Social Structure," in *Essays in Sociological Theory*, 188; and Karl Marx, *The Communist Manifesto* (New York: Penguin, 1967), 83. Note, too, the prescient comments: "The bourgeoisie has stripped of its halo every occupation hitherto honoured and looked up to with reverent awe. It has converted the physician, the lawyer, the priest, the poet, the man of science, into its paid wage-labourers" (Marx, *Manifesto*, 82).

operations of administrative offices in business firms: "Where technical competence, the technical impartiality of administration of an office, and the like are of primary functional importance, it is essential that particularistic considerations should not enter into the bases of judgment too much."[39]

What marks the professions as distinct is disinterestedness, or what Parsons later calls "collectivity-orientation." This is not to say that individual doctors or lawyers lack self-interested motivations or that they are altruistic; their institutional structures are oriented toward the fulfillment of collective purposes, and, therefore, certain forms of individual self-interested behavior are discouraged while collective-oriented behavior is rewarded. Professions organize and channel the self-regarding interests in the service of social ends. "The institutional patterns governing the two fields of action are radically different in this respect," writes Parsons, and "it can be shown conclusively that this difference has very important functional bases." "[M]any of our most important social functions . . . , notably the pursuit of science and liberal learning and its practical applications in medicine, technology, law, and teaching" are performed within professionalized institutions. The "maintenance" of the professional structure depends on more than the belief "in the importance of the functions themselves" and owes much to "a complex balance of diverse social forces" that reinforce the pattern variables and how they are expressed in professional organization.[40]

How, exactly, are social functions defined and their pursuit and fulfillment incorporated into professional identity? To answer such questions, Parsons's favored case illustration is medicine. The critical functions served by this profession, of course, are health and well-being. Low levels of these goods are dysfunctional for both individuals and society; from the macro perspective, social resources are "invested" in individuals and debilitating illness or premature death represent only a "partial return" on the investment.[41] The practice of medicine is institutionalized in the modern West around rationality, universalism, functional specificity, and collectivity-orientation. It is "organized about the application of scientific knowledge to the problems of illness and health, to the control of 'disease'" rather than being guided by traditional assumptions about illness and health. Technical training and competence expected in modern medicine "would not be possible in a relationship system which was structured primarily

---

39. Parsons, "The Professions and Social Structure," 192, 193.
40. Parsons, "The Professions and Social Structure," 196, 199.
41. Talcott Parsons, *The Social System* (New York: The Free Press, 1951), 430.

in particularistic terms." Modern Westerners expect meritocratic selection of candidates for professional training and expect impersonal, "objective" treatment. As for specificity, caring for the sick is not an "incidental activity of other roles . . . but has become functionally specialized as a full-time job." Rationality, universalism, and functional specificity reinforce one another since "intensive devotion to expertness in matters of health and disease precludes comparable expertness in other fields."[42]

These features of medical practice allow the doctor to do a job that makes unique demands on society and individual patients, not to mention on doctors themselves. To paraphrase Everett Hughes, doctors are professional deviants: they are allowed exemption from a range of social norms regarding the sacredness of dead bodies, the inviolability of the body, and the importance of privacy, among others. Apart from members of the clergy and undertakers, notes Parsons, physicians are one of the few groups that "in our society have regular, expected contact with death in the course of their occupational roles." In their training, doctors need access to cadavers, something that at one time had to be done in secret because it so violated social norms about the sacred.[43] Social norms about the body and privacy are also routinely violated by physicians: "To see a person naked in a context where this is not usual, and to touch and manipulate their body, is a 'privilege' which calls for explanation." The same can be said for the physician's "need of access to confidential information about his patient's private life," information the patient might not even be willing to share with her spouse or closest friend. Institutionalized normative patterns like universalism and functional specificity "enable the physician to 'penetrate' sufficiently into the private affairs . . . of his patients to perform his function. By defining his role in this way it is possible to overcome or minimize resistances which might well otherwise prove fatal to the possibility of doing the job at all."[44]

More than most other professional groups, medicine strongly aligns with a collectivity-orientation as opposed to a self-orientation. Parsons accounts for this in a characteristically functionalist way: because many social resources are at stake in medicine being done effectively, status, authority, and privileges directly related to the tasks performed are given to doctors as rewards; in return, so to speak, for these rewards, the critical social functions of health and well-being

42. Parsons, *The Social System*, 432, 454, 434, 435.
43. Parsons, *The Social System*, 445.
44. Parsons, *The Social System*, 451, 452, 459.

are served as a priority over the free range of self-interest on the part of individual practitioners.

> [T]he situation is such that it would be particularly difficult to implement the pattern of the business world, where each party to the situation is expected to be oriented to the rational pursuit of his own self-interests, and where there is an approach to the idea of "caveat emptor." In a broad sense it is surely clear that society would not tolerate the privileges which have been vested in the medical profession on such terms.[45]

For Parsons, both the authority and responsibility of social trustee professionalism depend on a functional equilibrium composed of a series of exchanges that lead, in short, to trust. The patient and his family, aware that the institutional expectation is for the physician to be guided by the patient's interests first and foremost, grant the access to his body and private information the doctor needs to perform her job competently. The doctor "earns" the compliance of her patient to "doctor's orders" or, in other words, is able to legitimate her authority by using it specifically to help solve the patient's problem.

From the perspective of the general social order, the authority and privileges given to physicians are rewarding and functional for both practitioners and society itself. The medical profession is quite strikingly in need of such legitimation. In few other professions is the client in as vulnerable and potentially exploitable state as medicine:

> [T]he sick person is not . . . competent to help himself. . . . But in our culture there is a special definition of the kind of help he needs, namely, professional, technically competent help. The nature of this help imposes a further disability or handicap upon him. He is not only generally not in a position to do what needs to be done, but he does not "know" what needs to be done or how to do it. . . . [H]e would, even if well, not be qualified to do what is needed, and to judge what needs to be done.[46]

The patient is not even in the position to judge the differences in technical competence between two or more physicians and must trust the judgments of the

---

45. Parsons, *The Social System,* 463.
46. Parsons, *The Social System,* 441.

profession itself. This "combination of helplessness, lack of technical competence, and emotional disturbance" makes the patient "a peculiarly vulnerable object for exploitation."[47] Given this potential for exploitation, it is striking that physicians are permitted the high degree of informal control they enjoy. Parsons explains that even though greater formal control, in the shape of legal constraints or state regulation, might be more "logical," considering the vulnerability of the patient to exploitation, informal control has its "functional significance." Like Durkheim, Parsons underscores the advantages of "informal control," such as the confidence it gives the physician to use "risky though well-advised procedures, which he would not be so ready to do in a more thoroughly bureaucratized situation."[48] In daily practice, the physician may make mistakes or come up short in terms of resources or technical ability. A heavy regulatory hand may make her more apt to follow the rules to avoid mistakes, but also may make her less willing to take chances that could possibly benefit patients. The trust society places in physicians to self-regulate, to separate out and sanction overly risky, foolish, or incompetent treatments and permit those that are risky but necessary, is evidence that it serves collective interests for doctors to take such risks. Informal control, even in the face of patient vulnerability, is a privilege that serves doctors' and public interests.

Another reason professions like medicine strongly align with collectivity-orientation has to do with their relationship to the modern university. Similar to law and engineering, for example, medicine "has been brought overwhelmingly within the university system," something that has resulted in "a complex pattern of interpenetration between the faculties of arts and sciences, on the one hand, and the so-called 'professional' faculties, on the other."[49] Such interpenetration fosters the transmission of cultural values and keeps alive traditional linkages between the professions and the "great tradition of liberal learning." Since academic professionals are closest to this tradition that "is the defining characteristic of a profession," writes Parsons, "the nucleus of the cluster of the professions is the profession of learning itself." Professional education, therefore, serves as "one of the most important channels by which the cultural heritage leavens the everyday social life."[50] By stressing the university's role in professional

47. Parsons, *The Social System,* 445.

48. Parsons, *The Social System,* 471. This is a strong theme that runs throughout Charles Bosk's *Forgive and Remember: Managing Medical Failure* (Chicago: University of Chicago Press, 1979).

49. Parsons, "Professions," 542.

50. Talcott Parsons, "Remarks on Education and the Professions," *International Journal of Ethics* 47 (1937): 367, 369.

education, Parsons significantly corrects the social trustee tendency held by both Durkheim and Tawney that professional values emerge without much cultural stimulus outside the professions. By contrast, Parsons held that the university served to enhance the cognitive rationality and applied skills of professions, but it was also to be a place of reflection and deliberation about professional values and the place of professions in society.

Parsons's version of social trustee professionalism portrays socially responsible or disinterested behavior reinforced by institutions granted exemptions from common social norms and given status and privileges. Professionals are expected to apply their technical skills and specialized knowledge primarily in the service of certain problem areas within society, not for self or profit. Doctors safeguard health and well-being, lawyers regulate order, engineers control physical processes.[51] Though not without danger, the significant autonomy professionals have been allowed in regulating their service and controlling its terms is the price the public pays for the high levels of rational and functionally specific competence it expects. Yet notice that under Parsons's version of the social trustee model, autonomy, authority, and other "privileges" are exchanged for competence, not granted outright as if to an ascribed role. Professionals cannot just say they serve vital social interests; they must in fact do so. Therefore, they are continuously subject to questions of legitimacy.

Indeed, social trustee professionalism raises legitimacy as a core problem and thus opens a door to later sociological critics who differ markedly from Parsons's guarded optimism about the positive function of professionalism. Parsons himself raises the issue with dramatic clarity when he describes the patient as one who needs help but cannot adequately judge the treatment offered and cannot even adequately judge between two different professional treatment recommendations. Such a relation of power and powerlessness makes professions vulnerable to the criticism that they are "disabling" on purpose—namely, to secure their own advantages.

Legitimacy issues are an effect of the social trustee model's general blindness to issues of power, or what I have called its "apolitical" tendency. As Table 1 illustrates, the social trustee model is apolitical in a number of respects, holding professions to be both critical to the functioning of modern society, yet in a significant sense removed from the steering mechanisms of modernity—the market and the state—that in their own flawed ways give voice to those affected by

51. See Parsons, "Professions," 537.

Table 1. The social trustee model of professionalism

Main characteristics of a profession are:	Knowledge, self-regulation, social responsibility
Social duties of professions flow from:	Group experience (Durkheim), functional purposes (Tawney), tacit exchange (Parsons)
Professionals' view of laypeople:	Clients, consumers, wards
Ideal role of professional in society:	Expert, specialist, guide
Professional ethics best fixed and overseen:	By professionals themselves
Political role of professions:	Protection for professional interests and social functions

professional services. Professions have carved out socially useful niches and provide service without much external regulation; they husband and nurture knowledge and skills that purportedly require a degree of protection from market and state pressures; and through their traditions, organizational norms, and peer cultures, nurture a spirit of professionalism both aloof from the lay public as well as indebted and obligated to it. Being blind to power is different from being callous; indeed, both healthy and unhealthy relations of power are underdefined and left unchecked by the social trustee model.

Contemporary social theorists of the professions hold little of the social trustee model's naive faith in ideas of service and social responsibility and are eager to challenge noble-sounding concepts such as professional honor. They are also more apt to point out unhealthy relations of power promoted by professions. Nonetheless, I will argue that contemporary social theorists share their social trustee forefathers' blindness to power. Though they break with the mainstream social trustee tradition and define professions less as moral institutions and more as examples of organized selfishness, contemporary social theorists collapse professional power into market power, thus neglecting both the negative and positive effects professions have and might have on the public culture of democracy.

Organized Selfishness and the Ideology of Service

By the end of the 1960s, the "assumptions about the moral superiority of professional careers that once enjoyed extremely wide acceptance," writes Thomas Haskell, had become nearly extinct.[52] No longer an ideal, the purported service

52. Haskell, "Professionalism versus Capitalism," 181.

orientation that scholars had been wont to use to distinguish professions from business occupations was now seen as merely an ideology. Far from being viewed as more ethical or more socially responsible, the professions were now judged to be more secretive, less responsive to social needs, and more self-interested than business occupations, which were, after all, open about their self-interests and were at least responsive to consumer needs. On its face, this was a dramatic shift in perspective that emerged from both liberal reformist roots, as in the work of Eliot Freidson, and from Marxist grounding, as in the work of Magali Sarfatti Larson.

Skepticism about the dominant values of professions, though, did not lead to much thought about the relationship, either positive or negative, between professions and democracy. Though skeptical of social trustee professionalism, these critical approaches entrenched more deeply the apolitical idea that professions had little to contribute to the public culture of democracy. When they did act in the political system, through interest group lobbying, this was merely to pursue their own privileges and protect their own interests. What separates professionals from other occupations is only the success professions have had in convincing outsiders that they are different, that their status and autonomy are deserved and underwrite high levels of knowledge, skill, and social orientation. In reality, professionals follow the same operating principles as business: self-interested market rationality. For contemporary social theorists, professionals are merely business occupations, albeit overprivileged and underregulated occupations.

Deconstructing Social Trustee Professionalism

A major attack on the social trustee model was launched by Eliot Freidson's *Profession of Medicine*. Challenging earlier interpretations of the origins of the status, autonomy, and service orientation of professions, Freidson underscores the prevalence of strategic rather than ethical behavior. He rejects, both empirically and normatively, the idea that professionalism can be theorized as a beneficial social exchange of status and autonomy for functionally specific expertise aimed at social purposes.

According to Freidson, the status, privileges, and authority of medicine were not earned as rewards for disinterested service, but were won through social and political tactics designed to ratchet up physicians' authority and diminish other occupations' claims to legitimate authority.[53] Professional authority, in short, is

---

53. Eliot Freidson, *Profession of Medicine* (New York: Dodd Mead, 1970), 72.

a political commodity. In the first place, Freidson makes clear that no objective characteristics held by the profession of medicine sociologically dictate the kind of authority it holds. Rather, the bounds of medical authority have been the result of a history of successful negotiations with elites and state agencies. Further, the medical profession has been able to maintain its status and privilege by keeping paramedical occupations like nursing in subordinate positions. Only physicians have the authority to define a medical problem—a power they have jealously guarded against usurpers.

What to make, then, of the claim to disinterested service? For Freidson and other critics, this has to now be seen as just that, a claim. Talcott Parsons and earlier social trustee theorists mistook formal norms and expectations of professions, such as those expressed by ethics codes and in the public discourse of leaders of professional organizations, with the actual operative norms of everyday professional life. Fueling such doubts is the lack of empirical evidence about whether professionals are more service oriented than self-oriented, what proportion of professionals share a service orientation, or whether professionals are more service oriented than other occupations. As a claim about institutional rather than individual tendencies, service orientation is something shared by paraprofessions, those occupations seeking to become professions. Freidson proposes that such claims are pieces of institutional rhetoric that some professions have been more successful than others at putting forward: "*The profession's service orientation is a public imputation it has successfully won in a process by which its leaders have persuaded society to grant and support its autonomy.*"[54]

The goal of such claims is autonomy, the prize any occupation seeking professional status wishes to obtain. "In one way or another, through a process of political negotiation and persuasion, society is led to believe that it is desirable to grant an occupation the professional status of self-regulative autonomy."[55] Now the social trustee defense of autonomy is to suggest that it is justified by special knowledge requirements and functional specificity of the professions. Autonomy is the price society pays for having specialized knowledge and practitioners who can provide useful services with it. Following this logic, more external regulation by the state and laypeople would mean a degradation of professional service. Taking aim at this argument in the very case of medicine Parsons had used to support it, Freidson claims that Parsons conflates four different

54. Freidson, *Profession of Medicine*, 82; italics in original.
55. Freidson, *Profession of Medicine*, 83.

aspects of professional medical work: theoretical knowledge of disease, classifi-catory work differentiating some conditions as "diseases," empirical study of illnesses and their treatment, and the organization and management of such treatment. The social trustee model treats all aspects of doctors' work as worth protecting by shielding them from external, lay scrutiny. Freidson, in contrast, holds that only the first—and most esoteric—element of medical professional work is worth shielding.

> *While the profession's autonomy seems to have facilitated the improvement of scientific knowledge about disease and its treatment, it seems to have impeded the improvement of the social modes of applying that knowledge.* It is precisely in applying knowledge to human affairs, I submit, where extensive professional autonomy is justified neither morally nor func-tionally. It is not justified morally because I believe that human beings, even if laymen, have a right to determine what their own problems are and to have a voice in how they are to be managed. It is not justified functionally . . . because it leads the profession to be blind to its own shortcomings and unable to regulate its practices adequately.[56]

With the other three features of professional work, normative, social, or indi-vidual judgments are closely intertwined with scientific judgments and there-fore deserve lay scrutiny. For example, "to designate something to be a disease is at bottom a moral understanding, with moral consequences. . . . Even assuming that there can be genuine experts in matters of morals in our society, clergymen and philosophers, not physicians and lawyers, come closest to being trained to be such experts." The diagnosis and management of treatment similarly involves both scientific and "social" knowledge: "[O]ne must distinguish between the purely technical activities of treatment and the social interaction and manipu-lation surrounding those acts, between the chemical, radiological, surgical, and other material elements of treatment, and the social organization or adminis-tration of such treatment."[57] Both are part of the practice of medicine, but the latter aspects of treatment do not justify autonomy; if anything, they raise ques-tions about the self-regulation of the medical domain.

Another mistaken element of the social trustee account is the faith that auton-omy will be "earned" by strict self-regulation of norm violation and enforcement

---

56. Freidson, *Profession of Medicine,* 371; italics in original.
57. Freidson, *Profession of Medicine,* 342, 343.

of norms that encourage a service orientation. Freidson points out that the medical profession has not, internally at least, done much to review the financial practices of its members. The only significant cost-control measures have been secured by external public and semipublic organizations such as health maintenance organizations. As for standards of service quality, the medical profession offers only weak self-regulation, mainly through the "minimal standards for medical education and licensing." For there to be truly effective self-regulation, "the social setting of practice must be organized to minimize isolation from colleague scrutiny and public accountability," but these "organizational forms" have been resisted by the profession.[58]

Another misstep of the social trustee account is the assumption that the authority of a profession is fixed by the functionally specific tasks it performs. Rejecting Parsons's claim that once the doctor leaves her clinic, her authority over nonmedical affairs declines to the level of the ordinary citizen, Freidson argues that professions are constantly seeking authority that is not functionally specific, or, put differently, tend to bring social issues and needs into their domain of authority that may not belong there. Medicine does serve needs the public has asked it to serve, but "it has also devoted itself to discovering and delineating new needs by developing its own moral conceptions of what men can or should ideally be." Indeed, Freidson argues, as medical institutions have become "increasingly independent of the public and organized by professional rather than by lay standards," medicine "has less and less come to reflect what the public asks of it and more and more come to assert what the public should get from it."[59] So, not only are doctors given unjustified self-regulated jurisdiction over many aspects of medical work, there are also no apparent natural, or functional, limits on what the medical profession can claim influence over if it can manage to define an issue as having to do with health or well-being.

Even if one grants that the professions are concerned with critical public goods such as health and well-being, justice and social order, truth and virtue, this does not mean that they ought to have the authority to determine just what of the many sorts or types of these goods to provide and how and to whom to provide them. "I myself do not believe that professions, no matter how beneficent their intent, have either the moral right or the special qualification to make such choices for the individual or for society. . . . When service to the community is

58. Freidson, *Profession of Medicine*, 365–66.
59. Freidson, *Profession of Medicine*, 350.

defined by the profession rather than the community," argues Freidson, "the community is not truly served." Though well meaning, writes Freidson, professional groups "are protected from the public by their organized autonomy and at the same time protected from their own honest self-scrutiny by their sanctimonious myths of the inherently superior qualities of themselves as professionals—of their knowledge and of their work."[60]

Professionalism as Ideology

Other major contemporary sociological accounts have filled out Freidson's account of how professions gain autonomy and authority in strategic ways that increase professions' commercial power but have only superficial connections to ideals of social responsibility touted by the social trustee model. One prominent approach takes a social conflict perspective that stresses the struggles of professions as they fought off competitors in the open market and fought to achieve standards within their own domains. Magali Sarfatti Larson's work is the standard bearer of this approach. "Professionalization," according to Larson, is "an attempt to translate one order of scarce resources—special knowledge and skills—into another—social and economic rewards. To maintain scarcity implies a tendency to monopoly: monopoly of expertise in the market, monopoly of status in a system of stratification."[61] From this perspective, the process of becoming a profession is a struggle for dominance over a particular economic market, a struggle that requires marshaling many different tools such as ideals of service, licensing, and university training.

Larson points out that the modern professions emerged during the nineteenth century, a period of major changes in economic and political organization as market capitalism expanded dramatically. Individual professions faced new challenges in establishing markets for their services and convincing outsiders that their members were respectable and worthy of a special status. For Larson, the professional project is thoroughly ideological: not just the ideal of service, but professionalism itself is a kind of rhetoric. Unlike some other forms of labor, professionals do not produce and market tangible goods. What is marketed, really, are their services, "things" that are "only formally alienable and . . . inextricably bound to the person and personality of the producer." This puts pressure

---

60. Freidson, *Profession of Medicine*, 351, 370.
61. Magali Sarfatti Larson, *The Rise of Professionalism: A Sociological Analysis* (Berkeley and Los Angeles: University of California Press, 1977), xvii.

on professionals to raise themselves and their profession up in the public eye: "[T]he producers themselves have to be produced if their products or commodities are to be given a distinctive form. [P]rofessionals must be adequately trained and socialized so as to provide recognizably distinct services for exchange on the professional market."[62] Otherwise, there is no market because there is nothing to sell.

For a professional market to be secure, one group's services have to be shown to be superior over a competitor's services. Larson indicates two aspects as critical to this process: standardization of professional services and elimination of competitors. Professions themselves had to take on the task of internal regulation in order to standardize, but they also depended indirectly on state support of professional education. Larson notes that the state plays a considerable role in the professionalization project by "sponsoring monopolistic education systems."[63] As for security against competitors, professions relied even more directly on various forms of state protection, such as licensing. Against Parsons, in Larson's view monopoly, not service, is exchanged for the sacrifices made by individuals undergoing professional training and education: "[A]t least a moderate guarantee that the [professional] recruits' educational investment would be protected had to be sought from the beginning. In a market situation, the guarantee against risks incurred tends to take the form of monopoly, or at least of special protection by the public authorities."[64]

Just because a profession manages to standardize its services and oust competitors does not mean that a market of consumers exists for these services. Monopoly of practice must be accompanied by "the parallel construction of a 'monopoly of credibility' with the larger public." Such credibility is advanced significantly by linking professions with education and, in particular, "a teaching monopoly on their specific tools and techniques," something Larson calls "cognitive exclusiveness."[65] These connections—to the state, educational institutions, the general public—are hard fought by professions and, once established, are maintained and updated with keen awareness of the costs to the profession's economic health of relaxing any monopolistic control.

Even though social trustee professionalism is viewed by Larson as ideological, this is not to say that it is false. Ideology is, after all, not a lie or a fiction, but

62. Larson, *The Rise of Professionalism*, 14.
63. Larson, *The Rise of Professionalism*, 18.
64. Larson, *The Rise of Professionalism*, 15.
65. Larson, *The Rise of Professionalism*, 17, 15.

rather a simplification of ideas with specific purposes in mind—in this case, the promotion of professional status and economic monopoly. In the case of medicine, for example, Larson admits that one reason state authorities stepped in to "facilitate monopolistic control over practice" was that the profession did appear to be healing patients, an important function and one with particular salience during a period of public epidemics: "The fact that medicine operates in an area of vital concern for the individual and for the community compels the state to intervene. Once scientific medicine had offered sufficient guarantees of its superior effectiveness in dealing with disease, the state contributed willingly to the creation of monopoly by means of registration and licensing."[66] The claims to service made by the medical profession were rhetorical, but they were unlikely to have been enough to secure and maintain privileges and autonomy without the "actual results" and public health activity of certain groups within the profession.[67]

Though they hearken back to a precompetitive capitalism period, the ideals of service and collegiality may not be as antimarket as they appear in social trustee accounts. Larson argues that since claims of disinterestedness and public service "deny the invidious implications of monopoly," they are especially useful in staving off "possible attacks" on the very monopoly they deny.[68] But here again Larson concedes that there are grains of truth in the social trustee account. Many doctors did for a time have graduated fees according to patient income, an expression of the service ideal. Additionally, standardization of professional services and meritocratic reforms in the medical school admissions process have benefited both those with professional aspirations and those who require professional services. So, while there is no doubt professionalization helped the professions secure what other occupations could only hope to achieve—namely, monopoly over a market domain—it is clear that some of the social functions heralded by the social trustee account were served as well. Still, Larson inverts the social trustee account: the functions served by professions are part of the professional project designed to show that the public could not possibly do without doctors, lawyers, engineers, and the like. Since function is also so closely related to the monopoly of practice pressed for by professions, suggesting that it existed independently of the professional project would be naive.

66. Larson, *The Rise of Professionalism*, 23.
67. Larson, *The Rise of Professionalism*, 39.
68. Larson, *The Rise of Professionalism*, 52.

The Competitive System of Professions

A third major contemporary theoretical challenge to the social trustee perspective views professionalism as an interoccupational struggle to claim certain social functions as tasks best served by a particular profession. In this interoccupational struggle, the terrain is defined by background cultural and political features and, above all else, by the competitors for service provision. Andrew Abbott, a pioneer of this approach, uncovers a buzzing competitive struggle for clients that is obscured by both the social trustee perspective and by critics like Larson and Freidson. While social trustee theorists assume that professions take up natural and given social needs such as health, mental well-being, and conflict resolution, Abbott shows how professions actually define and redefine these needs to suit their particular tools and approaches. While critics of the social trustee account like Larson assume that dominance over a social function is the end result of professionalism, Abbott holds that the conflict between professions over who deservedly should perform what function never ends. Temporary settlement, not dominance, is all professions can expect.

For Abbott, the connection to abstract knowledge distinguishes professional work, not commitment to disinterested service or any other such ideal. This knowledge "must require enough disciplined judgment to be uncommodifiable, . . . must enjoy enough success to generate continual demand, . . . and must be abstract enough to survive small market shifts, but not so abstract as to prevent monopoly." Professions are thus repositories of people with specialized knowledge who perform expert tasks, which the background culture deems appropriate to be handled by specific groups. Though some tasks, such as health care, seem to be professionalized in most cultures, Abbott notes that the range of professionalized tasks is quite variable: "[T]he human problems susceptible of this professionalized knowledge know few limits. Alcoholism, suicide, aging, building, ultimate meaning, financial advice, 'low sexual desire,' violence, the environment: all these have seen their professional embodiments."[69]

The "cultural logic" of professional practice revolves around three claims: "to classify a problem, to reason about it, and to take action on it: in more formal terms, to diagnose, to infer, and to treat." Diagnosis, inference, and treatment are aspects of professional work that are usually connected to a more abstract

---

69. Andrew Abbott, *The System of Professions: An Essay on the Division of Expert Labor* (Chicago: University of Chicago Press, 1988), 324.

body of knowledge that "formalizes the skills on which this work proceeds."[70] In most cases, this formal professional knowledge is housed in universities. Like Parsons, Abbott believes that universities provide a good deal of symbolic capital to professions and also connect professions to the "major cultural values" of "rationality, logic, and science."[71] Most day-to-day professional work, however, relies very little on formal knowledge.

Like Freidson and Larson, Abbott holds that a primary goal for professions is control over specific kinds of work and, whenever possible, expansion of the range of tasks under control. To accomplish this goal, a profession will make what Abbott calls "jurisdictional claims," or appeals to the larger society to accept it as the rightful and exclusive provider of those services. "In claiming jurisdiction," writes Abbott, "a profession asks society to recognize its cognitive structure through exclusive rights" such as "absolute monopoly of practice and of public payments, rights of self-discipline and of unconstrained employment, control of professional training, of recruitment, and of licensing," among others.[72] Critical audiences for jurisdictional claims are actors in the legal arena, such as legislators, judges, agency heads, and other regulators in the executive branch. These actors can help establish the barriers to competition and the control over the workplace that professions seek.

Perhaps an even more important audience for jurisdictional claims, especially in the United States, is public opinion. "In America," writes Abbott, "it is ultimately through public opinion that professions establish the power that enables them to achieve legal protection." Professions take great care to craft public images that validate and secure their claims to be the rightful group for diagnosing, inferring, and treating specific problems. Codes of ethics are public relations tools, and individual violations of ethics that tarnish the public image of the profession are taken the most seriously by the larger group. In the United States, public opinion is a particularly powerful force in validating jurisdictional claims partly because of the federal nature of American government, where claims for state protection must be made in fifty states, and partly because of the Jacksonian heritage of "free-market determination of professional boundaries."[73]

Issuing jurisdictional claims that are successfully validated by public opinion and make their way into formal validations such as regulatory rules and statutory

70. Abbott, *The System of Professions,* 52.
71. Abbott, *The System of Professions,* 54.
72. Abbott, *The System of Professions,* 59.
73. Abbott, *The System of Professions,* 164.

protections is neither the social exchange of service for trust imagined by social trustee theorists nor the monopolistic hegemony feared by critics such as Freidson and Larson. For Abbott, it is best seen as simply a settlement in a perpetual struggle between groups over occupational territory. Like other contemporary students of the professions, Abbott stresses the rhetorical nature of jurisdictional claims. Professions demand authority and exclusive rights on the grounds that they are the most fit to perform the service in question, yet there are no legally enforceable duties or obligations that follow from state-sanctioned professional authority and privilege: "Lawyers have a right to perform legal work as they wish, but only a hazy obligation to guarantee that all the needs of justice are served."[74] However, Abbott agrees with social trustee theorists that professions are committed to serving social purposes, at least to some extent. In a world where pediatricians attempt inroads into the treatment of child behavior problems, where psychiatrists battle psychologists for mental health clients, where accountants battle lawyers for financial services tasks, mere rhetoric will never be enough to attract and retain clients.

In Abbott's view, the vulnerability of professions—their need to renegotiate and revalidate jurisdictional claims—means they do not have the kind of commercial power asserted by critics such as Freidson and Larson. It is true that, at least for a time, incumbents of jurisdictions have many resources at their disposal to thwart more effective competitors. Mainstream medicine's definition of successful treatment, for example, is the standard against which competitors are judged. Professions often seek and receive state help in thwarting competition, as when medicine seeks to burden homeopaths with disadvantageous regulations. Still, even dominant professions like medicine are more vulnerable than contemporary critics believe. Even with their advantages, incumbents have historically lost work to adversaries: "the American lawyers losing trust work to trust companies, the neurologists losing neurosis to the psychiatrists, the solicitors losing bankruptcy to accountants. . . . While power clearly affects jurisdictional conflict, in the long run power alone does not suffice, even when buttressed with absolute monopoly. . . . If professions fail to deliver service, eventually clients go elsewhere."[75] In addition to being vulnerable to interprofessional competition, professions must be responsive to the demands of clients and payers, especially powerful clients and payers such as governments and large corporations.

---

74. Abbott, *The System of Professions*, 60.
75. Abbott, *The System of Professions*, 140.

Since jurisdictional contests are often decided by client choice, client power also restrains professional power, particularly when there are powerful clients or powerful payers, such as large commercial organizations or governments. As clients they purchase services from dominant professions. As payers they pay the bills that individual clients incur, as has been the case in American medicine. In either case, they confront dominant professions as powerful or monopsonistic groups that can overthrow their attempts to thwart jurisdictional competition.[76]

Further, though the state can provide barriers to competition for favored professions, it can also place limits on professional power. In addition to being a client of services that it wishes to have efficiently and expertly delivered, the state is itself a competitor in service delivery.

Along with social shifts in interprofessional competition and in state responses, professions face cultural shifts in the sorts of values they need to express in order to successfully legitimate their jurisdictional claims. From the nineteenth to the twentieth century, for example, the value of efficiency has trumped, though not replaced, earlier sources of legitimation such as tradition and learnedness. More important, Abbott notes a shift from "legitimacy of character to legitimacy of technique" in the twentieth century. "The major shift in legitimation in the professions has thus been a shift from a reliance on social origins and character values to a reliance on scientization or rationalization of technique and on efficiency of service."[77] What do you look for in professional service if you do not have professional training in the field? The nineteenth-century answer: look to professionals' "gentlemanliness," "courage," and "disinterest." The twentieth-century answer: look to their scientific training, their advanced degrees, and their university training. In addition to character and technique, a third source of legitimation is the social structure of professions itself—"examinations, licensing or registration, disciplinary committees, accreditation, and ethics codes."[78] This process of legitimation is strategic, self-interested, and rhetorical, as Freidson and Larson have also shown, but it also seeks to deliver both an image and reality of professional service that the public culture respects and desires. Professions are interested in the character—public image—of their members, the technical training of students and practitioners, and the organizational

76. Abbott, *The System of Professions,* 140.
77. Abbott, *The System of Professions,* 195.
78. Abbott, *The System of Professions,* 193.

ethics and norms of the institutions in which they work. To merely pay lip service to these sources of legitimation is to risk jurisdictional invasion by ever-present competitors.

Conclusion:
The Rise, Fall, and Persistence of Social Trustee Professionalism

In answering the questions of how and why professions are different from other occupations, leading social theories of professionalism develop four central themes. First, professions are distinguished by an other-orientation or collectivity-orientation that trumps, at least some of the time, traditional profit motives. Social trustee theorists such as Durkheim, Tawney, and Parsons hold that this orientation stems from the group life of professionals and from a division of labor in modern society, an exchange, so to speak, of status and privilege for self-sacrifice—the expenditure of time and energy in devotion to social goods such as health, justice, and knowledge. Post-Parsonsian critics such as Freidson, Larson, and Abbott all affirm that professions differ in terms of their collectivity-orientation, but they hold that this difference, at root, is strategic. Professions claim to be socially responsible in order to shore up their resistance to external regulation, competitors, and, more generally, market forces.

Second, this collectivity-orientation, whether real or ideological, is not to be understood as political. It is not a direct result of government regulation, nor does it stem from the pressure of public interests on professional cultures. Nor is this collectivity-orientation something that positively or negatively impacts the public culture of democracy. Indeed, these types of connections to politics would threaten the professional autonomy necessary to fulfill social purposes. Doctors would not take creative, time-sensitive risks if they were overly regulated from the outside. Lawyers' service to their clients takes a priority over any political or pragmatic obligations they may have. Professional domains may or may not serve the public, but they do not draw their values, norms, or purposes from social movements, political actors, officials, or institutions.

Third, professionals may work *for* the public, but they do not work *with* the public. Their collectivity-orientation is one way—just as a trustee works for his client, but in a way only partially understood by his client, so can much about the professional role only be judged by fellow professionals. Social trustee theorists view this as logically related to the specialized knowledge and skills held by and invested in professionals and by the larger society—years of training, advanced degrees, licensing requirements, and so forth. Post-Parsonian critics, on the other hand, see specialized knowledge and skills as jealously guarded and wielded by professions in order to secure protected markets for services; they are more badges of distinction than tools used in day-to-day professional work.

The fourth major theme in the social theory of professions is vulnerability. Professions are relics, holdovers of a precapitalist mode of economic organization. As such, they are in a struggle for existence against the pressures of efficiency, profit maximization, rationalized organization, and bureaucratization. Though they differ on whether the autonomy, status, and privileges of professions are deserved, both social trustee theorists and their critics agree that professions are constantly aware of their vulnerability to collapsing into strictly business occupations operating under the norms of contemporary capitalism.

Post-Parsonian analyses strongly contest the social trustee model's understanding of professional organization, action, and motivation. All the features of this model are still present in the rhetoric and actions of professionals, only now they are recognized as self-serving and symbolic rather than as evidence of an invisible exchange of trust for service. Do professions moralize their members? Yes, but in a manner hostile to social interests. Do professions perform important social functions? Yes, but through monopoly control that discourages potentially useful competition. Do professions offer professionals a semi-autonomous work life? Yes, but this self-regulation allows leeway for abuse of professional authority. So, the categories of analysis remain, but their meaning and larger social significance have become contested. The wall separating the business occupations dominated by self-interested rationality and the professions serving functional ends has been breached, never to be fully repaired.

This chapter began with the question "what about professions, professional organizations, institutions in which professionals work, and professionals themselves may make them receptive to a role as facilitators of public deliberation?" The social theory of the professions provides important, but for now inchoate, answers. Out of the social trustee tradition comes an account of professional domains as careful—or as the tradition's critics might say, jealous—of the kind and quality of knowledge and service, as concerned with the ethics of practice. These spheres of action and reflection are often involved with some of the most pressing and difficult human issues: justice, health, knowledge, and safety. It is a step, but not a large one, from caretaking and guarding such reflection to facilitating a more general and inclusive deliberation over these issues.

Out of the contemporary social theory critique of social trusteeism comes another answer to this leading question. The gap between professional domains and the public—whether the product of knowledge and skill differences or merely from the habits of group life—will always raise legitimacy issues. In other words, professional authority and privilege are always vulnerable to being revoked or being shifted to competing occupations. This vulnerability might make professionals more willing than others to close the gap by involving lay-people in professional affairs. If ignorance about professional authority breeds public distrust and public distrust makes it harder for professionals to redeem jurisdictional claims, then there is a clear motive to facilitate more public knowledge about professional domains.

For the purposes of understanding professionalism and its current connection to democracy, it is useful that contemporary critics puncture the idealism of the social trustee account by much more carefully examining claims to disinterested service and mechanisms of exchanging status, privilege, and autonomy for knowledge and skill. The upshot of contemporary social theory of the professions is not that social trusteeism is dead or false, but that it is on notice that professionals' claims—to privilege or jurisdictional control—must be redeemed only after close scrutiny by those affected by them.

Less usefully, contemporary social theorists perpetuate an apolitical frame of reference. Though they notice some macrolevel effects on society, as when professions seek economic gains or monopolies over certain tasks, they neglect a whole range of both positive and negative effects. Apart from such interest group activities, social theorists conceive professions as having no relation, good or bad, to democratic institutions or practices. Nevertheless, a number of persistent themes of social theory point the way to a more democratic conception of professionalism: a history and motivating ideal of self-sacrifice for the purpose of serving higher goods combined with a desire to retain status, privilege, and authority. Before these characteristics can be seen as building blocks to a political theory of professionalism, however, we need the assistance of some stringent political critiques of professions that raise the issue of professional power as a matter of democratic and not merely commercial importance.

3

PROFESSIONALS VERSUS DEMOCRACY:
THE RADICAL CRITIQUE OF TECHNOCRATS,
DISABLING EXPERTS, AND TASK MONOPOLISTS

I propose to call the mid-twentieth century the Age of Disabling Professions.
—IVAN ILLICH, *Disabling Professions* (1977)

Though social trustee ideas are still prominent, a critical discourse emerged in the late 1960s, drawing attention to the unhealthy relations of political and not just commercial power maintained and encouraged by professionalism. These arguments focus on a dimension of professional action left undertheorized by both social trustee thinkers and their critics within contemporary social theory. What I call the "radical critique" holds that professions manipulate and dominate the public, preventing citizens from taking up their rightful place in coordinating social action. The radical critique is a second descriptive and normative model for understanding what it means to be a professional and what aspects of professional life have relevance for the public culture of democracy. While critical of professional power as technocratic and overbearing, this model is not merely the destructive opposite of social trusteeism. The radical critique reflects everyday struggles between citizens and professions, between self-critical, reform-minded professionals and those more comfortable with existing norms, that have dramatically shaped current understandings of professionalism.

The radical critique shows how professions are inextricably connected to the public culture of democracy in ways that have strong relevance for issues of public deliberation. This chapter begins with a discussion of the persistent effects of social trustee thinking that obscure a wider view of professions and democracy. From time to time within political theory, this wider view is brought forward to challenge academic professional ethics, but, for the most part, professions and professional responsibilities are still seen as the academic subspecialties of sociology and philosophy. Three reasons for this are the somewhat general nature of radical criticisms of professions, their scattered trajectory across disciplinary boundaries, and their embedment in practitioner studies and unconventional academic projects. In the following sections, I draw from unconventional thinkers, such as Ivan Illich and Michel Foucault, who are only loosely rooted in specific academic disciplines, as well as those, such as Nils Christie and Frank Fischer, who are closely connected to practitioner studies such as criminal justice and policy studies. They offer the strongest arguments I have found articulating the radical critique of the counterdemocratic effects of professions.

Two arguments in particular have some force. The first considers professionals as technocratic barriers to popular influence on elected officials. The second charges professionals with actively disabling certain kinds of knowledge and skill that, if widespread rather than professionalized, would support a more participatory democracy. Though there are difficulties with each of these arguments, they bring forward the important idea of professionals as "task monopolizers" who exercise a form of authority over social needs, purposes, and problems that is different from the sort of commercial power stressed by contemporary social theory.

With few exceptions, radical critics offer only the barest of substantive alternatives to social trusteeism—or what they redescribe as technocratic professionalism. A kind of deprofessionalization, or, at most, a highly self-reflective practice that draws attention to the ways traditional practices and institutions block and manipulate citizens, is the only alternative presented by radical critics to reform-minded practitioners who might wish to be both professional and democratic. In response, I will argue that a certain kind of professionalism is required to enable the very citizen participation in public deliberation that radical critics endorse. In its own way, then, the radical critique points to how professions have democratic responsibilities—to enable rather than disable citizen participation within their spheres of professional authority—that stem from specific effects of particular professional norms and practices. It pushes us forward to a more positive understanding of professional power in democracy—the model of democratic professionalism.

Politicizing the Social Trustee Image of Professional Responsibility

Though contemporary social theorists have revealed strategic, self-interested motives behind the social trustee claims of professions, the apolitical view of professions as unselfinterested trustees of public interests has played a major role in how sociologists, philosophers, and professionals themselves have understood professions as being different from other economic actors and as having different responsibilities to both clients and the larger society.

As we have seen, the social trustee ideal holds that professionals have a more general responsibility than their fiduciary and function-specific obligations to their client base. Professionals are obligated, of course, to perform their tasks competently and not illegitimately deviate from the common normative standards of behavior that apply to all people regardless of occupation. But they also have broader responsibilities that stem from the trust clients place in them, the social status they have, and the market protection that the federal and state governments have permitted them through licensing and other regulations. To count as a profession, in Talcott Parsons's foundational account, an occupation must have a sense of such broader responsibility: "A full-fledged profession must have some institutional means of making sure that such competence will be put to socially responsible uses." In addition to healing particular clients, the medical profession contributes to larger social goals such as curing disease and other large-scale improvements in health and well-being. In addition to defending the rights and advancing the interests of particular clients, the legal profession embodies and upholds the social conception of justice, which Parsons calls "the moral consensus (incomplete as it is) of American society."[1]

As a practical ideal, social trustee professionalism emerged in the 1860s and was prominent in the century that follows for both established professions, like law and medicine, and for newer professions striving for status, like engineers and social workers.[2] As Steven Brint points out, the values that make up the ideal bear the marks of dominant social and political institutions: the value of "regulation by the occupational community in relation to high practice standards" was part of normal professional association practice, the value of "service in relation to the interests of public safety, convenience, and welfare" aligned with the regulatory state, and the value of "specialized expertise in a sphere of formal learning" resembled the division of the faculties in the university.[3]

---

1. Talcott Parsons, "Professions," in *International Encyclopedia of the Social Sciences,* vol. 12 (New York: Macmillan, 1968), 536, 544.

2. Steven Brint, *In an Age of Experts: The Changing Role of Professionals in Politics and Public Life* (Princeton: Princeton University Press, 1994), 5.

3. Brint, *In an Age of Experts,* 36.

Professionals were members of those occupations with such commonly appreciated values that were different from market values of efficiency and profit.

If social trustee professionals represented public interests, however, this representation was at a fairly high level of abstraction. Serving the "community" was not seen as something the community had much say in determining. "Community was understood as the aggregation of socially important functions, not as some more general kinship," writes Brint. "Each profession was understood to work on a single important sphere of social life—such as conflict resolution, health, design, education."[4] An economy of trust emerged: professionals earned social trust by performing such general social functions with a high degree of competence, and they spent it by insisting that they knew best how to govern themselves and establish their own standards of action.

The grip of the social trustee ideal has weakened, particularly in sociology, but it still has a hold on contemporary professionals and many of those studying them. In particular, it still has a grip on normative accounts of professional responsibilities. Consider contemporary bioethics, the study of professional responsibilities in the medical domain (the topic of Chapter 7). The dominant paradigm in bioethics, "principlism," conceives public interests in the medical profession in terms of four main values: autonomy, beneficence, nonmaleficence, and justice.[5] To serve public interests in health, argue bioethicists, the medical profession ought to be governed by such values. Their presumption is that the major social interests in medicine concern failures to live up to these values or with conflicts between the values in practice. For mainstream bioethicists, ethical problems that arise in medical practice and research can be resolved by thoughtful application of these principles. When the principles conflict, as they frequently do in the hardest cases of medical ethics, trade-offs must be made. Even methodological challengers to principlism, such as virtue ethics and philosophies of caring, stay within a self-defined domain and sketch alternative role moralities rather than open up the process of norm establishment—say, by inviting lay participation and deliberation over what counts as good health care. The upshot is that professionals, in particular those self-governed by particular values, are still idealized as protecting certain public interests from forces of the market, such as self-interested rationality, and from public ignorance.

4. Brint, *In an Age of Experts,* 7.
5. See, for example, Tom L. Beauchamp and James F. Childress, *Principles of Biomedical Ethics,* 4th ed. (New York: Oxford University Press, 1994), 37–38.

When political theorists focus on the normative discourse found in professional ethics, which they do only rarely, they are usually disappointed by the lack of attention to issues of power and authority. Peter Euben, for example, laments the "implicit acceptance of the existent structure of society" that follows from professional ethics' neglect of social structural analysis, and he notes the lack of "sustained questioning of professionalism and expertise" in that literature.[6] Stephen Esquith, putting the point even more strongly, holds that professional ethics "projects citizens into the confined ineffective roles of clients and consumers" and has "widened the political distance between citizens, thereby weakening them politically."[7] My view is that the persistence of the social trustee model may go some distance in explaining the apolitical nature of academic professional ethics. Whether they deal with individual-level matters of client autonomy or more macro-level matters of fair distribution of professional services and technologies, scholars tend to discuss the ethical problems and social responsibilities of professions in depoliticized terms abstracted from the already established, taken-for-granted social functions performed by the profession. Rarely do such scholars advocate any contribution from affected communities or any process of open public contention as necessary to define social functions or their related duties.

What I call here the radical critique strongly challenges the apolitical image of social responsibilities presented by the social trustee model and its adherents in philosophy and professional practice. Far from representatives of the public interest, under this critique professions are seen as impediments to the democratic expression of public interests. In this way, the radical critique shifts focus powerfully and immediately, making the problems, methods, and domains of professionals and those interested in their ethics the subject of political analysis. The radical critique asks what the relationship is between professionals and the ability of members of the lay public to recognize and act on their interests. A professional can be socially responsible and ethical under the apolitical Parsonsian or principlist standard (or the standards of virtue ethics or philosophies of caring) yet still be technocratic and domineering.

The radical critique needs to be considered carefully to determine just how professions are impediments. Radical critics discuss different problems and contexts when they write about technocratic and manipulative professionals, so it

---

6. Peter J. Euben, "Philosophy and the Professions," *democracy* 1 (1981): 118, 120.
7. Stephen Esquith, "Locating Professional Ethics Politically," *Centennial Review* 34 (1990): 133–34.

is necessary to disentangle arguments and prune away claims that no longer hold much weight. The radical critique is vitally important because it analyzes professions and their responsibilities in categories of democratic political theory—power, authority, representation, subjectivity—but it is too general to have had much effect on mainstream scholars interested in professions and their ethics. In addition, the critique has been largely unaccompanied by a positive reconstruction of professionalism. Just how can practitioners be both professional and democratic at the same time? Radical critics advocate a world devoid of professions or one populated by self-critical and acutely power-sensitive practitioners—positions that I will argue are self-defeating. After discussing some of the main arguments made by radical critics, however, I will show how they point not away from professions but toward a third way of looking at professional authority and professional ethics: democratic professionalism.

For a working definition of "professional," consider the features stressed by both social trustee theorists and their critics: knowledge, control over one's work, self-regulation, and some conception of a social purpose served by one's work. As Andrew Abbott stressed, there is competition over time over jurisdiction between established professions and between them and occupations wishing to become seen as professions by clients and the public at large. This means that who and what is professional is a dynamic process that will shift over time, becoming more and less inclusive. Further, not all occupations now considered professions or striving to become such maximize, so to speak, all the above characteristics. That said, a strong theme emerging from the social theory considered in the last chapter is that a necessary component of professionalization is a commitment to public purposes and declarations of such a commitment have been part of the competitive—some would say ideological—project of the professions.

We can follow sociologist Steven Brint's mainstream definition of professionals, which touches on most of the core features stressed in the literature while allowing flexibility on which occupations will be included: professionals are "people who earn at least a middling income from the application of a relatively complex body of knowledge" and "professional services" include "teaching, healing, advocating in court, building, designing, accounting, researching, or any one of a number of other activities requiring advanced training in a field of learning and non-routine mental operations on the job." Brint lists "doctors, natural scientists, engineers, computer scientists, certified public accountants, economists, social scientists, psychotherapists, lawyers, policy experts of various sorts, professors, at least some journalists and editors, some clergy, and some artists and writers" as professionals.[8] These are occupations that, at least to some extent, connect to some body of knowledge, have work autonomy and some degree of self-regulation, and express a commitment to social purposes. Though some figure more prominently than others, many are targets of the radical critique of professional power.

Professionals as Barriers Between Democratic Institutions and the Lay Public

A common version of the radical critique warns of the gradual takeover of political decision making by unelected technocratic professionals with expertise in the social and natural sciences. A response to social complexity and modernization, such technocratic professionals emerge as assistants for elected officials and democratically accountable administrators but eventually dominate the political agenda behind the scenes. Miguel Centeno, for example, defines "technocracy" as "the administrative and political domination of a society by a state elite and allied institutions that seek to impose a single, exclusive policy paradigm based on the application of instrumentally rational techniques."[9] Seen as a way of allowing a knowledge-elite to rule or, better put, manage in the best interests of the whole society, the technocratic state of affairs has been the subject of ideal political and social theory from Plato, Francis Bacon, Henri Saint-Simon, August Comte, and the American who coined the term "technocratic," William Smyth.[10]

Though a staple of critical and ideal theory, the argument that technocratic professionals rule has limited descriptive and analytical power. Its picture of government inaccurately describes the American system, for example, with its many complex layers of competition and stratification within the legislative and executive branches. In short, there is more diversity of opinion and interest at play than the picture admits and, therefore, multiple streams of political influence and power. Reviews of case studies of expert influence in national policy

---

8. Brint, *In an Age of Experts*, 3.

9. Miguel Angel Centeno, "The New Leviathan: The Dynamics and Limits of Technocracy," *Theory and Society* 22 (1993): 314.

10. John G. Gunnell, "The Technocratic Image and the Theory of Technocracy," *Technology and Culture* 22 (1982): 392–416.

making produce very limited evidence of technocratic dominance. In the first place, it is often "impossible to identify the particular group or individual who has had the decisive say in the development of the policy." Second, so-called technocrats "tend to have limited policy-making influence except on narrowly technical matters" that they do dominate, such as "the setting of produce and personnel standards in pre-set categories, the minor refinement of statistics of social and economic measurement, and the determination of whether particular drugs are safe enough to be released on the market."[11] Third, only in some contexts, such as when politicians are overloaded with responsibilities, do technocratic professionals have significant influence on nontechnical issues. It is difficult, then, to accept this critique of professionals' impact on democracy except in a few narrowly defined contexts. Two other versions of the radical critique of professionals, which I call the "barrier" and "disabling" arguments, have greater force.

A more nuanced critique of technocratic professionalism sees professionals as impeding the democratic expression of public interests by mediating between the lay public and elected officials. "Technocracy," under this view, is not rule by experts; it is an attitude, an "ethos," and institutional pattern that rejects popularly informed decision making in favor of expert-informed policy making. Discussions of this issue are definitive of classical social theory and the first sophisticated attempts to understand complex organizations in both public and private spheres.[12] In his recent book on technocracy, Frank Fischer argues that professionals such as policy analysts, management specialists, and other applied social scientists fit snugly into a "technocorporate" government consisting of three spheres: "a top echelon of political and economic elites, a technocratic strata of experts and specialized administrators . . . , and a largely depoliticized mass public." Professionals do not rule, but they do "mediate the policy decisions made by top elites, . . . direct their implementation," and, in some cases, especially in highly technical policy areas, "make the actual policy decisions."[13]

Under this view, technocratic professionals disempower democratic publics in a number of ways, reflecting their position as a buffer. First, their knowledge and their modes of analysis are treated by elected officials as superior to lay knowledge and analysis. Better versed in the economic, social, and technical details of particular policy domains, technocratic professionals have frequently

11. Brint, *In an Age of Experts*, 133, 136.
12. Max Weber, "Essay on Bureaucracy," in *From Max Weber: Essays in Sociology*, trans. and ed. H. H. Gerth and C. Wright Mills (New York: Oxford University Press, 1946), 196–243.
13. Frank Fischer, *Technocracy and the Politics of Expertise* (Newbury Park: Sage, 1990), 27, 110.

been seen in rosy light—as were Franklin Delano Roosevelt's "brain trust" and even some of John F. Kennedy's "best and the brightest." Like the machines that tell a physician more about the patient than the patient herself, technocrats are able to assess and address public needs for the purposes of policy makers better than members of the public could. Just as dialogue with patients has become more of a courtesy than a diagnostic tool for physicians, public deliberation need only take symbolic forms like televised "town hall meetings" since politicians already know the public's pulse from polls and other public opinion research.

Second, and related, technocratic professionals depoliticize issues by translating social problems into questions that can be solved by using the methods in which they are trained and over which they have greater command than the lay public. Armed with systems theory and policy analysis and focusing on means, costs, and benefits of pregiven ends, the technocratic professional spends little time on the fundamental substantive value questions that concern laypeople. In itself, this narrowing of focus is not a problem, but the technocratic ethos asserts the priority of some questions over others and relegates the fundamental substantive questions to the realm of the political or the subjective. As Fischer states, "[T]echnocrats see politics as a *problem* rather than a *solution*":

> Thus for technocrats the solution is to replace the "irrational" decision processes of democratic politics (group competition, bargaining, and compromise, in particular) with "rational" empirical/analytical methodologies of scientific decision making, or what has been aptly called "methodological decision-making." Nothing is more irrational to technocratic theorists than the disjointed, incremental forms of decision making (typically described as "muddling through") that result from a political commitment to democratic bargaining and compromise.[14]

Technocrats seek "technical solutions that sidestep the problematic social and political questions" raised by the central issues of the day.[15]

Third, their alignment with those at the top and with the organizational imperatives of the institutions that employ them helps reinforce and even exacerbate the already-existing counterparticipatory tendencies in American government. Peter deLeon puts this as a contest between "Madisonian" and "Tocquevillian"

14. Fischer, *Technocracy*, 22.
15. Fischer, *Technocracy*, 23.

tendencies: "[P]olicy sciences practitioners have enthusiastically applied the utilitarian tradition to Madison's republic of indirect democracy and, in so doing, even furthered his 'indirectness.'" By contrast, the "vast majority of analysts has . . . relatively ignored the de Tocqueville or participatory branch of American democratic theory." The technocratic professionals' "services to democracy come as an after thought to their primary fealty to their governmental agencies."[16] In deLeon's view, nontechnocratic, or Tocquevillian, policy analysts would reverse this tendency and serve the intermediary associations of civil society rather than the state bureaucracy.

The barrier argument does acknowledge the usefulness of technocratic expertise. By relying on policy analysts and organization specialists, officials, of course, short-circuit democratic public discourse with attendant risks I will shortly discuss, but apart from this the barrier argument is equivocal on the issue of technocrat's knowledge superiority. Fischer, for example, claims that the "technical knowledge and skill" of professionals "sustains the power of the top-level political and economic elites." Technocratic professionals "process the critical information essential to the stable and efficient operation of our contemporary institutions."[17] So, there is something "superior" about a technocratic professional's knowledge, yet we can still say it is disempowering because it is directed to elected and administrative officials and not to members of the public and because it serves system imperatives as distinct from social needs.

The risks of short-circuiting democratic public discourse are great, however, and outweigh the knowledge superiority of technocrats. One major risk is to legitimacy: precisely because a technocratic decision has been made outside the normative debates of ordinary politics, it may do little to address public concerns. Apart from threatening the electoral success of the officials who rely on technocratic experts, legitimacy problems can also affect the ability to implement policy. In the case of environmental policy making, for example, lack of citizen trust in expert authority can lead to deep skepticism about how experts have judged risks and impacts of public projects. This skepticism can form into the citizen resistance known as NIMBY (not in my backyard) and NIABY (not in anyone's backyard) movements.[18]

---

16. Peter deLeon, "Democratic Values and the Policy Sciences," *American Journal of Political Science* 39 (1995): 895, 896, 898.

17. Fischer, *Technocracy,* 27, 110.

18. See Frank Fischer, *Citizens, Experts, and the Environment* (Durham: Duke University Press, 2000), 130. See also Gregroy E. McAvoy, *Controlling Technocracy: Citizen Rationality and the Nimby Syndrome* (Washington D.C.: Georgetown University Press, 1999).

A second risk of short-circuiting democratic public discourse is substantive: decisions made by technocrats run a considerable risk of being hostile to public interests. Note, for a moment, Tocqueville's comments on the American public administrators he encountered in the 1830s. Unimpressed, he called them arbitrary, shortsighted, "unskillful and sometimes contemptible"—lacking, indeed, in the technocratic merits. He thought proximity to public participation and awareness caused the flaws of American public administration and resulted in mediocre policy—what he called "repairable mistakes." Yet repairable mistakes, in Tocqueville's view, were far preferable to the mistakes of an elite style of public management with which he was familiar from the French experience. Either out of blindness to class interests other than their own or out of self-confidence in their own powers, the elite style could produce irreparable mistakes: policy decisions with devastating consequences. "It is doubtless important to the good of nations that those who govern have virtues or talents; but what is perhaps still more important to them is that those who govern do not have interests contrary to the mass of the governed; for in that case the virtues could become almost useless and the talents fatal."[19] Tocqueville had in mind policies that created "miseries" for the already disadvantaged members of society. Fischer echoes Tocqueville when he blames the technocratic ethos for large-scale miseries such as the ecological crisis, technological miseries such as the Bhopal chemical leak and Chernobyl radioactive spill disasters, military miseries such as Vietnam, and social policy miseries such as busing and Reaganomics.[20] These expert failures are a result of professionals' remoteness from the ground-level situation, the limits of their methods for seeing the total problem, and their somewhat ideological commitment to certain ideas such as the "domino effect" or "trickle-down economics" that lacked a good deal of sensitivity and, therefore, applicability to particular cases.

The solution to technocratic professionalism under the barrier argument is, simply enough, to remove the barrier. But it is important to notice just who removes the barrier. Fischer advocates participatory policy research as an antidote to technocracy. Policy analysts interested in democracy rather than technocracy will seek to bring affected publics into problem-solving work. Democratic policy analysts, in Fischer's view, are to be inclusive, collaborative, and problem

19. Alexis de Tocqueville, *Democracy in America,* trans. and ed. Harvey C. Mansfield and Delba Winthrop (Chicago: University of Chicago Press, 2000), 214, 222, 223.
20. Fischer, *Technocracy,* 49; *Citizens,* 41.

oriented. They share power over the direction of research with their research subjects and they are motivated less by abstract scholarly goals than by the problems of their research subjects. Fischer's participatory policy analysts are to restrain their expertise, absorb local knowledge, and appeal to citizens for help.[21] To be democratic rather than technocratic, in deLeon's view, "public administrators would have to exchange the bureaucrat's tweeds (and mentalities) for educator's gowns. Policy analysts would need to expand their arsenal of methodologies to include survey instruments, facilitation, field work, and ethnography and to learn to listen as well as analyze, which, as we know, is anything but straightforward."[22]

Limits of the Critique of Professionals as Barriers

A chief problem with the barrier argument is that the substantive "miseries," the threats to legitimacy, and the depoliticization of key social issues all placed at the doorstep of technocratic professionals are probably better seen as the result of many other factors. As argued above, the American system embodies a number of complex layers of competition and stratification. It is a system with many internal barriers to popular influence—a fact praised by Publius in *Federalist No. 10* as he attempted to persuade the New York ratifying convention. It is probably true, as deLeon argues, that technocratic professionals can aggravate the counterparticipatory tendencies of the system. But it is difficult to place as much blame on technocratic experts for social policy miseries without significant qualifications and attention to specific contexts.

The barrier argument, though broad in its attribution of blame, does miss some well-justified targets by being primarily focused on the neopositivistic methods of technocrats. It is true that some experts focus on the technical sides of social and political problems and discount other dimensions. It is also true, however, that we have experts on the normative aspects of social and political problems and thus must worry about technocratic influence over debates about substantive values, not just process and methods. Consider the ethics commissions empanelled by Congress and the president to advise on normative issues raised by new health care technologies such as genetic testing and in vitro fertilization, and by medical research involving controversial new subjects such as stem cells. Seats on such blue-ribbon committees are reserved for medical

21. See Fischer, *Technocracy; Citizens;* and "Citizen Participation and the Democratization of Policy Expertise: From Theoretical Inquiry to Practical Cases," *Policy Sciences* 26 (1993): 165–87.
22. DeLeon, "Democratic Values," 902.

researchers, physicians, hospital and lab administrators, and lawyers, but also for specialists in health care ethics.[23] Though their methods are surely different from the systems theory and cost-benefit analysis of policy analysts, the authority of ethical experts is nonetheless real and its counterdemocratic effects apparent.[24]

The barrier argument also misses something important by being exclusively concerned with policy making. Even in the service of intermediary associations— namely, those with limited formal authority over collective decisions—tech- nocrats can be barriers to participation. If we are worried about nondemocrat- ically accountable influence on collective choice based on specialized knowledge and expertise, we need to cast a more general gaze. These criticisms notwith- standing, barrier critics have usefully pointed to the dangers of depoliticized technocratic decision making for the legitimacy of democratic institutions and protections against risky, immiserating policy choices. Social trustee theorists rarely hint at these real dangers.

Professionals as Disablers Affecting Public Confidence and Competence

While keeping the barrier effects of delegitimation and risky policy making in mind, we need to extend the barrier argument somewhat because we recognize technocratic effects in spheres outside government, we see blocks to participa- tion as being more subtle than the picture drawn by barrier critics, and we see claims of expertise resulting not just from the possession of neopositivistic meth- ods but also from the possession of substantive knowledge of, for example, pol- icy history and ethical issues. Borrowing from Ivan Illich, we need to consider the possibility that professionals disable the lay publics they purport to help.

Illich believed a number of socially prominent professions possessed what he called prescriptive power: "Professionals tell you what you need and claim the power to prescribe. They not only recommend what is good, but actually ordain what is right. Neither income, long training, delicate tasks nor social standing is the mark of the professional. Rather, it is his authority to define a person as client, to determine that person's need and to hand the person a prescription."[25]

---

23. Susan Cartier Poland, "Bioethics Commissions: Town Meetings with a 'Blue, Blue Ribbon,'" *Kennedy Institute of Ethics Journal* 8 (1998): 91–109.

24. See Albert W. Dzur and Daniel Levin, "The 'Nation's Conscience': Assessing Bioethics Com- missions as Public Forums," *Kennedy Institute of Ethics Journal* 14 (2004): 333–60.

25. Ivan Illich, *Disabling Professions* (New York: Marion Boyars, 1977), 17.

Illich saw that prescriptive power was the product of a nexus of interests among professional groups and states. States enable professions to have prescriptive power by granting exclusive licenses to perform certain tasks such as practicing law. This clearly benefits professions since they have protected and self-regulated markets for their services.

Prescriptive power disables, quite straightforwardly, by taking tasks away from laypeople. As contemporary social theorists such as Freidson, Larson, and Abbott have shown, professions have interests in gaining, maintaining, and extending occupational control over tasks and problem areas. This control lends authority to professional representations of both personal and political issues related to such tasks and problem areas. Illich's work on professional power in the medical domain describes how treatment tasks become not just the legitimate function of medicine but also become illegitimate when done by laypeople.[26] To a significant degree, laypeople cannot treat or medicate themselves without possibly being subjected to prosecution. Nils Christie, a critic of disabling professionalism writing about the criminal justice domain, claims that these "professional thieves" are task monopolists who have stolen the tasks of adjudicating criminal conflicts. "Many among us have, as laymen, experienced the sad moments of truth when our lawyers tell us that our best arguments in our fight against our neighbour are without any legal relevance whatsoever and that we for God's sake ought to keep quiet about them in court." And "treatment personnel" such as social workers, case managers, and others go so far as to convert "the image of the case from one of conflict into one of non-conflict."[27]

This crucial concept of task monopolization extends the issues raised by critics of professionals as barriers. Prescriptive power disables along a wide range of tasks involving more than instrumental rationality. The technocratic task monopolization that worries critics of disabling professionalism does not involve separating and discounting subjective elements of decisions from the objective means-ends reasoning in which professionals are trained. Social ends and values we wish to pursue are in fact subjects of expertise. The experts of the criminal justice domain—the prosecutors, defense attorneys, judges, case managers, and social workers—are not just working on the means to justice, they are defining what counts as justice. What is lost, writes Christie, are "opportunities for norm-clarification . . . opportunities for a continuous discussion of what

---

26. Ivan Illich, *Medical Nemesis: The Expropriation of Health* (New York: Random House, 1976), 41–43.

27. Nils Christie, "Conflicts as Property," *The British Journal of Criminology* 17 (1977): 4.

represents the law of the land."[28] When a harm is taken up by the state and prosecuted, the victim loses the chance to communicate to the offender and the offender loses the chance to seek forgiveness. More participatory forms of criminal adjudication, involving affected communities and oriented toward reparations and apologies rather than prison time, for example, are shut out as options because of the procedures followed by professionals.

In addition to being a barrier between the public and elites, for critics of disabling professionalism technocratic task monopolization shrinks the space of public decision in and out of formal institutions of collective choice. These critics see a range of social problems captured by professions: objective news about public issues captured by journalists, just social order captured by criminal justice professionals, humane health care captured by health care professionals. Not only do they provide these services, they in large part define what counts as satisfactory service provision. Giandomenico Majone, focusing on the public policy process, writes, "Far from waiting passively for the stipulation of public values to be served, policy analysts and researchers are often deeply involved in the process of norm setting."[29] Raising many of the concerns later taken up by deliberative democrats, Lawrence Tribe notes that "the whole point of personal or social choice in many situations is not to implement a given system of values in the light of the perceived facts, but rather to define, and sometimes deliberately to reshape, the values—and hence the identity—of the individual or community that is engaged in the process of choosing."[30] Such critics see such expert involvement and dominance over normative deliberation in all spheres of social life.

In addition to task monopolization, prescriptive power disables, more subtly, by making laypeople less confident in their own powers. Critics of disabling professionalism wonder whether professionals know us better than we know ourselves. As Bruce Jennings states, "The professions are powerful shaping forces in our culture. . . . They affect not only how individuals live and how institutions work, but also the way we think about how we should live and about the ends our social institutions should serve."[31] Illich writes of the "citizen-become-client"

28. Christie, "Conflicts as Property," 8.

29. Giandomenico Majone, *Evidence, Argument, and Persuasion in the Policy Process* (New Haven: Yale University Press, 1989), 24.

30. Lawrence H. Tribe, "Policy Science: Analysis or Ideology," *Philosophy and Public Affairs* 2 (1972): 99.

31. Bruce Jennings, Daniel Callahan, and Susan M. Wolf, "The Professions: Public Interest and Common Good," in "The Public Duties of the Professions," special supplement, *Hastings Center Report* 17, no. 1 (1987): 8.

inhabiting a "world-become-ward: . . . The language in which he perceives himself, his perception of rights and freedoms, and his awareness of needs all derive from professional hegemony." The result of "professional disqualification of lay opinion" is loss of both personal and political liberty understood as a self-confident responsibility for personal and collective choices.[32]

Prescriptive power would be disabling even if there were no layer of technocratic elites between the people and the officials. As Foucault famously observed, we must "cut off the king's head in political theory" to see how power enables and disables inside and outside formal channels of official authority. Foucault's monumental historical studies illustrate how the expert knowledge and specialized practices of professionals such as psychiatrists, criminologists, physicians, public health officers, urban planners, and others are joined to the interests and institutions of social control:

> [I]n the nineteenth century, there developed around the judicial institution—to enable it to assume the function of controlling individuals at the level of their *dangerousness*—a vast series of institutions that would enclose individuals in their bounds throughout their existence: pedagogic institutions such as the school, psychological or psychiatric institutions such as the hospital, the asylum, the police, and so on. This whole network of nonjudicial power was designed to fulfill one of the functions that the justice system assumed at this time: no longer punishing individuals' infractions, but correcting their potentialities. . . . This is the age of social control.[33]

The professional is supervisor, examiner, and service provider in this "vast series of institutions," placing the layperson not so much in a state of powerlessness as in a condition of dependency.

The disabling professional looms large in the space between citizens and the formal politics of lawmaking and regulation—the space I have been calling "middle democracy" and that Foucault argues is pervaded by a logic of "governmentality" inhabited by a "whole set of little powers, of little institutions situated at

---

32. Illich, *Disabling Professions*, 26, 28.

33. Michel Foucault, "Truth and Juridical Forms," in *Essential Works of Foucault, 1954–1984*, vol. 3, ed. Paul Rabinow and James D. Faubion (New York: The New Press, 2000), 57. There is a considerable overlap between what Foucault calls "disciplines" and modern professions. Disciplines are the knowledges developed and used by modern professionals. See Jan Goldstein, "Foucault Among the Sociologists: The "Disciplines" and the History of the Professions," *History and Theory* 23 (1984): 170–92.

the lowest level," and oriented toward the "management of population in its depths and details."[34] The professional is the one who counts, organizes, predicts, and manages all in the service of the health, welfare, and security of citizens now more consumers of services than participants in any form of collective sovereignty. The professional is given authority and credibility by the very governmentality that his actions, methods, and results support. To those who argue that such professionals have led to progressively better welfare for most moderns—safer streets, more hygienic water and sewage, more humane care for the sick—radical critics respond that disabling professionals do indeed serve this new kind of citizen as consumer and dependent. Yet, at the same time, the disabling professions have prevented other forms of well-being, of subjectivity, so to speak, from emerging.

To put this in perspective, consider the concept of "democratic trust"—the faith in the capacity of nonexperts to contribute to public choice. A negative consequence of deference to professional task monopolists is the risk that the general public loses such democratic trust, loses confidence in the competence of laypeople in making informed collective decisions about issues that relate to professional domains of action. Even the best intentioned of professions demand a vertical trust that threatens citizen-to-citizen horizontal trust.[35] Individuals, social movements, communities, and the "general public" all become reflected back by entrusted professions. Professions, along with providing services, mediate self, social, and political relations. Through the mediation of psychologists, lawyers, and public administrators, among others, citizens can lose

---

34. Foucault, "Truth and Juridical Forms," 86–87.

35. Most academic discussions of trust focus on the broader issue of reliance on others in the economic, social, political, and personal domains. Even scholarship on trust in the political domain tends to stress the importance of vertical trust between citizens and their representatives. See, for example, Valerie Braithwaite and Margaret Levi, *Trust and Governance* (New York: Russell Sage, 1998). Likewise, discussions of trust in the professions focus on fiduciary relationships between individual clients and professionals. See, for example, Edmund D. Pellegrino, Robert M. Veatch, and J. P. Langan, eds., *Ethics, Trust, and the Professions: Philosophical and Cultural Aspects* (Washington, D.C.: Georgetown University Press, 1991). What I mean by "horizontal" trust is quite specific: confidence in our ability to self-govern. For more on the vertical/horizontal distinction and on the importance of being able to trust other citizens, see Claus Offe, "How Can We Trust Our Fellow Citizens?" in *Democracy and Trust*, ed. Mark E. Warren (Cambridge: Cambridge University Press, 1999), 42–87. Students of trust have shown a decline not only in Americans' "vertical" trust in politicians, but also in "horizontal" trust in themselves and others: "the problem is not just that Americans are losing faith in politicians and other leaders. According to national surveys, Americans are also less willing now than in the past to believe that people in general can be trusted" (Robert Wuthnow, "The Role of Trust in Civic Renewal," in *Civil Society, Democracy, and Civic Renewal*, ed. Robert K. Fullinwider {Lanham, Md.: Rowman and Littlefield, 1999], 210).

trust in how capable they are as persons, how capable their neighbors are, and how they all are in collective action. In Foucault's terms, they lose the will to say "no" to being treated as consumers rather than citizens, "no" to their condition of dependency.

Limits to the Critique of Disabling Professionals

The argument about disabling professionals extends and makes more precise the concerns about professional authority raised by the barrier argument, but it has some weaknesses. In the first place, though critics of disabling professionalism are right to identify the negative impact of professional "thieves" and task monopolists on civic engagement, they overestimate the degree of impact. Contemporary scholarship on civic engagement and disengagement gives factors such as suburban sprawl, mass media consumption, historical generation effects, and national projects supported by the federal government the lion's share of the praise or blame for large-scale background conditions of civic engagement and disengagement.[36]

A consequence of inflating the negative civic impact of professions is the skepticism about any positive role for professionalism or the possibility of reconstructing professional powers along civic lines. Critics such as Illich, Christie, and Foucault hold that the solution to disabling professions is deprofessionalization. "[M]y project," explains Foucault, "is precisely to bring it about that they 'no longer know what to do,' so that the acts, gestures, discourses that up until then had seemed to go without saying become problematic, difficult, dangerous."[37] If the psychiatrist, for example, as a disabling professional "steals" the voice and ability of the patient diagnosed as mad, an antipsychiatrist is needed to return self-sovereignty to the patient and allow that voice to come forward, "giving the individual the right to take his madness to the limit, to see it through, in an experience to which others may contribute, but never in the name of a power that would be conferred on them by their reason or their normality." The antipsychiatrist liberates patients from their medical status, "freeing them

36. See, for example, Robert D. Putnam, *Bowling Alone: The Collapse and Revival of American Community* (New York: Touchstone, 2000), 283–84; and Theda Skocpol, "How Americans Became Civic," in *Civic Engagement in American Democracy,* ed. Theda Skocpol and Morris P. Fiorina (Washington, D.C.: Brookings Institution Press, 1999), 27–80.

37. Michel Foucault, "Questions of Method," in *Essential Works of Foucault, 1954–1984,* vol. 3, ed. Rabinow and Faubion, 235.

from a diagnosis and a symptomatology that had not simply a value of classification but also one of decision and decree."[38]

As Foucault suggests, for many radical critics, deprofessionalization entails more than avoiding certain practices. The proper role for the professional is to scrutinize and criticize his own knowledge and skills, especially insofar as they prevent lay citizens from speaking and acting for themselves—to, in Foucault's words, "struggle against the forms of power that transform him into its object and instrument in the sphere of 'knowledge,' 'truth,' 'consciousness,' and 'discourse.'"[39] This oppositional stance toward mainstream professional knowledge and practice seeks to clear the way for patients, prisoners, wards, and lay citizens to reestablish competencies and authority over tasks such as telling their own stories, policing their own behavior, and solving their own personal and social problems.

The deprofessionalization solution to the problem of disabling professionalism is more drastic than it needs to be. The critics of disabling professionalism, after all, are intellectuals and academics steeped in the original, or "ur-professional," university traditions of humanism and rational analysis. Their professional training did not erode their sensitivity to issues of power and authority or their commitment to share tasks with the lay public. This is not to tar radical critics with the charge of hypocrisy, but only with being insufficiently self-reflective about the resources internal to professional education and practice for a more democratic mode of professionalism. Additionally, though this is a crucial and valid concept, critics of disabling professionalism overstate the ways professional task monopolization is a kind of theft with the consequence of overestimating the lay public's willingness to take up such tasks in professional domains and in the public sphere. In the case of criminal justice, for example, as we will see later in Chapter 6, it has proven quite difficult for restorative justice reformers to return professional tasks to communities. Far from simply stepping aside, such professional reformers have had to actively mobilize and recruit lay participants.[40] Similarly, lay participation in health policy has tended to be seeded by reform-minded professionals aware of the importance of civic engagement.[41]

38. Michel Foucault, "Psychiatric Power," in *Essential Works of Foucault, 1954–1984,* vol. 1, ed. Paul Rabinow (New York: The New Press, 1997), 49.

39. Michel Foucault, "Intellectuals and Power," in *Language, Counter-Memory, Practice,* ed. Donald Bouchard (Ithaca: Cornell University Press, 1977), 208.

40. See Susan M. Olson and Albert W. Dzur, "Reconstructing Professional Roles in Restorative Justice Programs," *Utah Law Review,* no. 1 (2003): 57–89.

41. See James A. Morone, *The Democratic Wish: Popular Participation and the Limits of American Government* (New York: Basic Books, 1990), 253–321; and Bruce Jennings, "A Grassroots Movement in Bioethics," special supplement, *Hastings Center Report* 18, no. 3 (1988): 1–16.

The critique of disabling professionalism also neglects the ways that professionals can and should enable laypeople and even out the playing field. In the case of criminal justice, for example, it is hardly advantageous for victims to track down and prosecute offenders. In a social world with considerable asymmetries of physical force, social status, and financial power, the procedural symmetry provided by police, prosecutors, and judges cannot be gainsaid. One classic criticism of deprofessionalized informal justice made by law and society scholars is that the already-disempowered risk losing the very real advantages of procedural fairness.[42] In the profession of journalism, too, as we will see in Chapter 5, specialists in information gathering help even out the playing field by "comforting the afflicted and afflicting the comfortable." The critique of disabling professionalism points only to the risks of professionalism, but the advantages must also be acknowledged in order to make sense of the complex relationship between professionals and democracy.

Pruning and Reshaping the Radical Critique

Challenging the Social Trustee Model in the Right Places

Under the terms of the social trustee model, professionals serve the public through their commitment to high standards of practice, a normative orientation toward a specific and delimited sphere of social concern, and self-regulation. The model is held together on the basis of what I call an economy of trust: the public places trust in the professional to self-regulate and determine standards of practice, while the professional earns that trust by performing competently and adhering to the socially responsible normative orientation. Even though I have rejected some elements of the radical critique, in my view it effectively challenges the social trustee model and its economy of trust in exactly the right places: professionals can be barriers to public interests and they can disable the process by which the public determines its interests. It is not just by failing to live up to the social trustee model or merely appearing to be social trustees—

42. See, for example, Richard Abel, "The Contradictions of Informal Justice," in *The Politics of Informal Justice, Volume 1: The American Experience,* ed. Abel (New York: Academic Press, 1982), 267–320; Richard Delgado, "Fairness and Formality: Minimizing the Risk of Prejudice in Alternative Dispute Resolution," *Wisconsin Law Review* (1985): 1359–1403; and Christine Harrington, *Shadow Justice: The Ideology and Institutionalization of Alternatives to Court* (Westport, Conn.: Greenwood Press, 1985).

as through ethics codes that are rarely substantively applied to practice—that professionals block and disable. This is where the limits of contemporary sociological critics of the professions and applied ethicists become evident. The problem is not social responsibility as an ideology that cloaks commercial self-interest or as a weak promise that needs continual ethical analysis and advice. Rather, the economy of trust that makes the social trustee ideal work effectively excludes lay participation, allowing others—whether these are professionals or, as is increasingly common today, professional ethicists—to define the meaning of public service and determine what counts as breaches in ethical conduct.

We should take from the radical critique the focus on these specific negative consequences and potential negative consequences. Consider two concrete consequences it brings forward: delegitimation and disempowerment. In the professional domains of journalism, criminal justice, and medicine featured in Chapters 5, 6, and 7, evidence exists that technocratic and disabling practices that bar or undermine civic education and participation can lead to both the delegitimation of professional claims to status and authority as well as the disempowerment of communities affected by such actions. Very different sorts of task monopolization are taking place in these three domains, however, and the relationship between these domains and public deliberation over social choices is also different.

Jujitsu: Reprofessionalization, Not Deprofessionalization, as a Way to Remove Barriers and Enable Engagement

Radical critics illuminate how professions are political: they affect how public policies are shaped, influence the way members of the public conceive their interests and their ability to achieve their goals, and exert considerable power and authority over many social tasks within middle democracy. Yet having politicized the professions, radical critics seek to remove them from the political domain.

Deprofessionalization is a mistake, however, because to the extent that professionals serve as barriers and as disablers, they can also, if motivated, serve as barrier removers and enablers. Under modern conditions of complexity, professional skills and knowledge can help laypeople manage their personal and collective affairs. For fostering rational, respectful, and accountable public deliberation under contemporary civic conditions marked by apathy, distrust, and political ignorance, deprofessionalization is hardly the solution. Rather, a different kind of professionalization, one oriented toward public capabilities, is called for.

It is also a mistake to think of deprofessionalization as the answer when there is already a reservoir of support, albeit unstructured, within professions to reform practices so that they do not form barriers and disable. Chapters 5, 6, and 7 center around reform-minded professionals in journalism, criminal justice, and medicine who actively involve lay participants in professional tasks, build civic capacity, and foster public deliberation.

It will also be clear, however, that reformers run the risk of over- and under-shooting their goals because they lack an adequate positive account of post-technocratic and post-disabling professionalism. An overly general concern with the effects of traditional professional practice on civic disengagement and alienation, for example, can lead to what I call delusions of civic grandeur on the part of a reform-minded profession: the quixotic attempt to single-handedly, as it were, lead the public into a more deliberative mode. An overly general concern for empowerment can also lead to the uncritical acceptance of conventional morality. Such issues illustrate the need for a positive, but also more realistic, conception of nontechnocratic and nondisabling professionalism: democratic professionalism.

Indeed, a third reason why deprofessionalization is a mistaken response to technocratic and disabling professionalism is that contemporary professions are under significant threat from both market and state pressures. What Elliott Krause calls the "guild power" of professions to shape their associational life, their work-places, and the market for their services has eroded significantly in the face of encroaching market and state power:

> [P]recipitous increases in the costs to both capitalism and the state of the services provided by professions . . . [have] increasingly led capi-
> talism and the state to new working relations with professionals and further challenges to professional group guild power. The regulatory agencies, especially the Federal Trade Commission, have redefined pro-
> fessional work and professions as equally susceptible to regulation as all other forms of commerce, rescinding a long-held exemption. The payout agencies for professional services, especially the Department of Health and Human Services for health work, have taken on a new role in shaping practice by professionals. . . . The clear trend is for the key professions to lose guild power, while the marginal professions never developed any to begin with.[43]

43. Elliott Krause, *The Death of the Guilds: Professions, States, and the Advance of Capitalism, 1930 to the Present* (New Haven: Yale University Press, 1996), 33.

Though imperfect in ways that radical critics have stressed, professionalism at its best offers alternatives to market and state imperatives. What radical critics miss in their advocacy of deprofessionalization is how professions as intermediary associations can help disperse power over workplaces and offer ways of motivating innovation, service quality, and attention to social problems that are distinct from the ways and means of the market and the state.

Professions should retain a certain degree of separate authority and autonomy, albeit grounded in both the competence, skill, and social responsibility values lauded by the social trustee model *and* the participatory democratic values of the radical critique. Deprofessionalization is a self-defeating strategy if the goal is to empower the lay public and to secure linkages between formal institutions of democracy and informal public dialogue. In a contemporary polity marked by high levels of civic disengagement, that reform-minded professionals are seeking ways of mobilizing and including lay participants should be celebrated with at least two cheers. Yet, again, mere mobilization is insufficient. Lay voices ought to be respected, of course, but also subjected to the criticism of peers and to the criticism of those with more experience and training.

Conclusion: Toward a Democratic Professionalism

Professions are more political than many social theorists and applied ethicists who study the professions think. Professional norms detract from and contribute to democratic practice. Radical critics in America and Europe recognize this when they point to the detrimental effects of technocratic and disabling professional action in democracies. These critics argue that professions take over tasks that should be done by laypeople. Radical critics recognize that modern divisions of labor mean that for the sake of efficiency, productivity, not to mention innovation, differently talented and trained people do different things. What worries them is not modernity, not task distribution, but a task monopoly that blocks participation, shrinks the space of democratic authority, and disables and immobilizes citizens who might occupy that space. As Table 2 illustrates, the radical critique offers a striking challenge to mainstream social trustee conceptions of professionalism.

Professions shrink the space of democratic authority when they perform public purposes that could conceivably be done by laypeople. So, journalists provide information, doctors aid human welfare, and criminal justice administrators serve

Table 2. Social trustee model contrasted with radical critique of professionalism

	Social trustee	Radical critique
Main characteristics of a profession:	Knowledge, self-regulation, social responsibility	Power to define interests for the public
Social duties of professionals flow from:	Group experience, functional purposes, tacit exchange	Interest in retaining social authority and market security
Professionals' view of laypeople:	Clients, consumers, wards	Incompetent at high-level tasks
Ideal role of professional in society:	Expert, specialist, guide	Self-reflective critic of professionalism and expert task monopoly
Professional ethics best fixed and overseen:	By professionals themselves	By laypeople
Political role of professions:	Protection for professional interests and social functions	Disabling intermediary between lay citizens and democratic institutions

our needs for just security. Critics of disabling professionalism rightly stress that these services and products have public consequences: how they are done affects people not just as individuals but also as members of an ongoing collective. And as critics of professionals as barriers point out, sometimes professionals quite literally shrink the space of participation by deciding public issues in professional buildings and administrative complexes far from potential sites of participation.

Professions can disable and immobilize because, in addition to taking over these public-oriented tasks, professionals' sophistication in telling stories, healing, and sentencing makes people less comfortable with relying on their own devices for objective news, good health, and just security. Professions are professions by virtue of their application of abstract—not commonly shared—knowledge to serve social needs such as information, health, and justice. The status and authority of professional work depend on the deference of nonmembers—their acknowledgment that professionals perform these tasks better than nonmembers could. But with this deference comes the risk that members of the general public lose confidence in the competence of laypeople in making informed collective decisions about issues that relate to professional domains of action.

There are other, structural causes of civic disability, immobility, and contracted democratic authority, however. As John Dewey pointed out in his great discussion of democracy and expert knowledge, *The Public and Its Problems,* large-scale social and economic forces are the major factors in laypeople losing both

will and ability. Though radical critics are right that professionals are key intermediaries between the public and these forces, they have missed, first, how professionals can help or hinder the public's ability to understand and shape their
effects and, second, how professionals themselves are vulnerable to these same
large-scale social and economic forces.

How professional actors can help mobilize rather than immobilize, expand
rather than shrink democratic authority—what can be called the second face of
professionalism—is left largely unexplored in the radical critique. Critics such
as Illich, Christie, and Foucault lack a degree of self-awareness. Many critics of
technocracy emerged from the professional domain—in Illich's case, the clergy
and the academy; in Christie's case, criminology and criminal justice administration; and in Foucault's case, the ur-profession of the academy. Few recognize
much significance in the fact that those, like themselves, marshaling the call
for lay participation in sites of expert authority, are people trained for and even
occupying such sites. This suggests that there are internal resources available for
a new, more democratic mode of professionalism.

A number of contemporary reform movements within professions, in contrast with these critics, see both faces of professionalism. In seeking to change
key governing norms of practice within medicine, journalism, and criminal justice, they acknowledge the positive democratic potential of their domains. What
these reformers recognize that radical critics of technocratic professionalism miss
is the possibility that professionals might have a hand in reversing trends in democratic contraction and civic immobility. Contemporary reformers also see the
vulnerability of a merely commercial or merely technocratic professionalism. In
contrast, radical critics fail to fully appreciate the legitimacy problems of professions that are remote from the publics they serve.

Social trustee impulses need to be redirected, but they should not be extin-
guished. If anything, they need to be renewed at a time when professional
autonomy and normative orientation are under siege by market and state pressures on most professional domains. Professions can serve social interests above
and beyond individual client needs. The social trustee model fails, and fails mis-
erably, in recognizing the importance of opening up the process of defining
social interests to those affected by professional action. The radical critique makes
us aware of this failure by drawing attention to the harmful antidemocratic consequences of professional task monopoly.

The democratic professionalism model proposed in the next chapter is an
attempt to both absorb what is valuable in both social trustee professionalism

and its radical critics as well as go beyond these models. In the chapters that follow, public journalism, restorative justice, and the bioethics movement are examined as democratic professional movements. Though imperfect, these movements are trying to work out a better relationship between the tasks in which they specialize, the public that benefits from them, and the institutions of formal democratic and informal professional power that grant authority.

Democratic professionals are concerned about the effects of their expertise on the lay public's ability to make self-confident choices both inside and outside a particular professional domain. Though they retain the authority and at least somewhat privileged voice of people with experience and specialized training, they recognize that they may know only part of what is important in reaching a decision about a treatment plan, a service, or a public policy that relates to their domain. Above all, they seek to open their professional domain to other voices, other experiences. By mobilizing, actively recruiting, and including lay participants in both decision-making and agenda-setting capacities in news forums, on hospital ethics committees, in restorative justice proceedings, and elsewhere, democratic professionals may not solve the large-scale problem of civic disengagement, but they very well may encourage, incrementally, the norms and activities of public deliberation in the middle democracy within the reach of every person, lay and professional alike.

4

TASK SHARING FOR DEMOCRACY:
THEMES FROM POLITICAL THEORY

The possibility that professionals can serve as facilitators in a more active and engaged democracy is the central focus of the model of democratic professionalism. Just as task monopolists take away civic competencies, task sharers can help citizens gain competence or, equally important, help citizens understand when and why to hand over a job with public purposes to those with professional training and experience. Reformers can open spaces for public contribution within previously remote structures—the journalists of Chapter 5 share some of the authority for determining the news by taking cues from their communities rather than officials, the health care workers of Chapter 7 defer to laypeople over issues of clinical ethics policy, and the criminal justice administrators of Chapter 6 have devolved the task of sentencing some classes of offenses to citizen panels meeting in public-friendly places.

Only a third model of professionalism, one that builds on the insights of both social trusteeism and the radical critique, will help us understand why reform-minded professionals who have grown uncomfortable with the antidemocratic tendencies of their domains would seek to open up sites of authority that currently give them a good deal of power, status, and economic security. This model should comport with what reformers themselves think, but it will also put their actions in a broader web of meaning. Reforms will ebb and flow, perhaps mostly ebb, but theorizing the significance of these reforms may bolster such efforts and provide support for the next round of reforms over the long term.

In this chapter I draw on a sparse but important literature in political theory to construct a model of democratic professionalism that emphasizes the value of professionals sharing some of their space and competencies with members of the lay public. Following the lead of radical critics, I ask what the value of task sharing within the specific sites of professional authority is for the professions

themselves, the laypeople involved, and the active participation in public deliberation and collective decision making that is definitive of a more deliberative
democracy. Two canonical political theorists, Alexis de Tocqueville and John
Dewey, are useful guides in thinking about task-sharing professionals as important actors in American democracy.

Like radical critics and unlike social trustee thinkers, Tocqueville and Dewey
take seriously the democratic consequences of professional action. They emphasize the professions' intermediary role between individual and state, a role that
is misunderstood but critical to properly functioning democratic institutions.
Though aware of the political dimensions of professional power, Tocqueville and
Dewey show professions as intermediaries in democracy that can express healthy
forms of power and authority. Democratic professionals can facilitate and enable
civic engagement and public deliberation while also expecting lay citizens to
learn from professionals with greater training and experience in particular areas.
Tocqueville's and Dewey's characterization of a mutually deferential relationship between professional and citizen transcends the one-sided accounts of these
relations expressed by the social trustee and radical critique models of professionalism. While Tocqueville and Dewey share the social trustee view that professionals protect and exercise forms of knowledge and skill that are good for the
public even if they are not fully comprehended by the public, they share radical critics' view that professional domains are to be porous to lay involvement.

Turning from the canonical, this chapter considers two theorists who have
brought Tocqueville's and Dewey's thinking into contemporary times. William
Sullivan and Frank Fischer stress the continuing importance of professionals to
a public culture of democracy, though both are wary of current commercial and
technocratic trends. These contemporary theorists affirm central insights of Tocqueville and Dewey, but they also raise concerns about the viability of the democratic professional model put forward in this chapter and its potential for abuse.

Tocqueville: Task Sharing in American Democracy

Alexis de Tocqueville was no participatory democrat. He believed in natural
differences among people that marked special competencies for governing, and
he believed that the Americans of the 1830s wound up shortchanging themselves because of their resistance to elites.[1] He saw the egalitarian currents in

---

1. Elites are not necessarily aristocrats. Tocqueville was under no illusion about aristocracy; in his

American politics, such as an expanded electorate compared to the France or Britain of 1830; in American society, such as an assumption of moral equality regardless of family background; and in American economy, such as the operative principle of careers open to talents, as contributing to skepticism of the wrong sort about the professional authority of administrators and other officials. Also because of equality Americans were not skeptical enough in the right sort of way about centralized authority. Yet Tocqueville advocated the practice of sharing potentially professionalized tasks at certain levels of government and in civil society. Such task sharing would, in his view, mitigate against corrosive skepticism by building horizontal and vertical relationships of trust and deference.

Political Socialization Through Task Sharing in Township Government and the Jury

Liberty, for Tocqueville and for most political theorists, means that people ought to be free to conduct their lives, make their own mistakes, and learn from them. Tocqueville thought there was a political dimension to liberty as well: liberty means responsibility for one's self, as well as responsibility for one's society and government. To have full liberty is to be capable of bearing the responsibility for political decision making.[2] Just as someone who turns over their personal decisions to others is unfree in an important respect similarly is someone who turns over their role in political decisions unfree. One can be happy, more efficient, and more healthy if one turns over the burdens of self- and collective government to others, but one will be less free.

At its best, American democracy in the early nineteenth century offered many opportunities for the exercise of freedom. Tocqueville was impressed with how Americans shared governing tasks especially at the level of local or town government, that in Europe would be professionalized and centralized.

> It is . . . in the township that the force of free peoples resides. The institutions of a township are to freedom what primary schools are to science; they put it within reach of the people; they make them taste its peaceful employ and habituate them to making use of it. Without

---

view, ascriptive status, hierarchy, strict and exclusionary social codes of behavior, and limited social mobility were all well on their way to being dots in history's rear-view mirror.

2. For more on this "positive" understanding of liberty in Tocqueville, see Jack Lively, *The Social and Political Thought of Alexis de Tocqueville* (Oxford: Clarendon Press, 1965), 15, 227.

the institutions of a township a nation can give itself a free government, but it does not have the spirit of freedom. Fleeting passions, the interests of a moment, the chance of circumstances can give it the external forms of independence; but despotism suppressed in the interior of the social body reappears sooner or later on the surface.[3]

[I]n this restricted sphere that is within his reach [the citizen of the New England township] tries to govern society; he habituates himself to the forms without which freedom proceeds only through revolutions, permeates himself with their spirit, gets a taste for order, understands the harmony of powers, and finally assembles clear and practical ideas on the nature of his duties as well as the extent of his rights.[4]

Notice the term "habituate."[5] For Tocqueville, freedom is not just the right to vote and hold office even if you do not in fact vote or hold office. Freedom is an ability—indeed a self-recognized responsibility—and the task sharing of township democracy was one way Americans learned this ability. Also notice what Tocqueville anticipates as the risk of *not* sharing the tasks of governance: instability and despotism.

Nineteenth-century township government works, in Tocqueville's account, through direct democratic procedures and through numerous offices of public authority that are, at least in principle, open to all. Scattered power or task sharing spreads useful habits of active citizenship. Extrapolating from Tocqueville's discussion, one can say that task sharing encourages capabilities, interests, and norms of behavior needed for functioning democracy. By participating in governance, people learn how to hold a meeting, raise a point, and argue well with others. Their interest in attending to public issues and other people's views also increases. Last, but not least, they learn how to comport themselves in public as a public. They learn to curb desires for more time, responsibility, or credit than is due. They learn how to leave a lost dispute at the meeting house and do not seek street justice. Such capabilities, interests, and norms are endogenous to the practice of free institutions and civil associations. Though some may be

3. Alexis de Tocqueville, *Democracy in America,* trans. and ed. Harvey C. Mansfield and Delba Winthrop (Chicago: University of Chicago Press, 2000), 58 [1.1.5]. I have placed numbers representing the volume, part, and chapter of *Democracy in America* in brackets for easy access to other translations.
4. Tocqueville, *Democracy in America,* 65 [1.1.5].
5. George Lawrence's translation of *Democracy in America* (New York: Harper and Row, 1966) uses "accustom" and "gets to know," but my point about political socialization still holds.

exogenously formed in the private sphere of family life, it is doubtful that people could be fully "habituated" for the demands of orderly civic participation by dinner table arguments at home.[6]

Task sharing also allows Americans to express and temper their ambitions. Because of the limited opportunities available for the ambitious at the state and federal level, the township is the more likely stage for the dramatization of one's abilities: "It is in the township, at the center of the ordinary relations of life, that desire for esteem, the need of real interests, the taste for power and for attention, come to be concentrated; these passions, which so often trouble society, change character when they can be expressed so near the domestic hearth and in a way in the bosom of the family." Ambitions are also tempered in this process by the very fact that so many others are in positions of authority: "[H]ow many diverse offices, how many different magistrates, who all, within the sphere of their prerogatives, represent the powerful corporation in whose name they act! How many men thus exploit the power of the township for their profit and take interest in it for themselves!"[7] Americans defer and are deferred to in turn; these are healthy relations of authority.

Like the township form of government, Tocqueville views the American jury system as a kind of task sharing that leads to healthy relations of authority. The independent, self-confident American is socialized into orderly habits of formal decision making by taking part in formal decisions. Like participation in township governance, lay participation in the justice system helps Americans be free by cultivating habits of freedom—capacities, interests, and norms of behavior. "The jury," writes Tocqueville, "serves to give to the minds of all citizens a part of the habits of mind of the judge; and these habits are precisely those that best prepare the people to be free."[8] Habits of the judge's mind include an awareness and respect for procedures, the complexity of law, and the norm of impartiality.[9] As in his earlier discussion of township task sharing, the risk of not cultivating such habits is instability. The jury, for Tocqueville, "spreads to all classes respect for the thing judged and the idea of right. Remove these two things, and love of independence will be no more than a destructive passion."[10]

6. See the discussion of these factors in Robert D. Putnam's *Bowling Alone: The Collapse and Revival of American Community* (New York: Touchstone, 2000), 338–40.
7. Tocqueville, *Democracy in America*, 64 [1.1.5].
8. Tocqueville, *Democracy in America*, 262 [1.2.8].
9. Lively, *Social and Political Thought of Tocqueville*, 181.
10. Tocqueville, *Democracy in America*, 262 [1.2.8].

Just as participating in legislation and administration in the township is both a general political education and an education in the competencies of those domains, so jury duties teach both about government and about what is needed in the judicial sphere:

> It [the jury] teaches men the practice of equity. Each, in judging his neighbor, thinks that he could be judged in his turn.
>
> The jury teaches each man not to recoil before responsibility for his own acts—a virile disposition without which there is no political virtue.
>
> It vests each citizen with a sort of magistracy; it makes all feel that they have duties toward society to fulfill and that they enter into its government. In forcing men to occupy themselves with something other than their own affairs, it combats individual selfishness, which is like the blight of societies.
>
> The jury serves incredibly to form the judgment and to augment the natural enlightenment of the people. There, in my opinion, is its greatest advantage. One ought to consider it as a school, free of charge and always open, where each juror comes to be instructed in his rights, where he enters into daily communication with the most instructed and most enlightened members of the elevated classes, where the laws are taught to him in a practical manner and are put within reach of his intelligence by the efforts of the attorneys, the advice of the judge, and the very passions of the parties.[11]

Compare Tocqueville's task sharing defense of the jury with the similarly robust argument of the Anti-Federalist "Federal Farmer," who wrote that it was only by serving as jurors that ordinary citizens could "acquire information and knowledge in the affairs and government of the society" that would enable them "to come forward, in turn, as the sentinels and guardians of each other."[12] The Federal Farmer is primarily interested in power sharing and in keeping laypeople inside institutions of power as watchdogs on elites. Tocqueville, while certainly interested in task and power sharing, emphasizes the use of lay participation as

11. Tocqueville, *Democracy in America*, 262 [1.2.8.].

12. Federal Farmer, Letter IV, in *The Anti-Federalist: Writings by the Opponents of the Constitution*, ed. Herbert J. Storing and Murray Dry (Chicago: University of Chicago Press, 1985), 58–59.

a mode of socializing citizens to functional roles within government and to accept a degree of deference to those occupying higher roles.

Far from merely constraining the power of the judge, the jury system legitimates the power of the judge. Especially in civil trials, the judge "unfolds before them the various arguments with which their memories have been tired, and he who takes them by the hand to direct them through the turns of the proceeding; it is he who circumscribes them to the point of fact and teaches them the response that they ought to make to the question of law."[13] Indeed, the jury system consolidates the power of judicial officers both in the courthouse and in society at large. Like the respect for others' powers bred in the township, this healthy attitude toward necessary authority learned in the jury might just as aptly be called "democratic deference."

Tocqueville did not see lay participation either in township government or in the jury as necessarily leading to better administration and better justice. On the contrary, he thought township governance was merely competent and held that judge-dominated justice proceedings were probably better—if seen strictly from the perspective of justice.[14] Yet, though lay participation in the administration of justice and the administration of other governmental tasks may not be as efficient and may, at times, not be as fair or as intelligent as official-made decisions, Tocqueville thought the trade-off was well worth making because of its importance as a form of political education.

The Hazards of Democracy Without Task Sharing

Contrast the healthy relations of authority in the township and the jury with the dysfunctional relations Tocqueville finds in American electoral politics and prophesizes in the future development of the American federal government.

When Tocqueville writes about electoral politics, he wryly notes that merit is common among the governed but rare among the governors.[15] Common among the governed in part because public education under the American equality of conditions is a universal expectation. Now, given universal education—at least in principle—the question is why merit is not common among the governors. One would think the quality of candidates would rise and fall with

13. Tocqueville, *Democracy in America*, 263 [1.2.8.].
14. Tocqueville complains about the arbitrariness and lack of real administrative knowledge in New England selectmen. *Democracy in America*, 196 [1.2.5].
15. Tocqueville, *Democracy in America*, 188 [1.2.5].

literacy rates, but Tocqueville disputes this. His belief in natural inequalities in capacity leads him to argue that the enlightenment of the mass public has certain built-in limits.[16] Similarly, public education levels out the quality of education available so that naturally superior individuals have a more difficult time attaining excellence of mind.

In a related argument, Tocqueville claims that the mass public resents rule by the gifted. Americans, he writes, refuse meritocratic elite rule because they envy people who achieve greatness. Equality of conditions leads them not to esteem high achievers, but to resent the poor reflection their achievements cast on their less high-flying lives. Indeed, the gifted seldom seek office in the United States because they would be forced during elections to bridge the social distance that breeds resentment by pandering to the electorate.[17]

Even worse than the mediocrity of American electoral politics, though, is the vulnerability of American democracy to a new form of despotism. Traditionally, political theorists think of despotism as the takeover of government by some strong and charismatic leader as a response to some crisis or breakdown of institutions and as a condition of coercive power. Tocqueville, by contrast, warned of a kind of despotism in which citizens are free, the economy is strong, and there is widespread benevolence, security, predictability, and order.[18] Taking Montesquieu's clue that central powers can become despotic in the absence of intermediary political institutions or social orders that might provide counterweights, Tocqueville worries that the social-leveling effects of modernity could erode all barriers to freedom-consuming state authority.[19]

Tocqueville admitted that he had trouble even naming this new form of

---

16. Tocqueville, *Democracy in America*, 188 [1.2.5].

17. Tocqueville, *Democracy in America*, 189 [1.2.5]. Tocqueville mentions two "correctives" to this tendency toward mediocrity in selecting governors. In the past, the United States has been fortunate when great events, such as the revolutionary struggle, have lessened the resentment of the mass public and the reluctance of the elite so that the distance between them could be bridged at least temporarily. The second corrective to mediocrity is a "filtering system" in parts of American democracy that remove some members of government, such as judges and senators (at least in 1830), from direct popular selection (Tocqueville, *Democracy in America*, 190–91 [1.2.5]).

18. See the discussion of these points in Sheldon Wolin, *Tocqueville Between Two Worlds* (Princeton: Princeton University Press, 2001), 339.

19. Asserting the need for countervailing powers like the clergy under monarchies that threaten to become despotisms, Montesquieu writes, "Just as the sea, which seems to want to cover the whole earth, is checked by the grasses and the smallest bits of gravel on the shore, so monarchs, whose power seems boundless, are checked by the slightest obstacles and submit their natural pride to supplication and prayer" (*The Spirit of the Laws*, ed. Anne M. Cohler, Basia C. Miller, and Harold C. Stone [Cambridge: Cambridge University Press, 1989], 18).

despotism that came in the form of schoolmasters rather than tyrants. High above privatized, politically apathetic citizens, he writes, "an immense tutelary power is elevated, which alone takes charge of assuring their enjoyments and watching over their fate. It is absolute, detailed, regular, far-seeing, and mild." Unlike despotisms of old, this mild tutelary power "does not tyrannize, it hinders, compromises, enervates, extinguishes, dazes, and finally reduces each nation to being nothing more than a herd of timid and industrious animals of which the government is the shepherd."[20] Tocqueville's dramatic picture seems to have been meant as a prophetic warning rather than a prediction of where democratic government was heading. Put in simpler, less dramatic terms, democracy is vulnerable to a new kind of despotism where government is highly centralized, more powerful by far than any other organization, remote and less directly accountable to citizens, and intrusive in the lives of citizens.

Though a number of social forces and tendencies in American democracy make it vulnerable, the general logic of his argument is that when Americans shrink away from sharing tasks of government and turn merely individualistic in their pursuits and responsibilities, when they only participate in minimally deliberative ways, as in electoral politics, and when they are accustomed to conforming to majority opinion, they do not learn needed habits of freedom. Such civic atrophy erodes those intermediary institutions and countervailing powers that—like the counterweights to monarchical despotism of feudal Europe, the clergy and the nobility—could check centralizing administrative power in modern democracy in part by performing some of its service provision and governing functions. Without the habits of the judge, the legislator, and the executive, citizens in democracies come to rely on powers external to them for public services and goods and for making the "right" collective decisions. On the other side of the fence, eager administrators are willing to show how necessary they are for solving problems seemingly too complicated for laypeople.

Tocqueville perceptively noted how gradual social and political democratization in Europe was accompanied by centralization and bureaucratization of public administration: "[M]ore inquisitive and detailed; everywhere it penetrates further into private affairs than formerly; in its manner it regulates more actions, and smaller actions, and it establishes itself more every day beside, around, and above each individual to assist him, counsel him, and constrain him." In addition to the seeds of despotism sown by civic atrophy, Tocqueville warns of an

---

20. Tocqueville, *Democracy in America*, 663 [2.4.6].

unhealthy jealousy of authority that can develop if citizens are not practiced in ruling and being ruled in turn (to paraphrase Aristotle). Without the tempering effects of the right sort of deference, as experienced in the face-to-face relations of authority in the township and jury, democratic citizens' "immortal hatred" of privilege and even deserved inequality leads them to favor one big boss over a bunch of little bosses: "Man in democratic centuries obeys his neighbor, who is his equal, only with extreme repugnance; he . . . looks on his power with jealousy; he fears and scorns him; he loves to make him feel at each instant the common dependence of them both on the same master."[21]

Tocqueville writes that "in the democratic centuries that are going to open up, individual independence and local liberties will always be the product of art. Centralization will be the natural government."[22] My question is "whose art?" One answer, of course, is that this is the people's art. But it is also the art of the democratic professional—the person trained for administrative or judicial office who refuses to be a task monopolist, keeps open the possibilities for lay participation already in existence, such as town meeting and jury, and may even seek to open more. Tocqueville's democratic professional also respects and encourages, where possible, the handling of disputes and social problems in civil society rather than in government.

Like radical critics of professionalism, Tocqueville is frank about the disempowering effects of technocratic and disabling administrators, but he also stresses the necessity of democratic and enabling professionals—the judges and lawyers committed to supporting the jury process, the local officials and selectmen committed to the widespread "scattering" of political offices and powers, and the organizers of intermediary community organizations. Like social trustee thinkers, Tocqueville clearly believes that professionals have special skills and knowledge that serve social purposes; only he differs from them by recognizing that such attributes are meaningless and potentially harmful to democracy without task-sharing practices that teach laypeople enough about a professionalized domain to be both critical of illegitimate and deferential to legitimate uses of authority.

In Tocqueville, task sharing in contexts that could be professionalized produces valuable habits—competencies, interests, norms, and healthy relations of authority. Those spheres of democratic power that do not permit task sharing breed incompetence, apathy, suspicion of others, and unhealthy relations of

21. Tocqueville, *Democracy in America,* 653 [2.4.5] and 645 [2.4.3].
22. Tocqueville, *Democracy in America,* 645 [2.4.3].

power. The contrasting ideal-typic images of task sharing in the township and jury and task monopoly in dystopic future despotic central government are powerful guides to later thinking about the value of lay participation and the risk of technocratic authority.

Dewey: The Professional as Catalyst of Public Awareness and Competence

Civic Engagement and Freedom

Like Tocqueville, Dewey had a broad conception of American democracy as a "way of life." Both thinkers recognized that the democratic value of procedures and institutions of formal politics, such as elections, depends on an extensive civic environment marked by social equality, communication, collaboration, and reflection. To be interested in democracy, from their perspective, means to be interested in the realms that support the constitutions, offices, and elections of formal national politics. Closely akin to Tocqueville's thoughts on township governance and the jury, Dewey argued that the organization and direction of schools, workplaces, and other informal arenas where habits of thought and action are learned are integral to an active and reflective citizenship in the more formal arenas of normal politics.

Dewey believed that certain professions could serve as catalysts for a more civic environment. In *The Public and Its Problems* (1927) and in other writings, Dewey indicates a few key professions as intermediaries between a fragmented and underinformed public and a distant and increasingly complex political system. When he writes that the chief goal for contemporary democracy is "that of discovering the means by which a scattered, mobile, and manifold public may so recognize itself as to define and express its interests," he has in mind as "means" journalists, social scientists, and educators.[23] Dewey's democratic professionals were to provide analyses and information, encourage reflection about large-scale economic and political events, and, most important, to encourage self-recognition on the part of nascent publics formed around social problems. For example, the press, as we will see, was to be a "continuous, systematic and effective revelation of social movements."[24]

23. John Dewey, *The Public and Its Problems* (1927), reprinted in *John Dewey: The Later Works, 1925–1953,* ed. Jo Ann Boydston (Carbondale: Southern Illinois University Press, 1981–90), 2:327.
24. Dewey, "Practical Democracy" (1925), reprinted in *Later Works,* 2:219.

Progressive Era thinkers like Dewey saw the distance between citizens and the large-scale social and economic forces that impact them as the critical problem of twentieth-century democracy. Like Tocqueville, they worry about citizens lacking habits of freedom. Even though progressive thinkers favor terms such as "expert," "intelligence," and "knowledge," these are not just cognitive terms about the amount of information needed in industrial democracy; they refer to the spheres of action in which a person is accustomed (habituated) to participating. For Dewey, individual freedom can be ensured under contemporary social and economic conditions only if citizens are aware of these conditions and are able to act intelligently in the world.

Civic engagement is crucial for citizens to comprehend the social forces that affect them, but even more fundamentally for them to expand their range of freedom and prevent it from contracting. In other words, if not regulated through civic action, the social forces of industrial democracy threaten the ability of individuals to grow and respond to their environment. As in Tocqueville, one may be happy, comfortable, and healthy, but one cannot be free if political decisions that manipulate and constrain one's life choices are made by others. Dewey frequently frames his discussion in terms of the social intelligence of an active, collaborative society. Social intelligence allows people to alter their society to fit their needs rather than the needs of corporate actors.

Lay Participation and Professionalism: The Ideal of Associated Intelligence

Other Progressive Era thinkers, such as Herbert Croly and Walter Lippmann, saw a professionalization of policy making as a remedy to the problem of an increasingly complex civic environment. Public-minded professionals could lead and represent the public interest. Lippmann's realist argument held that the American public could not make rational contributions to the policy-making process because the time, ability, and interest levels of the average citizen were no match for the complexity of contemporary issues.[25] Lippmann believed the high expectations for public awareness held in classical democratic theory actually facilitated elite manipulation of the public through symbols and rhetoric. A realistic view of public capacities would lead to a chastened democratic theory that emphasized the professionalization of policy making. The public would

25. See Lippmann's *Public Opinion* (1922) and *The Phantom Public* (New York: Harcourt, Brace, 1925) for these arguments.

be left with the limited role of replacing one set of professionals with another in cases of clear policy failure.

Dewey thought Lippmann was right about the ignorance, remoteness, and privatization of the contemporary American public, yet he thought he had mistakenly seen these conditions as a natural feature of democracy rather than recognized what they were—effects of the patterns of economic, social, and political activity that emerged with industrial capitalism. Dewey affirmed Lippmann's argument that social problems are too complex to be handled by the public as it is presently constituted, but he put the argument in historical context:

> Indirect, extensive, enduring and serious consequences of conjoint and interacting behavior call a public into existence having a common interest in controlling these consequences. But the machine age has so enormously expanded, multiplied, intensified and complicated the scope of the indirect consequences, has formed such immense and consolidated unions in action, on an impersonal rather than community basis, that the resultant public cannot identify and distinguish itself.[26]

Further, Dewey argued that public incompetence is not, as Lippmann thought, simply a matter of a lack of individual intelligence or rationality. True, a large number of citizens are unable to cope with the issues affecting them because they lack the time, information, or analytical tools, but Dewey thought the underlying reason for this incompetence was a failure of social organization.

A growth in intelligence is needed, but Dewey saw that this must be social intelligence, or "associated thought," not the private intelligence of think tanks and policy experts.[27] "Dewey's call for scientific intelligence," writes Robert Westbrook, "was not a call for the rule of intelligent scientists but for the egalitarian distribution of the capacity for scientific thinking and its incorporation into democratic decision-making in the polity, workplace, and elsewhere."[28] The means used to close the distance between social and economic forces and the communities affected by them must themselves be fundamentally democratic, fostering democracy as a way of life—a set of norms governing a political culture that can master contemporary conditions. Opposing political and economic

26. Dewey, *The Public and Its Problems*, 314.
27. Dewey, *Individualism Old and New* (1929), reprinted in *Later Works*, 5:10.
28. Robert Westbrook, *John Dewey and American Democracy* (Ithaca: Cornell University Press, 1991), 187.

concentration and breaking through issue complexities require a different politics, a different society, and a different sort of professional—less hierarchical and pecuniary, and more cooperative. A rational public is a task-sharing public.

Democratic Professionals:
Sharing Tasks and Conveying the Value of the Scientific Method

Like Tocqueville's judges, who have specialized knowledge and appreciation for the procedures of justice, Dewey felt social scientists had specialized substantive knowledge and appreciation for the procedures of fact gathering and analysis. Just as jurors learn in Tocqueville's jury to defer in the right ways to the rule of law and to the legal principles presented to them by and embodied by magistrates, so Dewey's citizens come to learn to defer in the right ways to the rules of fact gathering and analysis brought before them by and embodied by social scientists.[29] Just as Tocqueville's judges defer to jurors in some important respects, Dewey's social scientists must also defer to lay participants even as they are deferred to by them.

Dewey thought Americans could master their collective fate if they became habituated to the scientific method. They could make better use of scientific analysis—this was one habit worth learning—but they could also constrain and guide their collective actions with valuable norms of scientific practice: willingness to submit claims to public examination, collaborate, experiment, and argue through fact and analysis. The mediation of social scientists, journalists, and educators was critical to this habit-forming process.

The model democratic professional for Dewey is the social scientist. Natural science, with its standards of evidence and argumentation, had accumulated a body of intelligence about the physical world that gave the lay public more control over their natural surroundings; so can social science help the public solve social problems. Dewey saw social science replacing circumscribed, particularistic, unsystematic, and conservative—unselfcritical—bodies of common sense knowledge about society in the same way natural science largely replaced traditional ideas about the natural world.[30]

29. In Sidney Hook's words, "The heart of Dewey's social philosophy is the proposal to substitute for the existing modes of social authority the authority of scientific method" (*John Dewey: An Intellectual Portrait* [New York: John Day, 1939], 151).

30. Social science is to play a key role in what Timothy Kaufman-Osborn calls "the reconstruction of the shared fund of accumulated meaning which currently constitutes our flawed medium of

For Dewey, though social scientists have a role as experts, their expertise is mainly focused on facilitating public engagement and public decision. Dewey's experts are not technicians who solve social problems; they are primarily concerned with presenting analyses of means to predetermined ends and pointing out conflicting values. "Inquiry, indeed, is a work which devolves upon experts," writes Dewey, "but their expertise is not shown in framing and executing policies, but in discovering and making known the facts upon which the former depend."[31] Notice that Dewey argues that the status and authority of experts actually depends on lay participation of some form. Experts in social policy do not remain experts long if their inquiry is not substantially reflexive, if their inquiry is engaged in the problems of specialists rather than the felt problems of the public.

> A class of experts is inevitably so removed from common interests as to become a class with private interests and private knowledge, which in social matters is not knowledge at all.
> The man who wears the shoe knows best that it pinches and where it pinches, even if the expert shoemaker is the best judge of how the trouble is to be remedied.[32]

When experts go beyond spelling out means and clarifying options, when they become task monopolists, they encourage a form of compliance to intellectual authority that Dewey saw as extremely unhealthy in a democracy. In weakening "personal responsibility for judgment and for action," expert task monopoly "helps create the attitudes that welcome and support the totalitarian state."[33] Dewey's democratic professionals are not, therefore, best seen as leaders or organizers of the public; they respond to social problems in a way that facilitates the organization of the public.

Dewey's social scientists promote the growth of critical thinking by challenging commonsense views, encouraging abstract thinking, and embodying certain habits of mind and character. Norms of social science, such as openness to opposition, fact-oriented debate, and willingness to work toward consensus, challenge

---

practical exchange in an insecure world" ("John Dewey and the Liberal Science of Community," *Journal of Politics* 46 [1984]: 1150).

31. Dewey, *The Public and Its Problems,* 365.
32. Dewey, *The Public and Its Problems,* 364.
33. Dewey, *Freedom and Culture* (1939), reprinted in *Later Works,* 13:184–85.

common public norms, such as reliance on tradition rather than empirical analysis and wariness of novel or unconventional perspectives. Though he does not specify where this challenge is to take place, it is clear that Dewey wishes it to occur at many levels: "The general adoption of the scientific attitude in human affairs would mean nothing less than a revolutionary change in morals, religion, politics and industry."[34] Dewey's social scientists are exemplars of intellectual habits, but they are also advocates who use these habits in public debate to challenge "the inertia, prejudices and emotional partisanship of the masses."[35]

Such engaged social scientists are not like Lippmann's experts in that they do not *represent* and act *for* members of the public. For Dewey, engaged social scientists can *facilitate* the public's solution to social problems. They can do this directly by providing analysis for motivated community groups, and indirectly by influencing the conduct of other professions.

Journalism was one democratic profession Dewey had in mind as a conveyer of the habits of pragmatic social science. He imagined a new journalist who was a hybrid of muckraker and social scientist. The "knowledge and insight" that could spark formations "of a democratically organized public," in Dewey's view, "does not yet exist." He thought journalists could draw on a more pragmatic social science for a body of research and established tools of analysis that could help the public comprehend "all consequences which concern it."[36] Like the social scientist, Dewey's democratic journalist joins facts together in order to help readers comprehend larger social forces. Like the muckraker, Dewey's democratic journalist is concerned with the impact of particular events on particular groups and seeks to broadly publicize their results.

Education was a third democratic profession Dewey had in mind. He directs educators to facilitate cooperative situations in the classroom in which "associated thought" and the democratic habits that go along with it can thrive. In Dewey's model schools, children are to be initiated into the participatory and deliberative mode of associated living characteristic of a task-sharing democracy.[37] Dewey was highly critical of the competitive individualism that reigned in many schools, where students learn little about how to work with others as equals. In

34. Dewey, *Individualism Old and New*, 115.
35. Dewey, *The Public and Its Problems*, 341.
36. Dewey, *The Public and Its Problems*, 339.
37. Westbrook describes Dewey's model school as a "community of full participation and 'conjoint communicated experience' in which social sympathy and deliberative moral reason would develop. Thus classrooms in a democracy had to be not only communities of inquiry but democratic communities of inquiry" (*John Dewey and American Democracy*, 172).

contrast, Dewey's democratic educators foster cooperation and creative problem solving by structuring the learning environment for students to work and deliberate together. Students are encouraged in group practice to place their beliefs into question, rely on evidence and argument for authority, be receptive to new perspectives and novel experience, and be willing to answer challenges. The learning environment that fosters this attitude places students in situations where difficult questions are asked and collectively resolved. Civics classes, for example, would involve deliberation about what values central public laws and policies embody and how students would resolve novel problems faced by established political institutions. Dewey's students learn about democracy by acting democratically; the very structure of their schools gives students a taste for collective self-determination.[38]

The schoolhouse, the newspaper, and the social science institute are forums and tools laypeople can use to learn about their own capacities and to work with others productively. Laypeople use these to gain habits of thought and collaboration and develop, hopefully, an active interest in other's perspectives and in the needs of larger group life. Those who stand at the sidelines facilitating, who create and maintain such forums and tools of associated intelligence, are democratic professionals.

Notice that Dewey's exemplary professionals are no less of a teacher, journalist, and social scientist for following and making manifest democratic norms. Rather, they have integrated these norms into professional practice and organizational life and achieved an enlarged view of professional purposes such as education, objective news, and social analysis. Without being political activists in the usual sense, they have sown the seeds of a more deliberative democracy in the institutions their professions influence every day by cultivating norms of equality, collaboration, reflection, and communication. Dewey's thought shows how professionals can be both devoted to their specialties as well as committed to democracy.

Like radical critics of professionalism, Dewey is sensitive to the potential for unhealthy relations of power fostered by a culture of experts or specialists who claim to serve the public good. Nonetheless, Dewey stresses the necessity of democratic professionals as intermediaries between publics that are "scattered, mobile, and manifold" and the forces of social, economic, and political power that shape everyday life. He insists that only those professionals whose knowledge and skill

---

38. Dewey, "The Challenge of Democracy to Education" (1937), reprinted in *Later Works,* 11:181.

are connected constitutively, and not merely symbolically, to affected publics have any real efficacy or legitimacy. By showing the mutual dependency between lay and professional—a relationship that demands porous institutions, task-sharing practices, and mutual respect among participants—Tocqueville's and Dewey's accounts overcome the dualistic separation of lay and professional cultures perpetuated by both social trustee and radical critique models of professionalism.

Contemporary Proponents of Democratic Professionalism

Two contemporary theorists, William Sullivan and Frank Fischer, both begin with the assumption that the ideal of democratic professionalism we see budding in Tocqueville and in full flower with Dewey has withered while technocratic and merely commercial professionalism have flourished instead. Accordingly, both focus closely on the risks of contemporary trends and the benefits of a more democratic professionalism for all sides.

William Sullivan's Civic Professional

William Sullivan's argument for a democratic professionalism explicitly builds on Dewey's work. Sullivan defines the role professions have in the functioning of democratic institutions as a form of civic responsibility: "[P]rofessionalism suggests how to organize the complex modern division of labor to ensure that specific functions are performed well and with a sense of responsibility for the good of the whole."[39] Professional responsibility is motivated by three values: integrity, security, and democracy. Integrity operates at the level of individual members of the professions; security comes in at the group level of professions; and democracy at the level of political society.

Integrity is what individual members have to gain from their professions when they are oriented toward public good rather than mere commercial gain. Professions are ways of life that further public purposes and therefore they are able to grant meaning to the work lives of individual professionals. This is not just a matter of status, but of personal fulfillment. A profession "is the kind of thing one can build a life around," writes Sullivan. "Providing counsel and care, curing

---

39. William Sullivan, *Work and Integrity: The Crisis and Promise of Professionalism in America* (New York: HarperCollins, 1995), 11.

illness, bringing justice, teaching: these are activities which provide more than jobs and satisfactions for individuals. By their nature they create goods which at some time are essential for everyone, and important for society as a whole."[40] Without public recognition, however, professions lose their ability to grant meaning. A profession that cannot be seen by the general public as responsibly serving key social needs is one that cannot fulfill individual professionals' demands for meaningful work lives.

Security is what professions as organizations have to gain from the right sort of relationship with the public. Professional work is particularly vulnerable to public recognition since it is often dependent on "public, legal acceptance of the value of services offered by the professional." The "security and negotiability of the professional's human capital exists . . . only as part of the public order of civil society. Even more than most other kinds of property, professional capital depends upon civil society's structure of legal procedures and reasonings." The authority and autonomy professions have to solve key social problems are based on reciprocal trust—something they earn by performing their tasks with social good, not just profit, in mind. The price of professional authority and autonomy is "the accountability of that group to other members of the civic community for the furtherance of publicly established goals and standards."[41] Security of legal authority is another explanation of why professions would seek to reinforce their public standing by representing themselves as serving the public in important ways. Groups unresponsive to social criticism not only risk loss of integrity, but also risk loss of the legal legitimacy they need to operate.

Sullivan's third reason for civic professionalism (the argument from democracy) holds that professionals can preserve democratic control of collective decisions against the pressures of technocratic control. Like Dewey, Sullivan sees the right sort of professionalism as a promising moral and political response to the modern division of labor:

> As new knowledge grows, and new instrumental systems expand, every society needs to restructure itself not only for efficiency but to improve equity, to reweave the bonds of trust and responsibility so that they encompass the emerging areas of human activity. Professions thus stand

40. Sullivan, *Work and Integrity,* 6.
41. Sullivan, *Work and Integrity,* 30, 145, 148.

on the boundary of interaction between systems of technical capacity and the moral and political processes which aim to integrate these powers into humanly valuable forms of life.[42]

These systems of technical capacity grant competencies to professions that can be concentrated, thus limiting democratic social coordination, or dispersed and aimed toward democratic competencies.

For Sullivan, the Progressive Era was marked by an ideal of professionalism that viewed professionals as critical to assisting and supporting "nascent publics in developing the understandings and institutions which could make the modern public viable." After World War II, however, professionalism became defined "in predominantly technical rather than civic terms, as rightly concerned only with improving the means by which individuals and groups could pursue their opportunities in an expanding economy."[43] Sullivan believes the technocratic model has real costs that have come to public awareness in recent years: the costs of failed social policies, instrumental, self-interested professional practices, and harmful social stratification. As the technical benefits of efficiency and competence are subjected to increasing public scrutiny, professionals and citizens alike are starting to recognize the virtues of a more democratic professionalism. Against technocratic authority that constrains democratically coordinated social action, civic professionalism can be counterpoised to promote the formation of engaged publics. Against technocratic authority that inadequately moralizes new systems, new technology, and the professionals who manage them, civic professionalism brings techniques and professionals "within the sphere of moral meaning."[44]

Sullivan is clear about the nexus of self- and collectivity interest that motivates the democratic professional, the judge, the administrator, the journalist, social scientist, or educator who opposes technocratic authority that constrains democratically coordinated social action and who promotes the formation of engaged publics. Professions are civic minded because this helps promote democratic citizenship and it serves the professional's interest in gaining the values of security and integrity that help the profession itself function. These are important contributions to the theory of democratic professionalism. Sullivan is less clear, however, on just how professionals are to be civic minded. His version

42. Sullivan, *Work and Integrity,* 145.
43. Sullivan, *Work and Integrity,* 101.
44. Sullivan, *Work and Integrity,* 144, 150.

of democratic professionalism retains too much of the social trustee model, pressing professionals to embrace the public good as they themselves recognize it. On this point, my own view of democratic professionalism is closer to the radical critique and would urge professionals to share tasks and involve the lay public in figuring out just what the public good is.

Frank Fischer's Dialogical Professional

Like Sullivan, Fischer recognizes that the Deweyean progressive model of professional action has failed to materialize. The public is as "scattered, mobile, and manifold" as it was when Dewey wrote those words in 1927. Even worse, professionals and experts in the information age are seemingly more removed in their methods and results from the public's ways of knowing. The information age is one of increasing remoteness of expert systems and their increasing incompetence at reducing some very serious risks to public well-being. Fischer notes that instead of the "associated intelligence" of the Deweyean ideal, current conditions might better be called alienated intelligence: the experts in their offices with symbolic knowledge, the citizens in their neighborhoods with their local knowledge, and an increasing distrust between the two groups.

The engaged, rational polity that Dewey imagined is nowhere to be found. Instead, we have the technocratic politics of a "hierarchical and asymmetrical decision structures of the corporate-bureaucratic state," a politics marked by citizen apathy and inefficacy in the face of expert systems of social coordination and control. As indicated in the last chapter, Fischer believes professionals and experts in technocracy play the role of buffers between citizens and elites by accommodating "the client's needs and problems to the structures of a larger system of domination and control."[45]

> Not only are experts socially situated between the elites and the public, but their technical languages provide an intimidating barrier for lay citizens seeking to express their disagreements in the language of everyday life. Speaking the language of science, as well as the jargon of particular policy communities, becomes an essential credential for participation. Indeed, in the cases of highly developed professions such

45. Frank Fischer, "Citizen Participation and the Democratization of Policy Expertise: From Theoretical Inquiry to Practical Cases," *Policy Sciences* 26 (1993): 167, 169.

as medicine and law, the credential is formally conferred and regulated by the state.[46]

Fischer agrees with the radical critique of technocratic professionals: "As the agents of expert discourses, the professions constitute the techniques and practices that disperse power and social control away from the formal centers of governance."[47]

Unlike other radical critics, however, and like the other democratic professional theorists we have been discussing, Fischer sees the technocratic model of professional action as fundamentally unstable and vulnerable to legitimation challenges. Though powerful, professionals and experts are much less competent as technocrats than as democrats. And though currently minimized both in public and professional imaginations, lay participation carries benefits for both sides. So, for Fischer, professionals are less competent and citizens more competent than we think. We currently *undervalue* citizen participation and *overvalue* expert contributions to viable social policy.

Lay participation in the policy analysis domain with which Fischer is primarily concerned is valuable, first, because it helps rebuild public trust. He notes that even though it only rarely takes the form of overt protest politics, there has been a significant decline in public confidence in professions and their technologies over the last generation. Far from the social trustee self-image of "a group of experts dedicated to the public good," many lay citizens see professionals as "a group more interested in increasing their own authority, power, and wealth."[48] In response to these widely shared perceptions, according to Fischer, reform-minded professionals have sought out ways to integrate lay participation into professional practice. For Fischer and these reformers, public trust is not a moral bonus, something professionals might work on once the real work of efficient, competent service is done. As Sullivan points out with his value of security, the trust lay participation brings is critical to the functioning of the profession itself.

Lay participation is valuable, second, precisely because contemporary civic competencies are weak or, better put, misdirected. Lack of public engagement, writes Fischer, is "often mistaken for public ignorance," but it could be that the public's "low level of activity only reflects the populace's limited opportunities to develop the interests and participatory skills required to engage meaningfully

46. Frank Fischer, *Citizens, Experts, and the Environment* (Durham: Duke University Press, 2000), 23.
47. Fischer, *Citizens*, 25.
48. Fischer, *Citizens*, 30, 32.

in public issues." Like Tocqueville, Fischer sees the lack of proper political social-ization as closely related to public apathy: "Americans are first and foremost socialized into the role of consumer rather than citizen. (And here, I think most would admit, Americans don't seem as ignorant or passive as they do in the pub-lic sphere. . . .) Missing . . . are well-developed political arrangements that pro-vide citizens with multiple and varied participatory opportunities to deliberate basic political issues."[49]

Professionals are less competent than people think, a point Fischer illustrates by noting grand "expert failures" such as Vietnam, Great Society (busing), and Reaganomics.[50] These expert failures are a result of professionals' remoteness from the ground-level situation, the limits of their methods for seeing the total problem, and their somewhat ideological commitment to certain ideas, such as the "domino effect" or "trickle-down economics," that lacked a good deal of sensitivity, and therefore applicability, to particular cases.

Professionals are also less competent in a different sense. The knowledge that they use in making judgments is usually not as dependent on their formal train-ing as we commonly think. Fischer holds that "contrary to their claims, pro-fessional analysts have no unquestionable knowledge advantage."[51] Most of social science knowledge, for example, is commonsense knowledge. Even most of the new knowledge produced by social scientists is generated in the same way lay-people generate knowledge. "To be sure, the social sciences have tested and re-fined important beliefs grounded in ordinary knowledge. But the actual amount of such knowledge that has been tested and refined is little more than a drop in the bucket. Moreover, on those occasions when policy analysts do possess such knowledge, the advantages of such knowledge can seldom be taken for granted."[52]

Unlike Sullivan, Fischer recognizes an ambiguity in the Deweyean ideal: Dem-ocratic professionals can represent and advocate the public's interest or they can push the public into serving as its own representatives and advocates. These are two very different roles that have very different consequences for democratic authority. In the context of environmental politics, professionals have often served as representatives. "Public interest" experts have emerged out of specific social problem sites, reflect and facilitate community awareness of the problems, and then wrangle with Washington agencies. This advocacy professionalism explicitly

49. Fischer, *Citizens*, 35.
50. Fischer, *Citizens*, 41.
51. Fischer, *Citizens*, 215.
52. Fischer, *Citizens*, 213.

represents interests of the powerless and unrepresented. Yet this is where Fischer sees a problem. Advocacy professionals do not really let people speak for themselves. Frequently, the local groups who were purportedly represented end up "feeling that the positions advanced by the experts did not really represent those of the group."[53] Worse, advocacy experts can get caught up in the "beltway" and take their cues from members of "policy networks"—other progressive interest group representatives, legislative aides, administrative analysts, and others—rather than their local base of support.

> [B]eyond a more progressive political commitment, the democratization of expertise requires new methodological orientations as well. . . . if citizens are to participate in the development of the policy decisions that affect their own lives, the standard practitioner-client model must give way to a more democratic relationship between them.
>   . . . Rather than providing technical answers designed to bring political discussions to an end, the task is to assist citizens in their efforts to examine their *own* interests and to make their own decisions.[54]

In the case of the environmental movement, Fischer notes how advocacy expertise has slowly given way to a more participatory model in large part because of lack of trust between advocates and their publics.

Fischer argues that lay participation is useful precisely in situations where policy solutions seem to be intractable because of their complexity. Complexity breeds distrust of experts, as frequently is the case with "not in my backyard" (NIMBY) reactions to the risk assessments of administrators and experts. In NIMBY cases, lay participation can provide more information about the risks of policy options to affected neighborhoods. It can also lead to a sense of "stake holding" in a decision and, therefore, more trust.[55] Far from being secondary to the more important process of expert analysis and decision, lay participation needs to be built into that process for it to be legitimate to affected publics.

Lay participation can also bring in important "local knowledge" to decision making. Building on Dewey's point about nonexperts knowing best where the shoe pinches, Fischer notes that there is a "different kind of rationality" that laypeople possess—more particularistic, more attentive to historical dimensions,

53. Fischer, *Citizens,* 38.
54. Fischer, *Citizens,* 39–40.
55. Fischer, *Citizens,* 130.

and more relationship and person oriented than expert knowledge. A process that makes use of local knowledge may create better decisions and surely reinforces the legitimacy of the decision.

For Fischer, democratic professionals play a facilitating role. They do not represent the public as advocates and they do not conceive of themselves primarily as educators. Rather, they seek to bring affected publics into problem-solving work. For example, democratic policy analysts, in Fischer's view, are to be inclusive, collaborative, and problem oriented. They share power over the direction of research with their research subjects, and they are motivated less by abstract scholarly goals than by the problems of their research subjects. Like the other theorists of democratic professionalism we have considered here, Fischer favors mutual deference between laypersons and professionals, but his ideal of democratic professionalism is the least assertive. Fischer's participatory policy analysts are to restrain their expertise, absorb local knowledge, and appeal to citizens for help.

Conclusion:
Moving from the Model of Democratic Professionalism to Case Analysis

The democratic professional model contains core elements of both the radical critique and social trustee models but alters them as it situates professionals squarely within the public culture of democracy. Like social trustee thinkers, the theorists of this chapter acknowledge the special responsibilities that guide and motivate practitioners and raise expectations on the part of affected publics. Lay publics and fellow peers rightly ask more of some professionals than that they have the knowledge and competence to do their jobs, that they do not cheat or violate the trust or privacy of their clients. For this third model of professionalism, however, this special role is conceptualized in democratic terms: seeking the public good *with* and not merely *for* the public. Like radical critics, democratic professional theorists are concerned that those with specialized knowledge, expertise, and skill are a seemingly inextricable part of how modern mass democracy solves social problems and reaches collective decisions and that they can potentially become technocrats who impede and disable citizen action. Though sharing these concerns, democratic professional thinkers have discovered mutual interests and values that link layperson and professional together in the realm of middle democracy and that support patterns of task sharing, mutual respect, and transparency.

As Table 3 summarizes, democratic professionalism is inherently collaborative. My definition of democratic professionalism is as follows: sharing previously professionalized tasks and encouraging lay participation in ways that enhance and enable broader public engagement and deliberation about major social issues inside and outside professional domains. The sharp distinctions between professional and layperson found in the other models disappear here. This does not mean that professional authority, status, privilege, and responsibility disappear as well, only that they are tightly connected to the empowerment of laypeople.

It is important to stress that democratic professionalism is not utopian theory, nor is it merely a democratic theorist's-eye view of ideal professionalism. The thinkers considered in this chapter draw out the concrete interests professions, citizens, and polity have in this collaborative, task-sharing model of professionalism.

On the part of professions, these concrete interests include the democratic deference earned by Tocqueville's selectmen, minor township officers, and judges;

Table 3. Models of professionalism contrasted

	Social trustee	Radical critique	Democratic professionalism
Main characteristics of a profession:	Knowledge, self-regulation, social responsibility	Power to define interests for the public	Commitment to knowledge, as well as to co-direction of professional services
Social duties of professionals flow from:	Group experience, functional purposes, tacit exchange	Interest in retaining social authority and market security	Professional training and experience, as well as from public collaboration
Professionals' view of laypeople:	Clients, consumers, wards	Incompetent at high-level tasks	Citizens with a stake in professional decisions
Ideal role of professional in society:	Expert, specialist, guide	Deprofessionalize, resist temptation to monopolize tasks	Share authority and knowledge through task sharing
Professional ethics best fixed and overseen:	By professionals	By laypeople	By both professionals and laypeople
Political role of professions:	Protection for professional interests and social functions	Disabling intermediary between citizens and democratic institutions	Enabling intermediary in realm of "middle democracy"

the concrete grounding and orientation provided to Dewey's social scientists, journalists, and educators by the problems faced by publics; the integrity of a public-spirited job well done and the security of the profession itself for Sullivan's civic professional; and the sense of helping rather than hindering democratic engagement and community empowerment for Fischer's participatory policy analyst. All the theorists agree that in addition to being indirectly threatened by the hazards of civic immobility and democratic contraction, professions dominated by the technocratic or market-oriented ideal face direct hazards, such as loss of integrity and public skepticism about professional authority, competence, and elite bias.

The phrase "democratic professional," though I have not used it this way, might also characterize citizens who participate in previously expert or professional-dominated domains. Again, none of the theorists considered here treats such participation as a moral bonus for citizens. Lay participation in these domains serves the concrete interests Tocqueville's citizens have in gaining public competencies, recognizing procedural rules, and respecting higher order principles; it serves the need Dewey's citizens have for comprehending their interests and the social, economic, and political forces that thwart them; it serves Sullivan's citizens' demand for public goods; and Fischer's citizens' need for purposeful self-determination.

At the level of the polity, each of the theoretical treatments agrees that democratic professionals can help reduce the paternalistic, centralized, remote, and minimally accountable dimensions of contemporary economic and political power. The language used by these theorists is strikingly similar: the benefit of democratic professionalism is a nonpaternalistic, decentralized, broadly socially grounded, accountable system of porous and rational authority. Though democratic professionals are not political activists, nor are their professional organizations political parties, they can encourage and enforce, so to speak, deliberative and democratic norms in those professionalized domains that interact with government institutions and even in those that do not do so directly.

The comparison of democratic professionalism with the other two descriptive and normative models of professionalism raises the question that if the model of democratic professionalism has the advantages stressed in this chapter, why is it only barely understood in academic discussions of professionalism and why, as both Fischer and Sullivan insist, is it losing ground in the "real world" to technocratic and market-oriented modes of professionalism? An obvious reply is that the latter fit neatly into the rationalized procedures and needs for predictability and control found in modern economic and political organization. Further, those trained for professions currently have minimal instruction in the democratic consequences of their professional domains. Applied ethics instruction abounds, of course, and more so with every passing year. Yet the explicitly democratic values of lay participation and task sharing discussed in this chapter are rarely part of the ethics seminars required in nearly all professional training curricula.

Another explanation for its current lack of competitiveness has to do with the demanding nature of the democratic professional ideal. As illustrated by Dewey's and Fischer's social scientist who must be both a competent researcher under the rules of the discipline and a reasonably good facilitator of community participation, the ideal is quite complex. Democratic professionals are in no way to give up their traditional occupational responsibilities to dedicated service, yet they must reframe and reorient their responsibilities as they collaborate with laypeople. In its demand that professionals both exercise authority and share it, democratic professionals face serious trade-offs, as in the case of Tocqueville's judges who know their solo decisions would be more just, yet they defer to the jury as a rule because of the political socialization and other benefits of lay participation. The ideal is also undoubtedly overly ambitious as shown by the hope that judges, social scientists, educators, and others can remedy serious structural deficits in the civic environment.

A central goal of the case-based chapters that follow is to see how reformers motivated by the ideal of democratic professionalism attempt to meet these demands of being both democratic and professional. Demonstrating that such beings as democratic professionals exist goes some distance toward making this model more prominent for academics and practitioners. How they manage to integrate the task-sharing, civic-empowerment aspects of their role with the more traditional features of professionalism and how they face market and state pressures will flesh out the practical dimensions—and limits—of the model. Revealing real-world examples of democratic professionalism, even if they are imperfect and show much room for improvement, will hopefully press those who study and teach professional ethics to broaden their horizons.

A major ambiguity in the democratic professional model also provides another important direction for the case-based chapters. What, exactly, are the limits of professional responsibility for enabling citizen competence and participation, and how are they determined? Are democratic professionals roving civic catalysts, educating and prodding the general public whenever and wherever this is appropriate? Or are democratic professionals people who are mainly interested in the democratic and undemocratic consequences of their professional domains and seek to empower and educate citizens in and about those domains by bringing them in? The former interpretation heightens the internal difficulties of democratic professionalism—makes it more complex, more prone to trade-off problems, and more ambitious. It also renders democratic professionalism more vulnerable to reasonable concerns expressed by the radical critique. Consider Sullivan's seemingly innocuous expectation that professions "behave as 'good citizens,' taking responsible, often leadership roles in the society's life."[56] By contrast, I share the view of radical critics that such an expectation may actually have the negative effect of diminishing the possibility that nonprofessionals behave as good citizens. It may be necessary, therefore, to sharpen focus and reject, at least as a primary expectation, the idea that professionals serve as general civic organizers pursuing valuable social purposes *for* the public.

Worries about immobilized citizens and contracted democratic authority may push one to require, as a baseline expectation, that professions do not hinder citizens' ability to solve social problems. Perhaps only after that expectation is met should one ask professions to facilitate, where possible, civic participation—including the expectation that they facilitate citizens' ability to better choose and monitor their professional helpers. Meeting these expectations entails self-restraint in entering the public domain with specialized knowledge claims and a concern for the protection of nonprofessionals' democratic confidence. Such a risk-averse way of conceiving democratic professionalism, however, has its own dangers and perhaps needlessly minimizes the positive civic impact of the professions. This was, after all, a key problem with the radical critique I raised in the last chapter.

The theory of democratic professionalism must keep in the foreground such questions about authority and the internal demands and tensions of the ideal such as its role complexity, need for trade-offs, and the potentially wide-ranging ambitiousness of its goals. Equally important, an adequate theory must stick close to cases of specific professions and the particular conflicts and possibilities that arise for real-life democratic professionals in their work settings and in the broader public arenas they influence. As these different cases of democratic professionalism are encountered in the next three chapters, I will describe as well as critique—engage the practitioners in virtual dialogue, as it were—about how they may better realize the ideal of democratic professionalism in their practices.

---

56. Sullivan, *Work and Integrity,* 221.

This chapter has used a few general themes and theorists to place professional activity within the concerns of canonical democratic theory and to articulate a third model of professionalism. It is now time to analyze the specificity—what Durkheim called the "moral particularism"—of professional activity in the life of a democracy. We will come to see professions such as journalism, medicine, law, public administration, and others as separate from other powerful economic and political organizations, as different from each other in democratically relevant respects, and as mediating among self, other, and group in ways that have both harmful and beneficial consequences for democracy.

5

PUBLIC JOURNALISM

The real problem of journalism is that the term which grounds it—the public—has been dissolved, dissolved in part by journalism. Journalism only makes sense in relation to the public and public life. Therefore, the fundamental problem in journalism is to reconstitute the public, to bring it back into existence.

—JAMES W. CAREY, *"The Press and Public Discourse"* (1987)

In this and the next two chapters, the theory of democratic professionalism is grounded in the practices of three reform movements within three different professions: the public journalism, restorative justice, and bioethics movements. Though in many ways success stories, this is not the reason they are considered here. Rather, they are three of the most prominent and most widespread examples of how professionals have changed their thinking about their professional roles to encompass the broader, more collaborative democratic professional identity. They are also three of the most theoretical, so to speak, in that the practitioners and interested outsiders have been active in thinking, writing, and arguing about these reforms—oftentimes in just the terms discussed in the last chapter. These movements are all ongoing, but they have been around long enough for there to be considerable debate among both practitioners and outsiders about their virtues and vices.

"Grounded" is meant, most generally, to give a face to the theory of democratic professionalism—show that there are real people doing real things that look like democratic professionalism. In particular, these chapters will describe the context and motivations of reformers, discuss internal debates, and relate how practitioners have managed internal tensions in the model to bear the burdens of a complex new role, make trade-offs, channel ambitions, and examine how they resolve, for better or worse, the ambiguities about professional authority raised in the last chapter. This kind of ground demonstrates the relevance— for practitioners and academics—of the concepts and arguments of democratic professionalism across a number of different professions. For each of these movements I will argue that greater clarity about democratic professionalism would help practitioners gain focus or redirect current assumptions and practices that cut against the spirit of the theory.

We should not expect different professions to be democratic in the same way. While democratic professionalism entails commitments to sharing authority and knowledge through task sharing and to being an enabling intermediary between citizens and the social and political institutions that affect them, these commitments will be manifested differently depending on the kinds of tasks that can be shared and the kinds of institutions within which democratic professionals have influence. The journalists and editors motivated by democratic professionalism in Chapter 5 have a direct potential impact on public knowledge and civic engagement regarding the broadest range of social issues. The criminal justice and health care professionals of Chapters 6 and 7, in turn, have a direct potential impact on public knowledge and civic engagement regarding a very narrow range of social issues, yet the issues of meaningful and appropriate punishment and fair and humane health care decisions are among the most difficult the contemporary polity faces. Though we do not expect democratic professionals to be political activists, we do expect them to engage and facilitate more deliberative publics—some larger and less specialized, as in the case of public journalism; others smaller and more engaged in specific tasks, as in the case of restorative justice and bioethics. To paraphrase Dewey, democratic professionals should be judged on their ability to enable publics to recognize themselves, but they should be judged on terms that are sensitive to their specific contexts and institutional homes.

Throughout these chapters, we will move back and forth using what we understand about democratic professionalism to raise questions about the cases while using what we know about the cases to better understand democratic professionalism. The methodological premise is that our developing theory can help clarify the democratic values articulated by these reformers while the tensions and problems they face can help clarify the theory. As they seek to reorient professional practices—making them more collaborative, more connected to participatory and deliberative publics—public journalists, restorative justice practitioners, and bioethics consultants make certain assumptions about their roles. Some of these assumptions are at present ambiguous and are capable of leading to both democratic professionalism and its opposite. A more developed and grounded theory of democratic professionalism will not completely remove these ambiguities, but it can focus constructively critical attention on them.

Public journalism is arguably the most significant reform movement in American journalism since the Progressive Era.[1] Beginning as a controversial series of experiments a decade and a half ago, public journalism techniques have become common practice in newsrooms across the country.[2] Closely influenced by the ideals of deliberative democracy, it advocates changes in techniques of news-gathering and reporting to foster more public deliberation and civic engagement. Theorists and practitioners of public journalism think the promotion of reasonable and informed dialogue among citizens should be part of the role journalists play in a democracy.

This chapter focuses on the context of public journalism, the motivations stressed by reform leaders, and the internal difficulties confronted by practitioners. For many mainstream reporters and editors, the democratic professional goal of encouraging and improving public deliberation is in deep conflict with traditional journalistic values. The major criticisms of public journalism relate closely to the internal tensions and ambiguities of the democratic professional ideal: trade-offs between competing values or purposes, complexity of a new role, and uncertainty about the dimensions of this role. Public journalists have shown how their stress on lay participation and public engagement has not meant unprofessional trade-offs with cherished traditional values of objectivity, independence, and fairness. They have less convincingly managed the complexity of the role and its dimensions. Journalism as a democratic profession has a role in promoting public deliberation, but it may very well have to be a different and more circumscribed role than public journalists have so far imagined.

Apart from putting a face to the theory of democratic professionalism, public journalism dramatically illustrates the model's problematic ambiguity about authority. The movement rightly places journalists at the center of problems such as civic apathy and public ignorance, thus focusing attention on the role of the profession in both blocking and disabling but also facilitating public deliberation.[3] However, many advocates see public journalists as central catalysts of a

1. Michael Schudson calls public journalism "the best organized social movement inside journalism in the history of the American press" ("What Public Journalism Knows About Journalism but Doesn't Know About 'Public,'" in *The Idea of Public Journalism,* ed. Theodore L. Glasser [New York: Guilford Press, 1999], 118).

2. Lewis A. Friedland and Sandy Nichols estimate that more than a fifth of all newspapers in the United States have implemented public journalism projects. Friedland and Nichols, *Measuring Civic Journalism's Progress: A Report Across a Decade of Activity* (New York: Pew Center for Civic Journalism, 2002), 4.

3. Peter Levine describes the public journalism movement as one key contemporary effort at putting the abstract ideals of deliberative democratic theory into practice. Levine, "Getting Practical About

more deliberative democracy, a role that significantly oversteps the resources and civic capabilities of the profession.[4] What I criticize as "delusions of civic grandeur" may be motivating for democratic professional reform movements, but I argue here that they raise serious problems regarding the ability of even the most democratic profession to represent, catalyze, and construct a "public." Public journalism, therefore, poses important lessons for democratic professionalism regarding the need to set limits and to admit fallibility, particularly when a profession seeks to enable a "public's" ability to give voice to its interests.

Journalism for a More Deliberative Democracy

Motivations for Sharing Journalistic Tasks and Prompting Civic Engagement

Public journalism attempts to put the ideals of deliberative democracy into the practice of journalism by making the promotion of public deliberation part of the journalist's role. This approach arose in the early 1990s mostly among a number of regional, medium-sized city newspapers such as the *Wichita Eagle, Charlotte Observer,* and *Virginian-Pilot* of Norfolk. Early corporate support of public journalism came from the Knight-Ridder organization under the leadership of James Batten. Foundation support from the Knight Foundation, Pew Charitable Trusts, Kettering, and others helped fuel reforms and guide research about public journalism.

One impetus to the movement was the perception that the American public had become politically alienated from government and politics. Editors such as Davis "Buzz" Merritt of the *Wichita Eagle* began to see the political domain as a "troubling moral environment," the pathologies of which were especially

---

Deliberative Democracy," *Report from the Institute for Philosophy and Public Policy* 19 (1999): 1–11. For more on deliberative democratic theory and public journalism, see Levine, "Public Journalism and Deliberation," *Report from the Institute for Philosophy and Public Policy* 16 (1996): 1–5; and John Durham Peters, "Public Journalism and Democratic Theory: Four Challenges," in *The Idea of Public Journalism,* ed. Glasser, 104–8.

4. Such limits to the role of journalism in deliberation may explain, though not justify, the short shrift the profession is given by deliberative democratic theorists. Amy Gutmann and Dennis F. Thompson, for example, devote only two paragraphs of *Democracy and Disagreement* (Cambridge, Mass.: Belknap Press, 1996), 125–26, to the role of journalists in relation to public deliberation. Jürgen Habermas, though he gave the profession considerable prominence in his early *Structural Transformation of the Public Sphere* (Cambridge, Mass.: MIT Press, 1989), spends little time on it in his current work on democratic theory.

noticeable during elections. The 1988 presidential campaign, in particular, marked by dismal turnout and highly calculated political discourse, reinforced a growing sense among journalists that a large part of the public had become alienated from politics.[5]

Alienation from politics was an economic problem for journalists because fewer people read papers when they are uninterested in public affairs. In his widely cited public journalism manifesto, *Getting the Connections Right: Public Journalism and the Troubles in the Press,* and elsewhere, Jay Rosen listed the "deteriorating economic base for journalism" as the first "alarm bell" signaling that American print journalism was in trouble. Rosen, a principal intellectual leader of the public journalism movement, cited a *Times Mirror* poll with dramatic evidence: "[O]nly 45 percent of Americans said they had read a daily newspaper the previous day, down from 58 percent in February 1994 and from 71 percent in a comparable study in 1965."[6] Edward Fouhy, director of the Pew Center for Civic Journalism, an early foundation supporter of the reform effort, stressed in a briefing on public journalism that it was a direct response to serious economic troubles in the press, including "alarming" declines in circulation rates for nearly all newspapers in the country and poor readership rates among women.[7]

One strategy pursued by newspaper organizations like Knight-Ridder in the face of these troubling numbers was a market-driven approach that sought to attract readers by making feature stories more prominent and increasing soft news stories. Once in effect, however, this strategy failed; it did not gain back lost readers and it posed a real threat to journalists' sense of professional identity. As Michael Schudson notes, "Market model journalism is anathema to journalists themselves. They may cite it in apology for what they do, to explain why their best efforts are often thwarted, but they never refer to it as an ideal or aspiration. It is the model of the business office, not the newsroom. . . . [I]t is the model that any self-respecting journalist fears and loathes."[8] Under the market-driven model, the pressure to write personality-oriented soft news drove many journalists to question the value of their work. "Two familiar refrains" heard during this period: "[I]f newspapers don't learn to listen to readers and

5. Davis Merritt, *Public Journalism and Public Life: Why Telling the News Is Not Enough,* 2nd ed. (Mahwah, N.J.: Lawrence Erlbaum Associates, 1998), 40, 83.

6. Jay Rosen, *Getting the Connections Right: Public Journalism and the Troubles in the Press* (New York: Twentieth Century Fund Press, 1996), 19.

7. Edward M. Fouhy, "Civic Journalism: Rebuilding the Foundations of Democracy," *Civic Partners* (Spring 1996): 1.

8. Schudson, "What Public Journalism Knows," 119.

adapt to the way they live, they'll die. And if newspapers treat their content as a mere commodity, they'll lose their souls. And damage democracy. And die anyway."[9] All this was recognized by James Batten, who in the late 1980s began to move his organization away from a market-driven "customer obsession" campaign and toward a different model that stressed the "customer" as citizen.[10]

Hard-boiled journalists may have looked askance at the civic language of public journalism reformers, but many realized it was better than the alternative market-driven model. Jim Walser, on the editorial staff of the *Charlotte Observer*, an early public journalism paper, asks, "Do you want to be in the business of delivering shoes to kids? Is that what newspapers should be doing? You can obviously take this to an extreme. But I personally think newspapers need to stand for something. In the eyes of a lot of people they've become just another big corporate money-sucking institution."[11] As many realized, infotainment was a risky strategy for news organizations: "They are locking themselves into a competition they are bound to lose. If the public is looking for pure celebrity or entertainment, it will go for the real thing. If public life continues to lose its claim on America's attention, so—inevitably—will journalism."[12]

Along with being an economic problem, public alienation from the political process was also a personal problem since many journalists themselves felt detached as public actors and as citizens.[13] Many journalists shared the belief that political campaigns had become meaningless and only minimally reflected key public interests. In a 1990 editorial that would galvanize public journalists, a frustrated David Broder wrote:

> It would be grotesque at such a moment to watch without protest the strangulation or distortion of democracy in the United States—which symbolizes successful and sustained self-government to so much of the

9. Michael Hoyt, "The Wichita Experiment: What Happens When a Newspaper Tries to Connect Readership and Citizenship," *Columbia Journalism Review* 31 (1992): 41.

10. Carmen Sirianni and Lewis Friedland, *Civic Innovation in America: Community Empowerment, Public Policy, and the Movement for Civic Renewal* (Berkeley and Los Angeles: University of California Press, 2001), 191.

11. Mike Hoyt, "Are You Now, or Will You Ever Be, a Civic Journalist? As the Theory Moves into Practice in More and More Newsrooms, the Debate Gets Sharper," *Columbia Journalism Review* 34 (1995): 31.

12. James Fallows, *Breaking the News* (New York: Vintage Books, 1997), 244.

13. Jan Schaffer and Edward D. Miller, *Civic Journalism: Six Case Studies* (Washington, D.C.: Pew Center for Civic Journalism/Poynter Institute for Media Studies, 1995), 2; Jay Rosen, *Community-Connectedness: Passwords for Public Journalism* (St. Petersburg, Fla.: Poynter Institute for Media Studies, 1993), 4.

world. . . . It is time for those of us in the world's freest press to become activists, not on behalf of a particular party or politician, but on behalf of the process of self-government. It is time to expose the threats to that process and support the efforts to get rid of them.

We cannot allow the 1990 elections to be another exercise in public disillusionment and political cynicism.

. . . [W]e must be far more assertive than in the past on the public's right to hear its concerns discussed by the candidates—in ads, debates and speeches—and far more conscientious in reporting those discussions when they take place. We have to help reconnect politics and government—what happens in the campaign and what happens afterward in public policy—if we are going to have accountability by our elected officials and genuine democracy in this country.[14]

Another impetus to the public journalism movement was the diminished public image of the press. One 1991 study of American political attitudes widely read by journalists reported that many people saw the press as part of a political class that was disengaged from the real concerns of communities.[15] Other large-scale surveys marked the decline in public respect for journalists and the increasingly common belief that "the media" were partially responsible for issueless elections and purposeless government. James Fallows, in *Breaking the News,* issued a scathing criticism of the bubble inhabited by political journalists, something that included political officials, pundits, other Washington celebrities but insulated journalists from their readers and viewers. Fallows endorsed public journalism as a way of breaking out of the bubble and regaining linkages between citizens' concerns and political journalism.[16]

Newspaper reporters rate near the bottom of Gallup's routine opinion polls of Americans' attitudes about professions. In 2004, only 21 percent of respondents marked them "very high" or "high" on honesty and ethical standards. This ranking is well below nurses (with 79 percent of respondents marking them "very high" or "high" on honesty and ethical standards), pharmacists (72 percent), military officers (72 percent), doctors (67 percent), police (60 percent), clergy (56 percent), judges (53 percent), day care providers (49 percent), bankers (36 percent),

14. David Broder, "Democracy and the Press," *Washington Post,* January 3, 1990, A15.

15. Harwood Group, *Citizens and Politics: A View from Main Street America* (Dayton: Kettering Foundation, 1991). This report was widely requested by journalists, according to the Kettering Foundation.

16. Fallows, "News and Democracy," in *Breaking the News,* 235–69.

mechanics (26 percent), local (26 percent) and state (24 percent) officeholders. Only business executives (20 percent), lawyers (18 percent), advertising workers (10 percent), and car salespeople (9 percent) rank lower than journalists.

The problem of diminished public image focused journalists on the linkages between their professional norms and their own role in contemporary democracy—their own political agency—in a way that the problem of political alienation alone would not have. As Michael Schudson has pointed out, the respect and status of the profession of journalism stands and falls based on how the public views politics: "The only part of journalism that consistently commands the serious attention of the public is political journalism. The symbolic center of the news media is politics. And that's the rub: politics itself is not dignified."[17] In his argument for reforming journalism toward more public norms, Rosen echoes these points about professional vulnerability by noting the "comparatively thin credentials of the journalist as a maker of professional judgments: no advanced training or licensing, no white lab coat, no obscure vocabulary to intimidate the layperson, no particular expertise in most of the subjects explored in the news, no scientific method or formal peer review."[18]

The motivations driving the public journalism reform movement closely reflect the logic of democratic professionalism I discussed in the last chapter. The writings of public journalists support the view that the movement is a reaction to economic threats to traditional professional norms—in particular, the dumbing down and infotainment pressures of a market-driven response to declining readership. To conceive the customer as citizen is to attempt to retain some of the traditional social trustee role—and concomitant status—of the journalist as an objective provider of critical information needed to uphold civic duties. The competitive advantage of newspapers over other news media is found in just this substantive area. Further, the special privileges of the press are grounded on this service to the public interest. "[I]f newspapers are solely a business," writes James Carey, "why do they need protection under the First Amendment, protections greater than those afforded other commercial enterprises?"[19]

Public journalists recognize that the social trustee model of professionalism is untenable and as problematic as a purely market-driven journalism. Under the social trustee model, "active roles were reserved for the state, the press, and

---

17. Michael Schudson, "The Profession of Journalism in the United States," in *The Professions in American History,* ed. Nathan Hatch (Notre Dame: University of Notre Dame Press, 1988), 146.
18. Rosen, *Getting the Connections Right,* 8.
19. James Carey, "In Defense of Public Journalism," in *The Idea of Public Journalism,* ed. Glasser, 50.

interest groups" while citizens were left out as spectators. The watchdog and adversary roles that are a part of social trustee journalism were plausible to the public as long as the press appeared "authentically their representative and therefore in a responsible and fiduciary relation to it," as long as the press did not appear to be "in cahoots with the state, and with the most powerful interest groups, or both," and as long as the press was seen as being able to convey a "reasonable, unbiased, true, and factual account" of the world.[20] Over the course of the last twenty-five years many citizens have lost faith in all these facets of the press as representative of their interests, something that was perhaps inevitable given the distance between the public and the press under the social trustee model.

Though connected to the self-interest of the profession in retaining status and respect, the recognition that the political environment is affected by certain norms and habits of newsgathering must be considered a separate, democratic motivation that is clearly present in the public journalism movement. The kind of status and respect sought by public journalists is defined by their role in fostering a more engaged, more reflective democracy.

Public journalism departs from traditional reporting practices by advocating public listening, by producing purposeful news, and by encouraging public debate. These democratic professional methods—the first a form of task sharing, the second a form of civic education, and the third a form of public engagement—are mirror images of traditional journalistic practices that are seen as contributing to widespread dissatisfaction with the media: an overreliance on elite or expert sources for news, an emphasis on conflict between opposing sides (often between elites), and a short time horizon that leaves some issues undercovered and others covered in a schizophrenic fashion.

Public Listening: Sharing the Task of Finding and Framing the News

As mentioned in the discussion of civic pathologies in Chapter 1, mainstream journalism frequently comes across as a domain of experts, celebrities, and political officials. James Fallows writes:

> Concentrating on conflict and spectacle, building up celebrities and tearing them down, presenting a crisis or issue with the volume turned all the way up, only to drop that issue and turn to the next emergency.

20. Carey, "In Defense of Public Journalism," 57.

They will make themselves the center of attention, as they exchange one-liners as if public life were a parlor game and make fun of the gaffes and imperfections of anyone in public life. They will view their berths as opportunities for personal aggrandizement and enrichment, trading on the power of their celebrity. And while they do these things, they will be constantly more hated and constantly less useful to the public whose attention they are trying to attract.[21]

Mainstream political journalism is dominated by official sources and a narrative that stresses conflict between extremes and emphasizes the gamesmanship and strategy of politics rather than the more dull, but potentially more important, business of governing and forming policies to address social issues.[22]

A key step in reconnecting with the public and promoting a more deliberative politics, according to public journalists, is to reconceive what counts as news. Instead of being driven by the agendas of office holders, party leaders, and other elite sources, news is to reflect the interests of citizens. This *public listening* involves finding out what is of concern in a community and then reporting on how those concerns are or are not being met.[23] Three early standard-setting examples of public journalism projects illustrate this process of task sharing.

One of the first and most prominent examples of public journalism was the "Your Vote Counts" election coverage by the *Wichita Eagle* in which the paper surveyed voters to determine the most important public issues and then regularly reported on how candidates addressed or failed to address these issues in their speeches and other public statements.[24] The groundwork for this 1990 experiment was laid in the frustrations of the 1988 presidential campaign, after which editor Merritt urged a new contract between the press, the public, and politicians:

The campaign just concluded showed at its frustrating worst the mutual bond of expediency that has formed over the years between campaigns and the media, particularly television. Together they have learned that feeding the lowest common appetite among the voters is safer, cheaper, and less demanding than running the risk, for the campaigns, and the expense, for the media, of providing in-depth information.[25]

21. Fallows, *Breaking the News*, 267.
22. Thomas E. Patterson, *Out of Order* (New York: Knopf, 1993).
23. Arthur Charity, *Doing Public Journalism* (New York: Guilford Press, 1995), chap. 2.
24. Merritt, *Public Journalism and Public Life*, 85.
25. Merritt, *Public Journalism and Public Life*, 84.

At the beginning of the 1990 Kansas gubernatorial race, the *Eagle* announced that it had a "strong bias": "The bias is that we believe the voters are entitled to have the candidates talk about the issues in depth."[26] The resulting "Your Vote Counts" project lasted the length of the 1990 campaign season.

The cornerstone of the *Eagle*'s project was an initial exercise in public listening. As Merritt puts it, "The thrust of the plan was a straightforward, unabashed campaign to revive voter interest backed by total focus on the issues that voters were concerned about as reflected in survey results."[27] The paper used a research consultant to interview five hundred Wichita residents to determine which political problems and issues were most important to them.[28] As a result of this public listening, it fixed on ten issues: education, taxes, economic development, health care, abortion, environment, crime, agriculture, social services, and state spending.[29] Each of these issues was then made the subject of long pieces published in the Sunday edition. In addition, the *Eagle* covered the gubernatorial candidates' responses to these issues—and their lack of response—every Sunday before the election in a feature called "Where They Stand." On October 7, 1990, for example, candidate Finney's response to the issue of agriculture was reported as: "Wants agriculture secretary elected by all voters. No other stated position on agriculture issue. This week: did not talk about it."[30]

Public listening at the *Eagle* allowed it to escape having campaign coverage dictated by what the candidates and what fellow journalists wanted to talk about. As managing editor Steven Smith notes, "[I]t took a while to reeducate ourselves to become aggressive about issues. We had become transcribers to political campaigns—getting A's statement and B's response and so forth."[31] Having done the public listening gave the *Eagle* license to press candidates harder on their positions than it otherwise might have:

> A startling insight occurred midway through as we struggled to pin down the candidates on issues. Abortion was a major one, and Finney's congenital, rambling abstruseness was making it impossible to understand her position. In frustration, we printed verbatim a press conference answer that was, in fact, incoherent. Outrage steamed from the

26. Merritt, *Public Journalism and Public Life*, 85.
27. Merritt, *Public Journalism and Public Life*, 85.
28. Hoyt, "The Wichita Experiment," 44.
29. Rosen, *Getting the Connections Right*, 36.
30. Hoyt, "The Wichita Experiment," 45.
31. Hoyt, "The Wichita Experiment," 45.

Finney camp that we would quote exactly what she said; they howled that it was unfair. The campaign later provided a translation, of sorts, although even that "position" was full of ambiguity.[32]

This approach is akin to the toughness of adversary journalism and investigative reporting, but it was driven by the specific interests voiced by citizens of Wichita. Indeed, the public listening framework became a driving source of news: as candidates altered their positions on issues in which citizens had declared an interest, these changes were reported as news.[33]

A second prominent example of public listening in practice comes from the eighteen-month "Taking Back Our Neighborhoods" public journalism project in which the *Charlotte Observer* polled and interviewed residents of some of the city's highest crime neighborhoods in order to, in the words of a mission statement, "bring the Charlotte area community together in an effort to understand the crime problem from the residents' point of view, to seek solutions, and to follow up with the people who make decisions on change."[34] After analyzing crime data it had obtained with some difficulty under Freedom of Information requests to the Charlotte-Mecklenburg police, the paper surveyed 401 citizens from ten of the highest crime neighborhoods to ask about the effects of crime on their lives and what possible changes might reduce crime in their neighborhoods. A community coordinator hired by the paper with funds provided by the Pew Foundation organized advisory panels made up of long-time residents, civic and business leaders in each of the ten neighborhoods, and an overarching "citizens' panel" made up of residents polled from all the neighborhoods.

In Seversville, the first neighborhood covered by "Taking Back Our Neighborhoods," the coordinator organized two public listening events that became models for how the project would proceed. The first, a gathering of the fifteen-member neighborhood advisory panel and the editors and reporters involved, shared information about the journalism project and gathered information about the neighborhood. This "discussion about crack houses, unemployment, and a desire for parents to take responsibility for their own children was credited later with influencing the *Observer*'s coverage." The second was a town meeting of more than two hundred citizens held in a neighborhood church and televised by the *Observer*'s main partner, WSOC-TV. Following these events, the *Observer*

32. Merritt, *Public Journalism and Public Life*, 86.
33. Rosen, *Getting the Connections Right*, 38.
34. Mission statement quoted in Schaffer and Miller, *Civic Journalism*, 9.

published seven pages of in-depth reporting on Seversville that included answers to frequently asked questions and the "needs list" generated by the public listening events.[35]

Public listening in Charlotte has been credited by the reporters and editors involved and later analysts with shaping the coverage of crime to focus on the felt problems of the neighborhoods themselves and to give credit to neighborhood solutions for these problems. *Observer* reporter Liz Chandler notes the importance of the concrete specificity of the community needs list put together in dialogue with the neighborhoods covered: "If we had written about it in generalities it would have been so overwhelming that people wouldn't know where to begin."[36] Cheryl Carpenter, assistant managing editor, recounts, "When the project started, there was a tendency to oversimplify the community's problems. When we went into the neighborhoods, we thought it was going to be a story about bad people. And then we realized it's a story about volunteer organizations and law enforcement and citizen groups and churches and landlords." Carmen Sirianni and Lewis Friedland write that the public listening efforts of the paper led to an emphasis on certain issues, such as absentee landlordism, that otherwise may not have earned prominence: "By listening closely to residents and providing them with public space to formulate what they felt were central problems, the paper and the follow-up reporting on television enabled several issues to come to the fore. By far the most important was the focus on absentee housing."[37]

A third example of public listening was initiated by the *Virginian-Pilot* of Norfolk, which held "community conversations" between reporters and a representative group of citizens to discuss public issues—an effort that produced a different sort of news than that emerging from official decisions and press conferences. Beginning in 1993, editor Cole Campbell moved the beat reporting structure of the paper away from covering typical institutions such as City Hall and specific geographical areas. Reporters were now clustered into teams oriented around readers' issue interests such as public life, education, criminal justice, public safety. The *Pilot* hired a public opinion firm to hold focus groups, or "community conversations," involving a professional facilitator, reporters, and a small number of citizens recruited through community networks or a call

35. Schaffer and Miller, *Civic Journalism,* 8–9.

36. Lynn Waddell, "A Different Way of Covering Crime," in *Mixed News: The Public/Civic/Communitarian Journalism Debate,* ed. Jay Black (Mahwah, N.J.: Lawrence Erlbaum Associates, 1997), 36.

37. Sirianni and Friedland, *Civic Innovation in America,* 219, 212.

for participation published in the paper. These conversations were deliberate attempts at public listening designed to reveal more depth and complexity in the community's views of public issues.[38] Unlike typical source interviews, these conversations allowed people to change their positions and express revised views over the course of an event where different perspectives were aired. As Thomas Warhover, the *Pilot's* public life team leader notes, "The conversation works best when group members ask questions of each other rather than simply let themselves be led by the moderator. At its core, a community conversation is about creating deliberation."[39] Sometimes parts of the conversations themselves made their way into news stories verbatim.[40]

Like the experiences in the *Eagle* and *Observer,* public listening by the *Pilot* reporters and editors allowed laypeople rather than officials and experts to help set a news agenda. After eight community conversations involving more than ninety people discussing the governor's 1994 proposal to get tough on crime by severely reducing parole options, for example, *Pilot* reporters discovered more than "what was missing in his [the governor's] plans (troubling questions of cost, among others), but also what was missing from the entire debate."[41] Juvenile crime, for example, emerged from these conversations as being an important issue for citizens even though it was not a part of the governor's plans or on the reporters' watchdog agenda. The impact of community conversations was an unsettling of *Pilot* journalists' assumptions about what was "news" for their readers:

> I remember one gathering at a Norfolk high school library—an event organized by the *Pilot's* education team with about twelve parents. Several reporters surrounded the residents but remained largely quiet for the next two hours. They listened. What they heard wasn't some policy debate. There was no "hot topic" to throw around. Instead, parents talked about how difficult it is to know when your kid is failing; how to deal with problem teachers; how to navigate an educational bureaucracy seen as impersonal and sometimes vitriolic. . . . As the parents filed out, the journalists dissected the discussion, looking for clues as to how they might do their jobs better. The education editor silenced

38. Chris Conte, "Civic Journalism," *CQ Researcher,* September 20, 1996, 823.
39. Thomas A. Warhover, "Public Journalism and the Press: The *Virginian-Pilot* Experience," in *Public Journalism and Political Knowledge,* ed. Anthony J. Eksterowicz and Robert N. Roberts (Lanham, Md.: Rowman and Littlefield, 2000), 51.
40. Sirianni and Friedland, *Civic Innovation in America,* 202.
41. Warhover, "Public Journalism and the Press," 52.

the group when she simply said: "You know, we're not writing about what they are talking about."[42]

For Warhover and other *Pilot* journalists, public listening events revealed stories that "were being missed entirely by our reliance on being watchdog to the official agendas of our school systems" and other institutions of government.[43]

Not uncommonly, *Pilot* reporters emerged from community conversations with a higher regard for citizen opinion. Discussing his public listening on crime and justice issues, reporter Tony Wharton remarks, "One thing that had struck me was the incredible human drama and power in their stories, and how easily it was cheapened by journalists and politicians alike talking about crime. I also saw the complexity of their feelings about crime, not the one-dimensional victim's cry for revenge that is so often depicted."[44] A new understanding of journalists' roles as co-participants in public conversations emerged in which the skills and expertise of journalists at information gathering and storytelling surely played a role, but not a dominant role in determining the shape, direction, and content of these conversations:

> We journalists can contribute ideas and information to that conversation, but mostly we must heed what ordinary citizens are saying, invite them back into the political dialogue we cover and reflect that in our newspapers and broadcasts. We can help order the flow of what's worth discussing immediately and what might wait for another day, as long as we see ourselves as partners with, and not cleverer than, the people and communities we serve.[45]

For Campbell and the other public journalists discussed here, public listening is just one part of a larger strategy to engage citizens in public affairs.

Purposeful News: Journalism as Civic Education

News is more than the information that the public wants. Public journalists make content and narrative choices based on what they think a citizen desiring

42. Warhover, "Public Journalism and the Press," 48.
43. Warhover, "Public Journalism and the Press," 48.
44. Jay Rosen, *What Are Journalists For?* (New Haven: Yale University Press, 2001), 140.
45. Cole Campbell, "Journalism as a Democratic Art," foreword to *The Idea of Public Journalism,* ed. Glasser, xxiv.

to be engaged in public affairs would need. They see their readers through a normative model of the active citizen who has become passive under the burdens of daily life: "Public journalism doesn't only aim to treat readers as citizens, it assumes that readers want to *be* citizens. By and large they're sufficiently serious about making their cities, states, and country work better that they would hammer out a smart agenda, ask experts and candidates smart questions, and strive for a smart set of solutions, *if* only they had the time, money, access, and professional expertise of journalists."[46] Without this normative model, the attempt to produce news that people find interesting runs the risk of reflecting existing market preferences and thus allowing "civic boosterism" or "infotainment" as seemingly legitimate examples of serving the public.

Public journalists, as democratic professionals, take cues from the public and in this way engage in task sharing. They are sharing the normally professionalized task of determining what is news, thus rendering their information provision authority more porous, more open to challenge and influence from outside. But to do all this, they are making assumptions about their public: that the public wants to be so empowered, wants to make these choices, wants to be more involved in the public sphere. These are leaps of faith that every democratic professional must make.

With the model of citizen-reader in place, public journalists have the justification for advocating what I will call "purposeful news." This includes reporting on long-term policy issues, such as environmental protection, that have important consequences for communities but involve policy choices that are too complex or drawn out over time to fit into normal news cycles. A good example of purposeful news is the "Facing Our Future" project taken up by the Binghamton *Press and Sun Bulletin* in 1995. As part of a project consortium involving television and radio partners as well as the local university, State University of New York–Binghamton, the *Press* examined the complex problem of economic development in a community seeking to recover from the loss of the defense and electronics industries that had supported it. "Facing Our Future" started with surveys and focus groups conducted in the fall of 1995 to solicit citizen views on the major problems facing Binghamton. Then the *Press* covered these issues with in-depth reports followed by coupons published in the paper that prompted people to join "action teams."[47] Eleven teams made up of around three hundred

46. Charity, *Doing Public Journalism*, 19.
47. Esther Thorson and Lewis A. Friedland, *Civic Lessons: Report on Four Civic Journalism Projects* (New York: Pew Center for Civic Journalism, 1997), 19.

citizens in total were formed in a televised town meeting in April 1996 and asked to study specific problems and write a report offering recommendations. Afterward, the *Press* published a story that summarized the reports written by the citizen action teams as well as a series of editorials on the teams' recommendations.

Purposeful news also encompasses civic information that helps people become involved in public debate. This can be basic information about the structures of government and the roles played by different office holders or more complex discussions of core values at stake in particular public choices. The "public life pages" of the *Virginian-Pilot,* for example, seek to give "how to" information to citizens. Organized thematically under the headings "Public Life," "Public Safety," and "Education," these appear once a week each in the metro section of the paper. The upper-left side of the pages convey practical civic information on subjects such as how to get official reports of city budgets and how to be involved in specific ongoing civic projects such as school improvement. The upper-right side of the public life pages covers official and civic events, such as city council or school board meetings, or a civic project. Between these "rails" are stories "designed to be working tools for citizens, quick and effective ways for them to locate themselves in public life, so that they can see how they are doing, what kinds of problems need to be solved, and what they can do to address them."[48] Such stories may involve follow-ups on the progress of projects, such as a proposed expansion of a community library, discussing in concrete detail problems and proposed solutions. Also between the rails is the "Neighborhood Exchange" that reports on numerous possibilities for readers to get involved in ongoing area civic projects and recognizes the activities of citizens involved therein.

Public journalists also publish meeting times and addresses for community discussions, calendars of public events, and timelines of political decisions and elections that affect the community—what public opinion scholars call "mobilizing information."[49] One dramatic example of this was the voter-registration drive promoted by the *San Francisco Chronicle* as part of its 1994 "Voice of the Voter" public journalism experiment. The *Chronicle* inserted postage-paid voter registration forms in five hundred sixty thousand papers distributed a month and a half before the election. A number of other Bay Area newspapers followed the example, resulting in forty thousand registrants using applications distributed by newspapers.[50]

48. Sirianni and Friedland, *Civic Innovation in America,* 205.
49. Merritt, *Public Journalism and Public Life,* chap. 7; Charity, *Doing Public Journalism,* 147–48.
50. Schaffer and Miller, *Civic Journalism,* 45.

Public Debate: Sparking Civic Engagement

More controversial than the reconceptualization of what is newsworthy—so that it includes nonelite stories and purposeful news—is the belief that to promote public deliberation, journalists must do more than report the news and should broaden their role to include helping the public convene and deliberate about public affairs. Though this is a remarkable addition to the traditional task of informing the public, holding community meetings can be seen as a natural outgrowth of the public listening that helps public journalists better cover their communities. Public journalists use two broad approaches that sometimes go hand in hand. One involves the newspaper as a virtual forum where the community can express and debate its problems and potential solutions; the other involves the newspaper as a catalyst and moderator of actual community forums where citizens can discuss issues in public.

An example of a newspaper serving as catalyst of community forums is the Maine Citizens' Campaign held between October 1995 and March 1998—one of the longest running public journalism efforts. Helped along by grants from the Pew Foundation, the Portland Newspapers Group in partnership with television stations initially brought together sixty residents of Sanford, Maine, to deliberate about politics in order to "focus coverage of the 1996 presidential campaign on the views of ordinary citizens and not rely on political insiders, pollsters and candidates' sound bites."[51] Planned only for one year, the project involved a diverse group of residents selected from a representative Maine town who would meet regularly to discuss the political issues that concerned them. News stories and editorials would regularly cover the small group deliberations and use some of the comments recorded as frames: "'What does it really mean to get a "B" in math?' asked a participant at last week's Maine Citizens' Campaign discussion of education in Sanford. It's the kind of direct, sharply focused question that lawmakers, educators, parents and taxpayers should be asking as they assess recommendations of The Task Force on Learning Results submitted to the Legislature last week."[52] Like other public journalism efforts, the paper used the small group meetings of the citizens' campaign to generate questions for political candidates during primary and general election campaigns: "At the group's

---

51. Mark Shanahan, "Volunteers Wanted for Voter Project," *Portland Press Herald*, November 20, 1995, 1B.

52. "Set Solid Learning Goals," *Portland Press Herald*, January 14, 1996, 4C.

first meeting in November, the participants selected education as their No. 1 concern. Here are some of the group's questions related to education. To get answers, the *Maine Sunday Telegram* sent the questions to the campaign staffs and examined candidates' recent speeches, published interviews and web pages on the Internet."[53] At the end of the year, members of the citizens' campaign were surveyed about their experiences, with special attention on how their positions might have changed as a result of group deliberation.[54]

Though the numbers of citizens involved in the project diminished over time, the interest was significant enough for the members to urge a continuation beyond the 1996 election year. In its second year, the campaign became more of an autonomous citizen-driven project than a journalism effort. "In part because they enjoy each other's company and in part because they have felt empowered by the experience of simply talking with one another, the group stayed together after the election."[55] Group members drafted an action-oriented mission statement to signal that they wanted to do more than serve as a study group: "Our mission is to talk politics and social concerns, educate ourselves and do something."[56] By the time the campaign ended, in the middle of its third year, another group, the "People's Forum," emerged to take its place.[57]

A second example, the *Tallahassee Democrat*'s "Public Agenda" project, is an effort that combines both actual and virtual public forums.[58] At the outset of the project, a week after the 1994 midterm elections, the *Democrat* used public opinion research firms to conduct focus groups and surveys to determine which issues were most important to community members. With that information in hand, the paper and other members of the "Public Agenda" consortium, which included a television station and two regional universities, set the stage for a series of community meetings by contacting community leaders and organizations. The newspaper hired and trained moderators who could lead group debates and publicized the rationale for the "Public Agenda" project along with interviews with citizens and information about how to be involved in the meetings.

---

53. Mark Shanahan, "Sanford Quizzes Candidates on Education," *Portland Press Herald,* February 25, 1996, 3C.

54. Mark Shanahan, "Participants Find Positions Shift Little but Understanding Deepens," *Portland Press Herald,* April 7, 1996, 3C.

55. Mark Shanahan, "Sanford Group to Branch Out," *Portland Press Herald,* June 18, 1997, 1B.

56. "Maine Citizen's Campaign," *Portland Press Herald,* March 6, 1997, 3E.

57. Mark Shanahan, "People's Forum Group Takes Up Where Citizens' Campaign Left Off," *Portland Press Herald,* April 9, 1998, 1B.

58. Schaffer and Miller, *Civic Journalism,* 24–29.

The early meetings led to the formation of subgroups that focused on specific issues, such as crime, "community and race relations," "jobs and the economy," and "children, values and education." These semiautonomous discussion groups were further subdivided with the aims of focusing more closely on specific issues and allowing more people to be involved in the "Public Agenda" project.

After encouraging community dialogue in a way that encouraged a good deal of autonomy in the way issues were framed and discussed, the paper opened a virtual forum called the "Public Agenda Page." It appeared after the first community meeting and was run regularly thereafter. The page included a section with citizens' comments on issues or dialogue from community meetings, a "Citizens Want Answers" section in which readers' questions and public officials' answers were printed, and a "Where Things Stand" section that charted the progress of public issue and policy debates and provided civic information on where citizens could get involved. The idea was to reflect the views of citizens in as unmediated a form as possible, to be interactive like the new media of talk shows while at the same time being focused and deliberative.

Facing the Tensions of Democratic Professionalism Posed by Traditional Values and the Complexity and Expansiveness of New Roles

Trade-Offs with Traditional Values:
Is Public Journalism Objective, Independent, and Fair?

The reforms of public journalism put pressure on traditional standards of journalistic independence and fairness. Public journalism has had many critics within the press, even among those who share the goals of reducing political alienation and increasing public deliberation. A chief criticism is the claim that public journalism assumes functions of government that it ought not assume if it is to be independent. This critique involves at least three separate arguments: (1) the sacrifice in news quality caused by public journalists' role confusion, (2) the loss of objective authority, and (3) the dangers of paternalism threatened by heightened press agency.

Some critics worry that promoting public deliberation through community meetings with trained moderators is costly in terms of financial resources as well as reporters' time and takes a toll on the basic functions of news reporting— the "elemental tasks of describing events and discerning their causes"—that are already underfunded.[59] Others are concerned with the loss of objective authority, which comes from the widespread belief that one is telling the truth rather than justifying one's position. No other institution does what journalism does— namely, "inform, monitor, and critique" public affairs. To the extent that papers and stations try to "fix government through journalism" or "substitute journalism for government" they depart from their unique duties to provide checks on government that are critically important to democracy.[60] A third argument involves a very different sort of problem. Once journalists become involved and critically interested in the deliberative quality of community discussions of public affairs, in clarifying public agendas and critiquing the way arguments are put forward in public forums by citizens or officials, they run the risk of crossing the line between activism and paternalism.[61]

One premise drives these three related arguments concerning the loss of press independence: public journalists are doing something different from traditional journalism when they set agendas and influence citizens rather than objectively report facts. This premise is strongly contested by public journalists, who insist that the only significant difference is that they are self-reflexive about their power to set public agendas and take self-limiting measures. "Can anyone seriously claim," writes James Carey, "given the heroic place of Watergate in the history of the press, that journalists do not convene and constitute communities of judgment, sort out virtue and vice, campaign against wrongs, pass moral judgments, direct the community toward needed legislation, and, incidentally, tell the truth along the way?"[62] In this way, even the most controversial element of public journalism, deliberative community forums sponsored by news firms, can be portrayed as a self-limiting measure—a way for the public to share the power of setting the news agenda—and not an attempt to exercise governmental power.

Public journalists have a heightened sensitivity to media power because of their belief that traditional journalism has contributed to the public's alienation. They see that the way journalists frame stories inevitably affects the way they are received by an audience. Public listening and other techniques to bring citizens into the news process are self-limiting remedies to the elite-centered frames that had previously excluded the public voice. As Davis Merritt points out, "The

59. Max Frankel, "Fix-It Journalism," *New York Times Magazine,* May 20, 1995, 30.

60. Carl S. Stepp, "Public Journalism: Balancing the Scales," *American Journalism Review* 18 (1996): 40.

61. Renita Coleman, "The Intellectual Antecedents of Public Journalism," *Journal of Communication Inquiry* 21 (1997): 73.

62. Carey, "In Defense of Public Journalism," 50.

inescapable fact . . . is that the way we do journalism has a strong effect on how people see themselves and their environment. If people see themselves as having no effective role in public life, as barred by circumstances from any control over their lives, they will continue to withdraw and democracy will be weakened."[63] Given that news stories always exercise a form of power—by highlighting some aspects of an issue over others, noticing some actors over others, and presenting some views and not others—it is tempting to say that traditional journalists present a false dichotomy when they distinguish objectivity from power. Most public journalists resist this temptation and simply claim that their practices serve the ideal of objectivity better by opening up newsgathering and agenda setting to a wider range of public influences rather than relying on traditional codes of journalistic practice. As Judith Lichtenberg has argued, the choice is not between objective and politicized news but between a naïve view of journalists as passive transmitters of news and a more realistic view of journalists as actors who must choose from a number of different ways of telling a story. Lichtenberg sees public journalism "as making a virtue of necessity, or rendering explicit what has been implicit: reporters do shape public discourse and guide public life, and therefore they might as well do these things self-consciously."[64]

One method of self-limitation involves self-reflexivity about the role of public journalists in agenda setting and openness to influence from their communities. When reporters ask community groups to comment on their paper's coverage of an issue—what has been left out or what has been shaded inappropriately—they are sharing power. Forums such as the *Tallahassee Democrat*'s "Public Agenda Page" render the paper more vulnerable to criticisms or requests for information by the community. Citizen oversight boards have been proposed to invite community criticism of news coverage.[65] These self-limitation strategies, if pursued systematically, help inoculate public journalists against being accused of assuming too much power.

Another self-limitation strategy used by public journalists is the conscious assumption of the neutral referee's role in public discussion. Of course, the metaphor is not entirely apt since referees do not influence the rules of the game and seldom urge the players onto the field. Like referees, though, journalists would immediately lose their particular role-based authority if they were to

63. Merritt, *Public Journalism and Public Life*, 111.

64. Judith Lichtenberg, "Beyond the Public Journalism Controversy," in *Civil Society, Democracy, and Civic Renewal*, ed. Robert K. Fullinwider (Lanham, Md.: Rowman and Littlefield, 1999), 352.

65. Charity, *Doing Public Journalism*, 147.

actively root for one side. Public journalists exert power, but it is the power of "proactive neutrality" directed toward the "broad public values" of promoting informed citizenship and focusing community debate but prescribing "no chosen solution" and favoring "no particular party of interest."[66] Papers and other news outlets are to be "fair-minded participants" who are necessary to the process of deliberation but do nothing to influence the outcome.[67]

There is a second main line of criticism coming from traditional journalists: a news outlet cannot be fair to all sides of an issue once it has helped convene community groups, moderated discussions, and reported the community's position on an issue. The fairness criticism focuses on two discrete issues that can be called the bandwagon and the conventionalism problems. The bandwagon problem occurs when, because the press wants solutions, it ignores disagreements within the community or glosses over hurdles that might depress community engagement. Reporters, for example, have complained that public journalism–minded editors have put a positive spin on stories concerning citizens' meetings that were nondeliberative and divisive.[68] The problem of conventionalism arises when the press reports what people are interested in rather than relying on reporters' judgments of what should be covered.[69] The more the press engages in public listening, the less willing it will be to report or discuss issues with which the public is uncomfortable, whether this is because it has not considered the issue before in its complexity or because its interests are threatened by the issue. A number of journalists see public journalism as undermining the critical perspective of investigative journalism. Rosemary Armao, a self-described investigative journalist "refugee" from the public journalism culture of the *Virginian-Pilot*, notes: "It's not courageous to go out and list the views of a whole lot of people without really writing what's at stake."[70] It is unlikely, traditionalists argue, that a publication such as *Newsday* would have published its series on segregated housing patterns on Long Island if it had publicly listened to its readers beforehand.[71]

---

66. Rosen, *Getting the Connections Right,* 13.

67. Merritt, *Public Journalism and Public Life,* 97.

68. Hoyt, "Are You Now, or Will You Ever Be, a Civic Journalist," 27.

69. Conventional attitudes may also reflect a history of news framing of "serious" concerns, such as crime and taxes, and earlier neglect of other possible concerns such as health care or economic inequality. See, for example, Robert M. Entman, *Democracy Without Citizens: Media and the Decay of American Politics* (New York: Oxford University Press, 1989), 75–89.

70. Quoted in Don H. Corrigan, *The Public Journalism Movement in America* (Westport, Conn.: Praeger, 1999), 114.

71. Hoyt, "Are You Now, or Will You Ever Be, a Civic Journalist," 30.

In response, public journalists argue that fairness is fostered, not jeopardized, by public listening that searches out a range of opinions and perspectives through representative polls and active reporting. The bandwagon and conventionalism problems arise from public journalism done poorly, not from public journalism per se. Though success stories and narration of community achievements can be useful in engaging an audience, public journalists recognize that they must be used with care precisely to avoid the bandwagon problem. As for conventionalism, public journalists point out that public listening done well picks up dissension and previously undercovered issues.[72] Turning the issue of fairness around to face traditionalist critics, public journalists question the picture of just and rational reporters challenging the benighted community. Even if a majority refuses to face up to an issue, such as racial discrimination, homelessness, or disparities in health care, numerous groups within the community are affected by the majority's neglect. Public listening does not mean translating majority opinion into news; it means discovering what concerns all of the publics that make up the public. In sum, public journalists reject the premise that reporters cannot promote public dialogue and listen closely to the concerns of their communities while at the same time confronting majorities with minority opinions or critical analyses.[73]

Managing Complexity: Struggling with a New Relationship Between Reporters and Lay Citizens

Public journalists advocate changes in the relationship between reporters and the public in somewhat ambiguous ways. They write about joint ownership of the news making, newsgathering, and reporting process; news is no longer a commodity but a "co-creation of journalists and the people; news is derived, in large measure, from their mutually defined relationship."[74] Rosen writes dramatically about the transformation at the *Virginian-Pilot:* "In 1991, readers were seen as a passive audience, on the receiving end of the news. By 1995 they are understood as active participants, partners with journalists in fashioning an understanding of events."[75] Community activities become stories that attract

---

72. Charity, *Doing Public Journalism,* 28–29.
73. Rosen, *Getting the Connections Right,* 63–64.
74. Rob Anderson, Robert Dardenne, and George M. Killenberg, "The American Newspaper as the Public Conversational Commons," in *Mixed News,* ed. Black, 99.
75. Rosen, *What Are Journalists For,* 147.

interest because citizen-readers have participated or could imagine participating in such activities. Citizens also make news through interviews and contributions to informational commons pages, and they can affect newsgathering and reporting by engaging with members of the press during focus groups or community meetings.

Public journalists have ambiguously characterized their reforms as opening up and leveling the field of political activity and deliberation so that citizens as well as elites can participate. Instead of sponsoring the elite-dominated debates, summits, and town-hall meetings so familiar to our political experience—where citizens can participate only marginally from the floor of the audience—papers and other news outlets are convening more inclusive forums. As Arthur Charity puts it, "[P]ublic journalists have set out to provide ordinary people with the same kinds of opportunities to meet and talk that these other papers provide officials."[76]

The difficulty with both of these characterizations is that the impetus and the agency for joint ownership and opening up are not coming from the citizenry but from the media outlets themselves. Public journalists are not responding to the immediate wants of their readers so much as what the journalists consider to be their readers' long-term, fundamental interests as citizens. By sponsoring real and virtual public forums, news outlets provide deliberative resources otherwise lacking in many communities, but they are doing so on the belief that this supply will ultimately encourage more demand for public debate.

The goals that public journalists advocate for their papers and stations go beyond the egalitarian goal of opening up or leveling the field of public affairs and nudging citizens onto it. Some advocates urge a transformative goal: the press can help readers want to be citizens and can help citizens deliberate in more thorough and public-spirited ways. Arthur Charity, for example, imagines a newspaper serving as a roving critic of public dialogue that asks "when, where, and how much citizens are practicing certain basic skills" and holds "public figures accountable for failing to 'actively listen' or 'negotiate.'"[77] Jay Rosen argues that public journalists who convene community meetings are to act not merely as facilitators but as cultivators of "civic dialogue," meaning that they hold citizens "to a respectable standard of discourse."[78] Others emphasize the importance of bringing people together across social and economic divisions so

76. Charity, *Doing Public Journalism*, 106.
77. Charity, *Doing Public Journalism*, 90.
78. Rosen, *Getting the Connections Right*, 55.

that dialogue about common interests can be joined. In their view, the newspaper can be a "forum in which citizens could be vulnerable to each other's cultural voices and political arguments."[79]

Some critics have asserted that public journalism is a "conservative" reform movement, a modified version of social trustee model of professionalism in which "journalists are to provide news according to what they themselves as a professional group believe citizens should know. The professional journalist's quest for truth and fairness, exercising sound and critical judgment as measured by a jury of peers, should dictate the shape of the news." Public journalists involve lay participants, but they in no way cede any real authority over the news. Schudson writes: "Public journalism exhorts journalists to put citizens first, to bring new voices into the newspapers, even to share setting the news agenda with individuals and groups in the community—but always authority about what to write and whether to print stays with the professionals."[80]

Though an apt reminder of how much more vulnerable journalists could be to public participation and how this could be done in more institutionalized forms—such as media review boards composed of citizen members—this critique misses its mark. The public listening, civic education, and public forums of public journalists are all open spaces, as it were, for lay participation. Professional skills are not abdicated in these open spaces, they are reoriented, redirected, and critiqued. As James Carey writes, "Against both the marketers and trustees, public journalism claims as its first task the necessity of making public life possible and cultivating an ethic of citizenship rather than cults of information and markets."[81] The real challenge for public journalists, as with all democratic professionals, is to accept the tensions of this role that demands both respect for lay participants and retention of the skills and expertise of professionals. Schudson too easily assumes that public journalists favor the latter over the former, but many of the self-reports of reformers show them to be struggling to achieve a balance.

The roles of civic educator and facilitator are certainly in tension: one assumes that citizens' voices must be heard along with official and expert voices; the other assumes that these voices must be informed and trained. This tension may

79. Anderson et al., "The American Newspaper as the Public Conversational Commons," 98; see also Lewis Friedland, "Bringing the News Back Home: Public Journalism and Rebuilding Local Communities," *National Civic Review* 85 (1996): 46.

80. Schudson, "What Public Journalism Knows," 120, 123.

81. Carey, "In Defense of Public Journalism," 51.

very well be a healthy one, however, under conditions that encourage respect for lay views even as they challenge them. *Virginia-Pilot* editor Cole Campbell's remarks express the kind of healthy tension I have in mind:

> [W]e have learned to respect citizens as partners in a continuing conversation about abortion, water supplies, neighborhood zoning, the Voting Rights Act, school prayer, political character and even the praying away of hurricanes by our neighbor, Pat Robertson.
>
> . . . We are learning to hold citizens accountable, not only by asking to reconcile their beliefs with contradictory evidence but also by asking them to spell out their own responsibility for the health of their community.
>
> . . . We are holding public figures and institutions more accountable to the concerns of the citizens they serve by making explicit in our coverage what those concerns are.[82]

Campbell's remarks reflect an important insight about the complexity of the relationship between professional and lay participant: under conditions of mutual respect, experts can be vulnerable to lay input, and lay participants can be open to requests to inform and clarify their positions. Still, healthy or not, the tension between the journalist as civic educator and as public listener is ever present. Self-assessments of journalists and their readers' responses will determine whether they have been too vulnerable to lay participation and not aggressive enough in pursuing stories that push readers to consider new or difficult information. As Dwayne Yancey reflects on his public journalism experience at the *Roanoke Times*, "Perhaps our biggest concern . . . as we analyzed our own coverage, was a fear that some of it had been too thin. Because we spent so much time finding citizens to fit the format we had devised, we didn't leave enough time for real reporting on the proposals the candidates had advanced."[83]

In addition to the general tension between educator and facilitator, there are practical tensions involved in being both a reporter or editor and facilitator: money, time, and training. There is little doubt that public journalism experiments would have been much less widespread and much less ambitious without the considerable funding put forward by Pew and Knight and other foundations.

---

82. Rosen, *Getting the Connections Right*, 17.
83. Dwayne Yancey, "Is Anybody Out There? The *Roanoke Times* Experience," in *Public Journalism and Political Knowledge*, ed. Eksterowicz and Roberts, 74.

In a number of the cases discussed in this chapter, outside consultants were brought in to train reporters in public listening, to conduct focus groups, and perform surveys. Sometimes, as in the case of the *Observer's* "Taking Back Our Neighborhoods" project, a community facilitator became part of the newspaper's staff for a time. Having someone on the staff in charge of the lay elements of the project may reduce some of the tensions in being both reporter and facilitator, but it costs money and it may lessen the vulnerability of traditional reporting techniques and routines to laypeople. The larger the project—the bigger the town meeting event, for example—the more costly and the more likely it is there will be a division of labor between reporters and facilitators hired specifically for such events.

Being a facilitator and a reporter is not easy to manage logistically, which is reflected in comments from editors and journalists engaged in public listening events. Making time, "slowing down the news-gathering process in the middle of it," seems to contradict "common sense for most working journalists" but is necessary in order "to hear the public conversation without forcing it into a fixed set of habits or reflexes defined by traditional news gathering."[84] Yancey of the *Roanoke Times* writes, "[A] citizen-based approach takes a lot of time and preparation. Campaign offices have known locations, and candidates have campaign managers and press secretaries to speak for them. Finding citizens willing to take the time to be interviewed was a much more difficult task."[85] The experience at the *Virginia-Pilot* was similarly challenging:

> [Community conversations] . . . are difficult to sustain. Every hour of conversation requires at least four of preparation. Second, it is difficult to find citizens to commit to two or more hours, and to find people who are not "the usual suspects." A third issue is what to do with the conversations. Early on, some were run verbatim in large chunks, but reader feedback convinced editors that this format was much less helpful than utilizing the conversations to identify issues and frame coverage.[86]

These logistical tensions will likely be present in any democratic professional reform. Indeed, they are evidence that professionals are modifying established habits that have traditionally kept laypeople at arm's length.

---

84. Sirianni and Friedland, *Civic Innovation in America,* 219.
85. Yancey, "Is Anybody Out There," 74.
86. Sirianni and Friedland, *Civic Innovation in America,* 202–3.

Managing the Dimensions of Democratic Professionalism:
Fighting Delusions of Civic Grandeur

Public journalists can escape traditionalist criticisms that their methods erode press fairness and independence, and they have been able to manage the complexity and changing relationships inherent in democratic professionalism. Less clear is how carefully their goal of promoting public deliberation has been articulated and executed. In their ambitious critique of traditional norms, public journalists may have assumed more responsibility for the character and quality of public life than is reasonable to think organizationally possible to fulfill. Though such delusions of civic grandeur may have been useful for mobilizing support, they can lead to both democratic professionalism and its opposite. It is one thing to involve more laypeople in the professional domain of journalism. Though it is complex and somewhat ambiguous, this sort of task sharing has been accomplished quite well in many public journalism experiments. However, it is another thing to conduct "public" forums that claim some authority as representing "public" views on pressing political issues. A democratic professional would not shirk from conducting the forums but would certainly be wary of claiming representativeness.

One pressing issue faced by the movement is that too much counts as public engagement. Theorists of the movement admit that some experiments have been mistaken, yet they have difficulty explaining just what standards obtain for determining what counts as legitimate public journalism. Rosen, for example, criticizes an unnamed television outlet for targeting public forums at likely Nielsen neighborhoods because this is a commercial and manipulative view of public engagement. Likewise, he criticizes the *San Jose Mercury News* for encouraging voter registration in low-income neighborhoods because this public journalism project appears partisan and overly involved in the electoral process.[87] Clearly, the public journalism movement needs standards of public engagement to determine which projects are suitable for the organizational capacity of news firms and for the role of journalists in a democracy.

A powerful component of democratic professionalism is the attempt to legitimate professional authority on social grounds as well as skill or expertise qualifications. The public listening and public forums of public journalism open up

87. Rosen, *What Are Journalists For,* 252–57.

the process of journalism—defining what is "news" and what is needed information—to lay voices. In doing so, public journalism empowers these voices, encourages an understanding of the news-making and news-writing process, and secures a new kind of respect and social standing.

"Public" listening and "public" forums must be accompanied by a tough-minded awareness of the nondeliberative threats to democratic values and an admission of considerable fallibility on the part of anyone claiming to have listened to the "public." These qualities are not always present in public journalism efforts. The 1996 "Your Voice, Your Vote" election coverage by a coalition of six North Carolina newspapers and nine broadcasters was widely criticized by members of the mainstream press for limiting the public debate. The coalition conducted polls to determine the most important issues and then chose four of the top-ranking issues: crime and drugs, health care, taxes and spending, and education. They used these issues to frame interviews with candidates, and they produced "issue packages" that were published with some modification by each partner.[88] Critics such as Jonathan Yardley of the *Washington Post* argued that this was an "attempt to control the political agenda rather than to report on the candidates' activities and positions."[89] Other critics complained that such polling pandered to readers rather than challenging them to think about important public issues—race, for example. Though I think the mainstream rejection of poll-driven framing of political coverage is mistaken, what is correct are the "insidious possibilities for twisting the public debate."[90] Polls must be reported with many grains of salt. Public listening projects may need to be more porous to changes in opinion over time, more dynamic, more open to dissident views rather than just the mainstream opinion.

A more democratic profession of journalism may actually play a more circumscribed and different role in promoting deliberation than public journalists imagine. Why more circumscribed? When we look at the multifaceted demands of improving public engagement and public deliberation raised in Chapter 1, we see that no single institutional actor could play the dominant role of democratic catalyst. To paraphrase Benjamin Page and Robert Shapiro, we find that a division of deliberative labor is needed.[91] The normative demands of public reason—

88. Seth Effron, "The North Carolina Experiment," *Columbia Journalism Review* 35, no. 5 (1997): 12.
89. Yardley, "'Public Journalism': Bad News," *Washington Post*, September 30, 1996, C2.
90. Effron, "The North Carolina Experiment," 13; Yardley, "Bad News."
91. Benjamin I. Page and Robert Y. Shapiro, *The Rational Public: Fifty Years of Trends in Americans' Policy Preferences* (Chicago: University of Chicago Press, 1992), 365.

that deliberation be rational, respectful, accountable, inclusive, and fair—can only be met when a number of social and political institutions are performing their particular tasks well.

Why criticize public journalism for taking on too broad a role when more democratic dialogue is preferable to less? There is a big difference between a paper or media outlet conceiving itself as a public forum rather than simply as one institution that helps public forums function well. When it characterizes itself as a public forum, a paper assumes functions of democratic deliberation that it cannot meet in a substantive way.

Public journalists underestimate how difficult it is to foster the rigorous and representative deliberation that would offer a clear view of community interests—both practical and ethical. This requires more than simply being open to the community by public listening or public forums. Without systematic attention to existing deliberative inequalities, public journalists can give unrepresentative views an undeserved normative weight.[92]

Consider the values of inclusion and fairness. As important as public listening and fostering public deliberation, any journalist committed to these democratic values must take up the role of criticizing the accessibility of any such process and the deliberative resources available to citizens. This means taking a sociological, and perhaps even historical, view of the constraints on participation manifest in the polity so that light can be shed on those who are not involved in the process of public debate.

Though a public forum may be inclusive in that its participants are not constrained by lack of deliberative resources and abilities or blocked from entering by a lack of civic information, it can still be unfair. Marginalized groups, communities, or associations that have been the subject of historical discrimination may be included in all the ways mentioned above while still lacking equal opportunity to influence the policy debate.[93] Dominant groups that have been the beneficiaries of historical discrimination can have a greater opportunity to influence the policy debate simply because of their past ideological success. Business interests in the United States have an unequal political voice not just because they have more deliberative resources and abilities and more political access—though they do possess these advantages—but also because of an ideological

92. For a version of this argument made more generally against ideal deliberative democratic theory, see Lynn M. Sanders, "Against Deliberation," *Political Theory* 25, no. 3 (1997): 347–76.

93. Iris Marion Young, *Justice and the Politics of Difference* (Princeton: Princeton University Press, 1990), 151–91.

environment that is oriented toward market capitalism.[94] Of course, fairness does not mean that all people should have the same degree of influence over the policy outcome. As Ronald Dworkin has argued, equality of influence—as an ideal—would contradict the purpose of democratic deliberation because it would lead one to conclude that people with better and more persuasive reasons or arguments are acting unfairly.[95] Fairness means equal *opportunity* to influence deliberation, which demands the removal of unreasonable influences on deliberation—such as threats or rewards offered by socioeconomic elites—that unjustifiably allow some interests a louder and more effective voice than others.

Also consider the values of rationality and accountability. The forces of strategic manipulation of information combined with the degree of public ignorance in American political culture make public forum events problematic. For those with self-interested motives, there is an incentive to indirectly pursue their interests by manipulating the flow of information about alternative proposals. Rational deliberators need accurate, nonstrategic information about policies and their implications in order to clarify their practical and ethical interests, and this information may not always be provided by their fellow participants. Important sources of nonstrategic information, in addition to officials or lay citizens, are academics and other members of nonpartisan, scholarly associations. The news media can disseminate expert reports, broadcast the results of deliberative polls, and engage the general public in a widespread debate.

The flow of information between citizens and officials and among citizens themselves can be distorted in many ways. In taking account of their constituents' positions, officials can be misled by vocal and active minorities and organized interests who characterize the majority view in self-serving ways or who manipulate public opinion through political advertising.[96] In taking account of officials' positions, voters can be misled by the same actors, but they are also vulnerable to the misinformation provided by their representatives' electoral opponents. Because of the incentives and opportunities for strategic use of information, the electoral process itself is not sufficient for making representatives and voters more positively vulnerable to each other's views.

Undistorted communication is even more important for the accountability

94. Page and Shapiro, *The Rational Public*, 117–70.

95. Ronald Dworkin, "What Is Equality? Part 4: Political Equality," *University of San Francisco Law Review* 22 (1987): 1–30.

96. Susan Stokes, "Pathologies of Deliberation," in *Deliberative Democracy*, ed. Jon Elster (New York: Cambridge University Press, 1998), 123–39.

of official decision making. Journalists are the key to making representatives vulnerable to public rather than organized interests—by reporting policy positions and breaking through official language that obfuscates the nature of debate, among other activities. Journalists are also the key to rendering citizens vulnerable to the reality of official decision making—for example, by reporting on budgetary constraints or conflicts with existing law.

Journalists have two roles vis-à-vis these democratic values: conduit and critic. As a conduit, the news media can maintain the fairness of widespread deliberation by resisting the influence of better-organized and better-funded interests. This resistance can take the form of constraining politically motivated advertising, perhaps by providing equal space for opponents or requiring self-revelation of advertising sources. As a critic, the media can raise questions about the way interests are represented in public dialogue and address prejudices or other ideological barriers to the equal opportunity of deliberative minorities to influence deliberative majorities.

My worry about delusions of civic grandeur differs from the traditionalist concerns about press independence and fairness. The point is not about press power or press bias but about press naiveté: public journalists construct public forums without protecting against strategic manipulation or deliberative inequalities—two obvious threats to democratic deliberation in contemporary politics.

Public journalists could insist that it is wrongheaded to complain about journalists being democratic catalysts when few others seem to be serving that function in contemporary politics. They could argue that by convening community meetings and creating public forums in the pages of their papers, they are filling a deliberative democratic vacuum. In response, I suggest that instead of acting as public forums or sponsors of such forums, papers can apply pressure on institutions and social groups that may actually be able to enforce the substantive requirements of democratic deliberation—namely, state institutions and office holders and civil associations and their members and leadership.[97] As Thomas Patterson writes, "The press is in the news business, not the business of politics . . . its norms and imperatives are not those required for the effective organization of electoral coalitions and debate."[98] When significant public issues are being ignored, however, editorial pressure can be applied on state institutions,

---

97. Schudson is right to suggest that public journalists have overlooked the importance of city and state government in fostering community engagement. Schudson, "What Public Journalism Knows," 129.

98. Patterson, *Out of Order,* 36.

relevant civil associations, community groups to set up nonpartisan committees and release funds for adequate public deliberation. Public journalists can then monitor these forums to see that they are rational, accountable, inclusive, and fair.

Ideally, journalists would play not just a more circumscribed role but also a role different from that favored by public journalists. Public journalists downgrade a unique and important democratic role of the press: the role of critical watchdog. Any deliberative process has gaps where bias can occur. The press is well suited to shed light on gaps of *rationality* by investigating whether significant ideas or policy positions are not being represented in expert or public debate. The press can remedy gaps of *accountability* by drawing attention to attempts at manipulating public opinion. And it can publicize gaps of *inclusion* and *fairness* by inquiring into barriers to participation and unjustifiable inequalities in the opportunity to influence others in the public forum.

The role of critical watchdog embodies, in part, an adversarial attitude that public journalists have wanted to avoid. This attitude, which, according to recent studies, is held by only a minority of journalists today, sees one function of the press as a democratic check on business leaders and government officials.[99] Being an adversarial check on powers that may encroach on public deliberation is not incompatible with public journalism, but, at least at this time, the two roles fit uneasily. Some evidence supports that papers having a culture of public journalism in the newsroom score lower on indicators of adversarial attitudes than more traditional papers.[100] This may be so because the history public journalists tell themselves links adversarial attitudes of the press to public disengagement.

Journalists interested in promoting deliberation would ideally combine the adversarial attitude with the communally engaged standpoint of public journalism. From the adversarial attitude they would draw keen attention to moves of political strategy and attempts to manipulate the flow of public information. Such attention is needed to assess formal declarations of deliberative norms, such as "I believe this policy is in the best interests of the community, not just my supporters," in political contexts where formal declarations are less costly than attempts to actually live up to the norms. From public journalism they would draw the use of nonelite sources for news and engagement in the community.

---

99. David H. Weaver and G. Cleveland Wilhoit, "Daily Newspaper Journalists in the 1990s," *Newspaper Research Journal* 15 (1994): 2–21.

100. John Bare, "A New Strategy," in *Assessing Public Journalism,* ed. Edmund B. Lambeth, Philip E. Meyer, and Esther Thorson (Columbia: University of Missouri Press, 1998), 102–4.

Such engagement is needed to determine what and who is left out of public discussions and official decisions. We can name the combination of these "the role of democratic watchdog."

The more closely public journalists view the very goals they are trying to promote, the more focused their practice will become. If they recognize the broad and complex demands of rationality, accountability, inclusion, and fairness, public journalists can tailor their projects in ways that link up with state agencies, civil associations, community groups, and other professions. Though it is a mistake to think that news outlets can foster a more deliberative public opinion and deliver it back to the public and legislative arenas, as democratic watchdogs they can focus attention on gaps and successful achievements in an expanding deliberative process.

Newspapers are not public forums, but they can help public forums become more rational, accountable, inclusive, and fair. By orienting their experiments more closely toward these democratic values, public journalists can avoid doing too little or too much for public deliberation. As the movement has been marching through the institutions of journalism, it has become more focused. A study of public journalism efforts between 1995 and 2000 shows a move away from sponsoring election projects and grand public forums and toward deepening coverage of specific community issues and closer engagement with specific public projects.[101]

Equally important as aggressive attention to critical democratic values such as inclusion and accountability is the self-awareness and public expression of fallibility seen in some of the best public journalism efforts. In these, editors and journalists reveal the limits of their coverage of news, officials, and citizens. An example of this *public fallibility* comes from the *San Jose Mercury News*. During the heated debate over affirmative action and what was to be called Proposition 209 in California in the mid-1990s, the *Mercury News* sponsored and facilitated deliberative forums on the topic and even wrote a discussion guide for the events. The forums did not produce any clear-cut "public voice, pro and con" on affirmative action, but they revealed multiple perspectives—concerns that overlapped as well as conflicted. The editor responded to this complexity by admitting fallibility: "No one—not Bill Clinton, not Pete Wilson, not Jesse Jackson or Louis Farrakhan, and certainly not the editor of this newspaper—knows precisely how to frame the questions and make the conversation useful.

---

101. Friedland and Nichols, *Measuring Civic Journalism's Progress,* 9.

I ask your help and advice."[102] Editor Rob Elder redesigned the *Mercury News* editorial page to include—with the same font size and same space as "official" editorial and op-ed stories—public opinions drawn from letters, interviews, and the like. This kind of expression of public fallibility goes a long way in reducing the risk that what is only partially the "public" voice is lauded as such.

Another good example of fallibility, though unintentional, is instructive of how the norms of public journalism make it more vulnerable to the public than mainstream journalism—even if public journalism efforts are not perfect from a democratic standpoint. After a presentation by Dennis Hartig, an editor at the *Virginian-Pilot,* on public journalism to members of a local League of Women Voters, the league decided to examine how well the paper was living up to its standards. Members were asked to read articles from the paper on the topic of crime, an issue the league had been studying. Then the members met to discuss how well the theory of public journalism they had heard from the editor matched up with the paper's practice. Though mostly positive, league members felt the *Pilot* missed opportunities to give citizens information that would empower them to do something about crime—in particular, "more community-oriented reporting," "coverage of people working to find solutions."[103] In a published response to this audit, managing editor Campbell endorsed the league's goals and reaffirmed the paper's commitment to covering grassroots efforts. This exemplifies a constructive feedback loop that is possible only when journalists are listening to public voices.

Conclusion: Lessons for a Theory of Democratic Professionalism

As an example of democratic professionalism, public journalism shows both the concrete relevance as well as some of the difficulties of the ideal. The motivations, purposes, and values expressed by the theorists and practitioners of the movement match up with what the model of democratic professionalism presented in Chapter 4 argued: caught between two professional role alternatives—the market-driven model and the social trustee model—that have harmful consequences for the economic viability, social standing, and practitioner sensibilities of journalism, reformers sought an alternative kind of role. Public journalists' critique of mainstream journalism echoes the democratic professionalism claim

---

102. Quoted in Rosen, *What Are Journalists For,* 107.
103. Barbara Ballard, "A Community View of Public Journalism: League of Women Voters Chapter Grades Norfolk Newspaper Project," *National Civic Review* 85, no. 1 (1996): 30.

that professional skills and authority are ultimately quite vulnerable to delegit-imation without strong linkages made to active publics, without an explicit component of lay participation and task sharing. Further, at its best, public journalism shows how the open, socially grounded authority that is produced actually reaffirms the special power of the professional that was under stress, helps regain a sense of integrity on the part of the practicing professional—the sense of contributing to a better public world.

A critical lesson for a theory of democratic professionalism is the importance of drawing limits—seeing the professional domain as not being coextensive with the public domain and admitting fallibility at conceiving public interests. This may be a particularly difficult habit for journalism to break. After all, from the muckraking journalists of the Progressive Era to the investigative journalists of the Watergate era to today's adversary reporters, the motivation is to serve the public by exposing fraud, waste, and corruption. In Bill Moyers's words, "[N]ews is what powerful people want to keep hidden; everything else is publicity."[104] Such a strong social trustee motivation to serve the public has to be nourished as a part of democratic professionalism. Yet as important are expressions of fal-libility, even as journalists share the tasks of newsgathering and storytelling with members of the lay public.

It is not surprising that public journalists may not be living up to their own ideal of promoting a more deliberative American democracy. This is a demand-ing and powerful ideal that no institution in our society has adequately achieved. The concerns about public journalism expressed here do not stem from its fail-ure to live up to an ideal, however, but more precisely from its attempt to single-handedly accomplish what it would take a coordinated effort of a number of professions and institutions to accomplish. This discussion of public journalism shows how important it is to open up further analysis of how different profes-sions, institutions, roles, and practices fit into the complex division of deliber-ative labor needed to achieve more adequate public deliberation.

104. Bill Moyers's farewell to *NOW,* PBS, December 17, 2004.

6

RESTORATIVE JUSTICE

Modern criminal control systems represent one of the many cases of lost opportunities for involving citizens in tasks that are of immediate importance to them.

—NILS CHRISTIE, "Conflicts as Property" (1977)

This chapter focuses on a second case of democratic professionalism in practice: restorative justice. Like public journalists, restorative justice advocates seek a different mode of professionalism that involves citizens as partners rather than consumers and contributes needed "associated intelligence," as Dewey would put it, to the public culture of democracy. Also like public journalists, restorative justice advocates have had to confront practically the complexity, trade-off issues, and ambiguities about the roles of both practitioner and layperson under the democratic professional model.

Beginning with a brief discussion of the history and practice of restorative justice, this chapter reveals the main motivations for democratic professional reforms within the criminal justice domain. Like public journalism, the restorative justice movement affirms the relevance of integrity, professional efficacy, and civic concerns as motivations for reform. This chapter turns to examine the dialogue within the movement about the values of lay participation and task sharing. This dialogue provides a good deal of support for collaboration between professional and layperson within the criminal justice domain, emphasizing the professional efficacy, civic empowerment, and public education benefits of such a collaboration. It also raises a number of interesting questions of interpretation regarding the meaning, purpose, and scope of lay involvement that have relevance for democratic professionals in this and other domains.

To show how restorative justice practitioners have settled some of the internal difficulties of democratic professionalism, this chapter briefly considers a "best case" example, Vermont Reparative Probation—one of the most participatory restorative justice programs in the United States. Vermont Reparative Probation shows how democratic professionalism reforms in criminal justice need not come at the cost of important traditional professional values that protect individual rights.

Restorative justice provides another face of democratic professionalism and both supports and complicates the theory. The sophisticated division of labor between layperson and professional built into Vermont's and other states' programs shows how this sort of collaboration can take place even in highly sensitive areas such as criminal justice. Like public journalism, though, restorative justice raises the issue of how "the public" is to be understood. Different from the problem of whether and how professionals can represent or give voice to the public, restorative justice advocates wonder about the status of lay participants within criminal justice, what they represent, exactly, and how their beliefs and norms are to be treated by professionals. Along with obvious sources of contention between professional and lay values, beliefs, abilities, and norms, this chapter shows that in the background of democratic professional efforts may also be a contest about what the values, beliefs, abilities, and norms of lay and professional really are and whether and how they should change. Lay involvement and task sharing, then, may be continuously contentious not merely because they pose challenges to professional cultures of specialized knowledge and expertise, but in themselves, as democratic professionals and lay citizens struggle to define what it means to be a citizen, a member of a public responsible for life-altering measures such as punishment.

Opening Criminal Justice to New Voices

History and Practice of Restorative Justice

Restorative justice is a practitioner-led reform movement calling for changes in the criminal justice domain that place greater emphasis on communication and reconciliation among victim, offender, and community. In North America, restorative justice is the product of informal justice experiments in the 1970s, such as victim-offender reconciliation and neighborhood justice programs, and reflects the frustration with mainstream criminal justice experienced by victims' rights groups, prison reformers, and other activists.[1]

1. John Braithwaite, *Restorative Justice and Responsive Regulation* (New York: Oxford University

The birth of the restorative justice movement in North America has been traced to the victim-offender mediation projects in the mid-1970s in Kitchener, Ontario, and Elkhart, Indiana, run by members of the Mennonite Central Committee in collaboration with probation officers.[2] The prison reform efforts of the American Friends Service Committee in the 1960s and 1970s also contributed to the movement.[3] These religiously based reformers found kinship with other reform-minded critics, such as victim-advocates who were calling for restitution-type penalties, expanded victim services, and a more active role for victims in criminal justice proceedings. Restorative justice experiments also appealed to many criminal justice professionals as a way out of the pendulum swings of criminal justice policy between rehabilitative and retributive models of crime control. In the "nothing works" era of the 1970s and 1980s, critics asserted that neither rehabilitative treatments nor retributive penalties effectively curbed crime or increased the public's sense of security.[4]

Activists frustrated with the dominant rehabilitative and retributive models of criminal justice began to call for a new "lens" through which persistent problems such as recidivism, victim dissatisfaction, and punitiveness on the part of the public might be seen more clearly.[5] Nils Christie, Howard Zehr, and other early proponents of restorative justice argued that the criminal justice process should shift its focus away from "fixing" or punishing the offender and devolve responsibility for resolving conflicts and redressing harms from the state to affected communities. A less mediated process would empower the victim to address the offender, hold the offender accountable for his actions, and enlist the support of community members for both victim and offender. Rather than "punish" or "rehabilitate"—both offender-centric targets—the new programs would "restore" what was lost to the victim and affected community and, ideally, would "restore" the offender's status as a norm-abiding citizen.

In the last decade, restorative justice found support across the political spectrum.[6] Liberals are attracted by the humanistic, nonpunitive elements of

---

Press, 2002), 8–11; Daniel Van Ness and Karen Heetderks Strong, *Restoring Justice* (Cincinnati, Ohio: Anderson, 1997), 16–23.

2. Howard Zehr, *Changing Lenses: A New Focus for Crime and Justice* (Scottdale, Pa.: Herald Press, 1990), 158–59; see also Van Ness and Strong, *Restoring Justice,* 21.

3. Van Ness and Strong, *Restoring Justice,* 22–23.

4. David Garland, *The Culture of Control: Crime and Social Order in Contemporary Society* (Chicago: University of Chicago Press, 2001), 61, 104.

5. Howard Zehr, *Changing Lenses,* 181.

6. Sharon Levrant, Francis T. Cullen, Betsy Fulton, and John F. Wozniak, "Reconsidering Restorative Justice: The Corruption of Benevolence Revisited?" *Crime and Delinquency* 45 (1999): 3–27.

restorative justice and see in these a potential for broad social change. Conservatives, seeking more justice for victims, more responsibility for offenders, and less cost for communities, recognize the limits of contemporary criminal justice in securing these goals and lean toward restorative justice as a promising alternative. Restorative justice programs, however, are rarely the subjects of political campaigns. Although there are some grassroots efforts, most are advocated by reformers in city and county prosecutors' offices, departments of corrections, legal defender's offices, and probation services departments.[7] These reform-minded professionals seek innovation for various reasons, but a strong motivator is the desire to share responsibility for the costs and other social consequences of criminal justice institutions.[8] As for the nonprofessionals involved, there is some evidence that victims, offenders, and lay facilitators and board members from the community appreciate their expanded roles in the process and the opportunity to have their voices heard.

For example, a four-site study of victim-offender mediation programs for juvenile offenders in the United States found that victims in mediation programs were more likely to be satisfied with the criminal justice system than similar victims who went through traditional proceedings (79 percent compared to 57 percent); victims in mediation programs were less fearful of being revictimized; and offenders in mediation programs were more likely to complete their restitution agreement (81 percent compared to 58 percent) and less likely to reoffend (18 percent compared to 27 percent).[9]

A critical review of research on Australian and New Zealand restorative justice programs found significant benefits for victims: "Drawing from the victim interviews in 1998 and 1999, over 75 percent of victims felt angry toward the offender before the conference, but this dropped to 44 percent after the conference and was 39 percent a year later. Close to 40 percent of victims were frightened of the offender before the conference, but this dropped to 25 percent after the conference and was 18 percent a year later. Therefore, for victims,

7. For more on administrative stakeholders, see Susan M. Olson and Albert W. Dzur, "Reconstructing Professional Roles in Restorative Justice Programs," *Utah Law Review*, 2003, no. 1: 57–89, and "Revisiting Informal Justice: Restorative Justice and Democratic Professionalism," *Law and Society Review* 38 (2004): 139–76.

8. Gordon Bazemore, "Community Justice and a Vision of Collective Efficacy: The Case of Restorative Conferencing," in *Criminal Justice 2000*, vol. 3 (Washington, D.C.: National Institute of Justice, 2000), 239–42.

9. Mark S. Umbreit, *Victim Meets Offender: The Impact of Restorative Justice in Mediation* (Monsey, N.Y.: Criminal Justice Press, 1994).

meeting offenders in the conference setting can have beneficial results." Kathleen Daly found that compared with offenders in mainstream court procedures, those attending restorative conferences have a stronger sense that they were treated fairly and a greater respect for the police and the law. Not much research has yet been done on community perspectives, but there is some evidence that lay participants experience a good deal of satisfaction.[10]

In the United States, the principles of restorative justice are put into practice through four types of programs. The most common is victim-offender mediation, in which victims meet with offenders in a structured dialogue facilitated by a trained mediator who is typically a volunteer rather than a court professional. Next most common is the community board, in which a small group of citizens meet with victims and offenders. Community boards are also called "neighborhood accountability boards," "neighborhood" and "community" panels, and, in Vermont, "reparative boards." Family group conferencing—based on Maori practices of handling disputes and conflicts and a fixture of juvenile justice in Australia and New Zealand—is present but less common in the United States. Family group conferences conduct discussions among victims, offenders, and people close to them such as family and friends, in which all are invited to participate by a trained facilitator. Least common, but indigenous to the United States, is the circle sentencing form of restorative justice that draws on traditional practices of Native Americans. Sentencing circles gather victim, offender, friends, family, and community members together and allow each to speak about the offense, in turn, as a "talking stick" is handed around. Though the number of participants varies—from the usual three participants in victim-offender mediation to the half dozen or larger groups in the other programs—there is a similar commitment to healing and amplifying the voices of affected parties outside the formal procedures of the court.

Restorative justice is fast becoming a common practice in the United States with 393 victim-offender mediation programs, 227 community board programs, 93 family group conferencing programs, and 17 sentencing circle programs across the country. Though widespread with at least one restorative justice program in each state, the distribution is uneven. California, Pennsylvania, Minnesota, Texas, Colorado, Arizona, New York, Ohio, and Alaska have the highest numbers of restorative justice programs, while some other states are experimenting

---

10. Kathleen Daly, "Restorative Justice: The Real Story," *Punishment and Society* 4 (2002): 71. See also Olson and Dzur, "Revisiting Informal Justice," 162–63.

with only a few small-scale programs. Most counties are not currently using restorative justice programs, with only around 14 percent reporting them; Vermont, Alaska, and California lead the way with 86 percent, 70 percent, and 50 percent of their counties served.[11] This kind of distribution is common under American federalism, where state and local governments have autonomy as "laboratories of democracy." So, there is considerable variation in how, where, and to what extent restorative justice programs take root within the criminal justice establishment of states, counties, and municipalities. In Vermont, for example, planners in the Department of Corrections are primarily responsible for restorative justice reforms, while in Salt Lake City the city prosecutor has been the principal actor. Statutory authority for restorative justice exists in twenty-nine states, and in most of the other states restorative justice principles are endorsed in policy statements.[12]

The criminal justice process falls into two stages: the determination of guilt and the penalty phases. The victim-offender mediation programs, community boards, family group conferences, and circle sentencing groups in use across the United States typically take the place of traditional penalty-stage proceedings. Offenders enter restorative justice programs in different ways depending on the way a particular program was established and who established it: by a referral from judges, prosecutors, defense attorneys, or police. Some programs send offenders to restorative proceedings only after guilt has been established by the court; other programs divert cases from traditional prosecution to restorative proceedings with the caveat that the offender successfully complete the requirements there. Because acknowledging responsibility is such a key value for restorative justice, some programs only permit offenders who have pled guilty. Vermont Reparative Probation and Salt Lake City Passages Program are variations on the same theme. In Vermont, low-level offenders are sent to restorative proceedings postconviction. In Salt Lake City's restorative justice program, on the other hand, defendants are offered a "plea in abeyance." They plead guilty to the offense, but

11. These data are drawn from the most recent and most comprehensive study of restorative justice programs nationally: Gordon Bazemore and Mara Schiff, *Juvenile Justice Reform and Restorative Justice: Building Theory and Policy from Practice* (Devon: Willan Publishing, 2005), 101, 105. For another survey, see Leena Kurki, "Restorative and Community Justice in the United States," *Crime and Justice* 27 (2000): 283.

12. See Elizabeth Lightfoot and Mark Umbreit, "An Analysis of State Statutory Provisions for Victim-Offender Mediation," *Criminal Justice Policy Review* 15 (2004): 418–36. See also Sandra O'Brien and Gordon Bazemore, "Introduction to the Symposium: Communities, Organizations, and Restorative Justice Reform," *Public Organization Review* 5 (2005): 280.

the prosecutor then requests that the court dismiss the case once the conditions established for the defendant by the restorative justice panel have been met.[13]

Offenders thought suitable for restorative justice have, in some but not all programs, been restricted to juvenile offenders; few programs in the United States accept repeat adult offenders or violent offenders.[14] Most have tended to focus on young offenders who have committed nonviolent crimes, such as shoplifting. In Salt Lake City, for example, adult offenders were considered candidates, although felony offenders, offenders with a history of violence, or those with a history of failure to appear for court hearings were excluded.[15] Rather than appear before a judge or jury for the penalty, an offender faces a mediator, community panel, and the victim. Together they work out a mutually satisfactory agreement through a process that aims to generate reflection about the harm caused by the offense, the means by which that harm can be compensated or rectified, and the ways such offending can be avoided in the future. An agreement may involve an offender in writing an essay on the offense, apologizing to the victim, some hours of community service, payment of restitution, and the like.

Restorative Justice as Democratic Professionalism

Democratic professionalism is a core part of the background normative theory of restorative justice that has inspired and, in turn, has been inspired by the experiences of reformers over time and across a variety of concrete practices. Advocates wish to replace the one-sided formal procedures of treatment and punishment with a many-sided communicative process outside standard criminal justice institutions, free from the domination of procedures and professionals, where victims can communicate with offenders, offenders can acknowledge wrongdoing and accept responsibility, and community members can help reintegrate offenders. Restorative justice pioneer Nils Christie describes a village mediation session in Tanzania he offers as exemplary:

1. The parties . . . were in *the center* of the room and in the center of everyone's attention. They talked often and were eagerly listened to.

13. Olson and Dzur, "Reconstructing Professional Roles," 68.

14. Gordon Bazemore and Mark Umbreit, "A Comparison of Four Restorative Conferencing Models," *Office of Juvenile Justice and Delinquency Prevention Bulletin* (Washington, D.C.: U.S. Department of Justice, 2001), 8; see also Kurki, "Restorative and Community Justice," 290.

15. See Olson and Dzur, "Reconstructing Professional Roles," 69, and "Revisiting Informal Justice," 155.

2. Close to them were relatives and friends who also took part. But they did not *take over.*

3. There was also participation from the general audience with short questions, information, or jokes.

4. The judges, three local party secretaries, were extremely inactive. They were obviously ignorant with regard to village matters. All the other people in the room were experts. They were experts on norms as well as actions. And they crystallized norms and clarified what had happened through participation in the procedure.[16]

Advocates of restorative justice believe it to offer more justice to victims, offenders, and affected communities because it involves laypeople in resolving their own problems and focuses on the issues that have most meaning for the stakeholders of the offense rather than what is most relevant to criminal justice professionals.

Advocates characterize their process and values as being distinct from and a rejection of retributive and rehabilitative models of criminal justice, but it is more accurate to see them as being a hybrid and modification of those theories.[17] Like retributive justice, it seeks to censure the offender for past behavior and to levy sanctions that are proportionate to the offense. With rehabilitative justice, it shares the goal of curbing future offending behavior. The major difference between mainstream and restorative justice is the devolution of traditional procedures and values so they can be taken up by those most affected by a criminal offense.[18]

Like public journalists, restorative justice reformers understand that conventional professional practices have effectively excluded lay voices and lay participation. The distance between public and profession has come under increasing scrutiny in the last few decades of mutual frustration. In both cases, civic involvement is seen not as an ideal or a moral bonus so much as a necessary component in rebuilding social trust in a professional domain. In both cases, lay participation and task sharing are ways of regaining social trustee–like authority under cultural conditions that could not possibly embrace social trustees. Not merely reflective

16. Nils Christie, "Conflicts as Property," *The British Journal of Criminology* 17 (1977): 2.

17. Albert W. Dzur and Alan Wertheimer, "Forgiveness and Public Deliberation: The Practice of Restorative Justice," *Criminal Justice Ethics* 21 (2002): 3–20.

18. Kathleen Daly, "Revisiting the Relationship Between Retributive and Restorative Justice," in *Restorative Justice: Philosophy to Practice,* ed. Heather Strang and John Braithwaite (Burlington, Vt.: Ashgate Publishing, 2000), 33–54.

of the wishes of the public for a different kind of news and a different kind of justice, these reform movements seek to catalyze new ways of thinking about news and justice.

Consider one of the most participatory restorative justice programs in the United States, Vermont's Reparative Probation program, which is used throughout this chapter as a "best case" for examining the democratic professionalism of restorative justice in practice. Begun in 1995 and continuing to grow statewide, Vermont Reparative Probation empowers citizen review boards made up of five or six citizens to meet with offenders and impose sanctions on them such as community service, victim reparations, and formal or informal apologies. Reparative probation is a large-scale reconstruction of Vermont's criminal justice system led principally by the Vermont Department of Corrections with the support of the courts, state's attorneys, and defense attorneys. A major motivation for the reconstruction, on the part of the Department of Corrections, was to find a way out of an incoherent politics of criminal justice policy.[19] Public fear of crime and dissatisfaction with early release of offenders led to "get tough" legislation that increased incarceration and imposed more rigorous parole recommendations. At the same time, the limited resources for prison expansion created overcrowding and pressures for early release of offenders. Although crime rates, arrests, and convictions had dropped, the incarceration rate—the number of convictions sentenced to prison—was up and parole rates were down. Reparative probation that offered intermediate sentencing options between incarceration and probation was a way out of this vicious cycle.[20] Public opinion research sponsored by the Department of Corrections supported the idea that community members could become more involved in sentencing nonviolent offenders.[21] This idea appealed to Vermonters surveyed because they believed citizens could handle nonviolent offenders better than the criminal justice system.

The reasoning behind the Vermont program as expressed by its founders closely reflects the motivations stressed by the model of democratic professionalism presented in Chapter 4. Reform-minded professionals within the Department

19. John G. Perry and John F. Gorczyk, "Restructuring Corrections: Using Market Research in Vermont," *Corrections Management Quarterly* 1 (1997): 26–35.

20. Michael Dooley, "Restorative Justice in Vermont: A Work in Progress," in *Community Justice: Striving for Safe, Secure, and Just Communities* (Washington, D.C.: National Institute of Corrections, 1995), 31–36.

21. Doble Research Associates and Judith Greene, *Attitudes Towards Crime and Punishment in Vermont: Public Opinion About an Experiment with Restorative Justice* (Englewood Cliffs, N.J.: John Doble Research Associates, 2000).

of Corrections came to realize that the conventional professional practices were not the most effective response to at least some sorts of criminal offenses.[22] In addition, they came to see that involving lay citizens in dealing with such offenses could "free up scarce court and correctional resources to meet the more urgent priorities of determining justice and providing sanctions and services in cases involving more serious crimes."[23] Further, such civic involvement in a professional domain could give power and responsibility back to citizens. In the words of John Perry, director of planning for the Vermont Department of Corrections, "There's a hunger for local control over justice. We've done a pretty good job of taking justice away from the local communities. This process allows it to go back to the level that it probably ought to be at."[24]

Like public journalists, restorative justice professionals are *professionals,* they need to retain a certain degree of separate authority and autonomy grounded in both the competence and skill values of the social trustee model. As *democratic* professionals, they share the radical critics' concerns about the effects of their expertise on the lay public's ability to make self-confident choices both inside and outside their professional domains. Though they retain the authority and at least somewhat privileged voice of people with experience and specialized training, they recognize that they may know only part of what is important in reaching a decision or providing the best public service possible. Above all, they seek to open up their domains to other voices and other experiences by mobilizing, actively recruiting, and including lay participants in both decision-making and agenda-setting capacities.

Reasons for Lay Participation and Task Sharing in the Criminal Justice Domain

Of the three cases of democratic professionalism in practice considered in these chapters, restorative justice reformers have done the most theorizing about the role of the community in a professional domain. Like public journalists, restorative justice reformers have had to directly confront pressing issues involving "the public" or "the community." What is the value of such involvement, exactly, for

---

22. Perry and Gorczyk, "Restructuring Corrections," 32.
23. Dooley, "Restorative Justice in Vermont," 33.
24. Emily Stone, "Winooski's Justice Board Completes First Year," *Burlington Free Press,* May 28, 2001, C3.

the particular professional responsibilities with which they are charged? On what sorts of issues should the professional defer, and on what should the lay citizen defer? Like journalists, who see themselves as trustees of objective information about public events, criminal justice professionals are keenly aware of the values over which they stand watch: fairness, humane treatment, public safety, and the constitutional protections of both innocent and guilty alike. Because of these important responsibilities, restorative justice advocates have done a good deal of thinking about the value of lay participation and task sharing. This thinking is marked by some significant interpretive differences that raise important issues for the model of democratic professionalism.

Crime, Punishment, and the Relation Between Communities and Their Criminal Justice Systems

Crime, for advocates of restorative justice, means more than violation of state laws and more even than harm to victims. To paraphrase Nils Christie, crime is a dysfunctional way of saying something, and punishment, for restorative justice theorists, is an equally dysfunctional way of answering.[25] Crime *and* punishment have spillover effects on communities: fear and insecurity even among nonvictims, loss of wage-earning family members, weakened social ties, among others.[26] Nevertheless, the idea that the public has a stake in an offense—that apart from direct victims a larger social network might also be a harmed party—is incorporated in mainstream criminal justice practice only in abstract, highly formalized ways.[27] The prosecutor and judge may proclaim the voice of the public, but apart from participation as silent jurors and as witnesses on request, community members do not, themselves, speak out in criminal justice proceedings to address the harm an offense such as shoplifting or personal assault has caused to a larger social network. In response to this neglect, restorative justice proponents call for more public participation in the criminal justice process so that the harm to community is more clearly brought to the attention of the offender.

Yet harm to community is a notoriously vague idea, as critics of restorative justice have frequently pointed out.[28] In addition, the simple fact that a criminal

25. Nils Christie, *Limits to Pain* (Oslo: Universitetsforlaget, 1981), 11.
26. Brenda M. Baker, "Improving Our Practice of Sentencing," *Utilitas* 9 (1997): 106.
27. Zehr, *Changing Lenses*, 186.
28. Andrew von Hirsch, "Penal Theories," in *The Handbook of Crime and Punishment*, ed. Michael Tonry (New York: Oxford University Press, 1998), 675.

offense spills over to indirectly affect a larger group does not explain why that larger group must represent itself in the criminal justice system. Just as modernity has brought division of labor to many social tasks, it may be a reasonable trade-off for efficiency that a formal representative such as prosecutor or judge addresses communal harms. Because in many jurisdictions both prosecutor and judge are held accountable to the public through elections, the public does have an opportunity for making sure the indirect effects of crime are acknowledged in court. The restorative justice critique of the status quo, therefore, is best seen not merely as an argument for more attention to community harm, but as a call to change the relationship between communities and their criminal justice systems. More particularly, restorative justice calls for a shift in the "essential role of the citizen from service recipient to decision maker with a stake in what services are provided and how they are delivered," a focus on how the community can be an active participant and resource rather than a "client" of professional services.[29] Rather than the general claim that "communal harm" needs to be addressed, the strongest reasons for public participation link community participation to a better functioning criminal justice system or some other specific benefit to the community.

Restorative justice advocates offer three more precise reasons for participation, most frequently expressed in the context of criticism of mainstream criminal justice practices. Pointing to professionalism, proceduralism, and the social distance between the agents and institutions of the criminal justice system and the communities they serve, advocates argue that the lack of public participation causes criminal justice procedures to be ineffective at deterring crime, "restoring" victims, and reintegrating offenders; to undermine community authority and self-governance; and to exacerbate public fears and misinformation. Put positively in the spirit of reconstructing criminal justice practice, they stress the following reasons for participation:

Efficacy: Laypeople are better than criminal justice professionals at certain key tasks, such as reprobation and reintegration of offenders and communicating sympathy for victims.

Empowerment: The more the public participates, the more it takes back the authority for social control ceded to the state.

29. Gordon Bazemore, "The 'Community' in Community Justice: Issues, Themes, and Questions for the New Neighborhood Sanctioning Models," in *Community Justice: An Emerging Field,* ed. David Karp (Lanham, Md.: Rowman and Littlefield, 1998), 334.

Education: By participating, people learn more about offenders, victims, the criminal justice system, and their own social norms, and they may come to have more rational demands on the criminal justice system.

Most restorative justice advocates hold all of these to be reasons for more community involvement in criminal justice practice but differ, as we will discover, on how these reasons are to be interpreted. This interpretive wriggle room allows restorative justice to be a platform shared by both political liberals, who agree with the progressive interpretations of these reasons, and conservatives, who side with the more traditionalist interpretations.

Efficacy: The Strengths of Informal Social Control

The efficacy argument is based on the strengths of informal as opposed to formal social control. For restorative justice advocates, the informal monitoring of criminal activity has deterrence effects unmatched by the formal efforts of the police. Community members have a better sense of who is doing what, when, and where in their neighborhoods. In addition, citizens can be more intrusive into their own lives than state officials. They are a "more powerful agent of social control, if for no other reason than the fact that parents, teachers, or neighbors provide a level of surveillance that can never be matched by the police in a free, democratic society."[30] "Uncle Harrys" who can take car keys away from an alcohol-abusing friend or relative for a week or a month or a year have at their disposal "a more plural range of incapacitative keys they can turn than a prison guard who can turn just one key."[31] Social intimates also have many other informal sanctions besides incapacitative ones, such as social ostracism.

In addition to deterrence effects, public participation produces positive effects on offenders and victims. Though restorative justice advocates do not want to focus narrowly on offenders—something they see as a flaw of mainstream criminal justice practice—they do have high hopes for transforming offender attitudes through face-to-face dialogue with victims and community members. In restorative justice programs, community members are thought to represent social mores violated by offenders. They "speak the same language" as the offender and are

30. Todd Clear and David Karp, *The Community Justice Ideal* (Boulder, Colo.: Westview Press, 1999), 18.
31. John Braithwaite, "Restorative Justice: Assessing Optimistic and Pessimistic Accounts," *Crime and Justice* 25 (1999): 67.

therefore thought to communicate disapproval better than criminal justice professionals, who might be seen as "part of the system." In my experience as an adviser to and observer of a restorative justice program in Salt Lake City, this idea of a shared language between offender and community representative was a very common assumption among community volunteers and the professionals involved. As John Braithwaite puts this point, "It is not the shame of police or judges or newspapers that is most able to get through to us; it is shame in the eyes of those we respect and trust."[32] Such reprobative effects of public participation are seen as good for victims as well since in shaming an offender, the community is standing with the victim, reaffirming the wrong done by the offender and reaffirming the moral order of the community. Merely dyadic communication between victim and offender is less powerful for affirming that the victim did not deserve to be harmed and treated as less than equal. Public support of the victim's perspective, then, shores up the victim's fractured sense of social order.

Public reprobation puts pressure on offenders to recognize the harm of their actions, acknowledge responsibility, and distance themselves in a productive way from their actions. As important, reprobation is to be accompanied by reintegration—something members of the public are again seen as better able to perform than professionals.[33] Successful resolution for offenders means joining the victims in criticizing criminal activity. Gestures of reprobation are followed by "gestures of reacceptance into the community of law-abiding citizens. These gestures of reacceptance will vary from a simple smile expressing forgiveness and love to quite formal ceremonies to decertify the offender as deviant."[34] This is a tricky business, since for public reprobation and reintegration to be effective, offenders must feel they have a stake in the community and belong to the social order.[35] So community members must keep in mind, even when they are reprobative, that the offender is to be treated as a member of community who just temporarily violated its norms. Though this mode of communication is quite clearly complex, restorative justice advocates see laypeople as better able to accomplish it than professionalized members of the criminal justice system.

32. Braithwaite, "Restorative Justice," 40.

33. Braithwaite, "Restorative Justice," 40.

34. John Braithwaite, *Crime, Shame, and Reintegration* (Cambridge: Cambridge University Press, 1989), 55.

35. Clear and Karp, *The Community Justice Ideal*, 118–19.

Empowerment: Community-Building Through Public Participation

A second virtue of public participation in criminal justice practice is its potential to strengthen communities. By being included in a restorative justice program, "[t]he community is given a forum through which it can exercise its responsibility for its members rather than suffer crime passively and depend entirely upon the coercive power of the state for protection and order."[36] When the public is more involved in the criminal justice system, people meet one another, neighbors are no longer strangers, and informal social control is increased. Seen this way, empowerment is an indirect good produced by participation, just as disempowerment is an indirect evil produced by criminal justice professionalism. Todd Clear and David Karp write:

> The criminal justice system is built on the professional administration of justice, providing few avenues for citizen participation and usurping community-level opportunities for the exercise of informal social control. Lawyers speak for their clients; the true stakeholders are excluded from the process. Defendants are expected to deny culpability, victims are expected to be tough and not to forgive, community residents are expected to be the "eyes and ears" of the police but not to resolve their own conflicts. A community justice model reverses these expectations, vastly increasing the roles and responsibilities of victims, offenders, and other members of the community in the pursuit of public safety and justice.[37]

Participation ideally strengthens the social ties that empower community members to deter crime and shame and reintegrate offenders. Though this is a circular argument, it is neither vicious nor sociologically implausible. People do learn by doing, and, over time, community members might realize a source of pride in their ability to solve social problems—something that may, in turn, help them solve those problems.

Some restorative justice advocates also see empowerment as good for its own sake—the good of self-government, independent of any indirect effect on deterrence, recidivism, or victim satisfaction. From this perspective, restorative justice

---

36. Francis J. Schweigert, "Moral Education in Victim Offender Conferencing," *Criminal Justice Ethics* 18 (1999): 33.

37. Clear and Karp, *The Community Justice Ideal,* 81.

programs are similar to small experiments in direct and deliberative democracy.[38] Though restorative justice proceedings deal with local issues and are quite narrowly focused on individual criminal acts, they can link to macrolevel social relations and general issues of democratic politics. Participation at the local community level in restorative justice proceedings can help citizens address the pieces of larger social problems that intersect with the criminal act being discussed. Braithwaite writes, "I have known restorative justice conferences where supporters of a boy offender and a girl victim of a sexual assault agreed to work together to confront a culture of exploitative masculinity in an Australian school that unjustly characterized the girl as 'getting what she asked for.'" Participation in criminal justice proceedings, like restorative justice conferences, can also school people in broader democratic competencies. Braithwaite states: "We hope that citizens are learning in [restorative justice] conferences how to deliberate respectfully in the face of the greatest of the provocations of daily life. If they can learn to deliberate wisely and respectfully in the most provocative contexts, then they are citizens well educated for democracy."[39] By taking some responsibility for crime control, people become better democratic citizens, which has positive effects in social domains other than criminal justice.

Whether empowerment is a direct or indirect good, as a reason supporting public participation in the criminal justice process it is an important element of restorative justice thinking. One chief criticism of restorative justice by hardheaded realists is that community-based approaches may only work in places with low violent crime rates and high levels of social trust and communal feeling.[40] Critics point out that restorative justice may have a role to play in countries such as New Zealand and Australia and in states like Vermont, where indeed it has flourished, but not in more urban areas where community is fractured and crime rates are high. The possible empowerment effects of public participation give restorative justice advocates a way of responding to this charge. Restorative justice does not presuppose "a geographical community that may not exist," but

---

38. John Braithwaite has called restorative justice programs "micro-institutions of deliberative democracy that allow citizens to discuss the consequences of criminal acts, who is responsible, who should put them right and how" ("Survey Article: Repentance Rituals and Restorative Justice," *The Journal of Political Philosophy* 8 [2000]: 128). Nils Christie believes more participation in bureaucratic systems like criminal justice is necessary for a fully democratic society: "[C]onflicts represent a *potential for activity, for participation*" ("Conflicts as Property," 7; italics in original).

39. Braithwaite, "Restorative Justice," 37, 79.

40. For other questions about restorative justice from a realist perspective, see Dzur and Wertheimer, "Forgiveness and Public Deliberation," 11–18.

"looks for community on many and any bases."[41] If communities are simply where people come together to resolve social problems, then restorative justice procedures can be said to build community and depend on community ties— albeit under development—at the same time.

Education: Affirming and Developing Social Norms Through Participation

Like empowerment effects, the educational effects of participation in restorative justice programs are other frequently understated links in the larger argument, which tends to emphasize efficacy effects as the strongest reasons for implementing restorative justice programs. Yet a core restorative justice critique of mainstream criminal justice practice is that it is overly retributive and punitive. Though not usually stated in a formal, analytic fashion, this critique points to the motivations behind designating an act a crime and attaching a punishment to it. As Joel Feinberg has noted, though not endorsed, "[P]unishment generally expresses more than judgments of disapproval; it is also a symbolic way of getting back at the criminal, of expressing a kind of vindictive resentment."[42] Punishment relieves retributive sentiments that naturally arise from the relations of dominance inherent in most crimes.[43] Even if natural, however, retributive sentiments can produce seriously flawed criminal justice policy. Punitive criminal justice policy, writes Brenda Baker, can be "a kind of mythologizing that supports a belief that 'they' are completely different from 'us.' It precludes the one really effective way to break down such alienating tendencies, namely, personal interaction on a day-to-day basis through which concrete knowledge of others as individuals and relations of trust can develop."[44] For restorative justice thinkers, contemporary methods and justifications of punishment are rooted in bureaucratically resilient professional practices and natural, understandable, but ultimately dysfunctional public sentiments about crime and criminals.[45]

Restorative justice advocates have two different ways of understanding what

41. Braithwaite, "Repentance Rituals and Restorative Justice," 122.

42. Feinberg, "The Expressive Function of Punishment," in *Doing and Deserving: Essays in the Theory of Responsibility* (Princeton: Princeton University Press, 1970), 100.

43. See J. G. Murphy, "Forgiveness, Mercy, and the Retributive Emotions," *Criminal Justice Ethics* 7 (1988): 3–15.

44. Baker, "Improving Our Practice of Sentencing," 103–4. Braithwaite echoes this point when he claims, "Punishment erects barriers between the offender and punisher through transforming the relationship into one of power assertion and injury" (*Crime, Shame, and Reintegration*, 72).

45. Zehr, *Changing Lenses*, 58–59, 195.

the public learns from participation in restorative justice proceedings. On one interpretation, the public learns what it has already known all along—namely, that it has certain constant standards of behavior. "Participation in expressions of abhorrence toward the criminal act of others," writes Braithwaite, "is part of what makes crime an abhorrent choice for us ourselves to make."[46] Through participation, then, communities reaffirm their normative orders. On another interpretation, the public modifies its standards, changes its normative order to be more rational, more inclusive, or more effective. "This understanding," writes Gordon Bazemore, "moves beyond changing the offender to focusing on interventions and outcome standards for the justice process that give equal emphasis to community change; this focus implies a vision of justice as 'transformative,' as well as ameliorative or restorative."[47]

Though these seem like exclusive interpretations, some restorative justice thinkers hold both at the same time. Clear and Karp write:

> [T]he community is obligated to clarify local normative standards, expressing to the offender in particular what is and is not acceptable behavior. Certainly there is room here both for moral education and for democratic discourse about the legitimacy of a given standard. Most important, however, is the collective process that reminds all parties of the significance of the standards in the face of a concrete manifestation of harm wrought by transgression.[48]

One way to explain how these different views can be held simultaneously is to say that restorative justice advocates see participation as having moral education effects, meaning that the community learns about both the strengths and weaknesses of its own moral resources. As Francis Schweigert puts it, "[A]ll have a stake in learning ways of interacting that will reinforce positive behavior and attitudes and reduce harmful behavior. Ultimately, the educative aim of criminal justice is to achieve more resilient and peaceful communities."[49]

Different views of educative effects are harder to reconcile if emphasis is placed on the public becoming less retributive and more rational about crime, criminals, and conflict resolution—more rational meaning more self-aware and

46. Braithwaite, *Crime, Shame, and Reintegration,* 74.
47. Bazemore, "The 'Community' in Community Justice," 337.
48. Clear and Karp, *The Community Justice Ideal,* 91.
49. Schweigert, "Moral Education in Victim Offender Conferencing," 33.

deliberate about criminal justice policy choices. Strong versions of each inter-pretation are incompatible. If the public needs to learn to be less punitive and more rational, then the educative effects of restorative justice proceedings can-not simply be matters of reaffirming community norms. What Christie writes about the need to stage "a political debate in the court" is difficult to square with traditionalist confidence in the moral order.[50] The "competency development" that Clear and Karp think mainstream community members require to "over-come the temptation to exclude deviants from their midst" would be difficult under conditions designed merely to resurrect, affirm, and apply community standards.[51] So, those restorative justice thinkers worried about "othering" and exclusion would strongly resist the idea that expression of unreconstructed social morality, such as "get tough" legislation, would be good in and of itself as an exercise in norm affirmation.

Traditionalist versus Progressive Interpretations of the Meaning, Purpose, and Scope of Community Participation in the Criminal Justice Domain

Though most striking in the restorative justice understanding of moral educa-tion, interpretive differences mark the understanding of efficacy and empower-ment as well. Under the traditionalist view, the source of community volunteers' efficacy is their membership in a moral order external to a forum of restorative justice. In contrast, under a more progressive interpretation, efficacy flows from the volunteers' social ties and relationships—including their relationships as citizen-strangers with all members of their community—that become imbued with meaning in such forums. As for empowerment of communities through participation in restorative justice, this too can be understood in very different ways. Traditionalists conceive the ends or purposes of empowerment quite nar-rowly—as focusing on crime control and response—while progressives see em-powerment broadly—as contributing to civic responsibility and competence that would be useful in many different domains of democratic politics.

Simply characterizing these interpretive differences as "liberal" and "conserva-tive" is not accurate. Though it is fairly clear that most liberals would favor pro-gressive interpretations as good reasons for supporting restorative justice programs and most conservatives would see more of the former as good reasons, the "liberal"

50. Christie, "Conflicts as Property," 8.
51. Clear and Karp, *The Community Justice Ideal,* 110.

and "conservative" labels distract from some of the nonideological, or more general theoretical, grounds of these interpretive differences.[52] The terms "traditionalist" and "progressive" are thus better suited for labeling these differences.

Traditionalist and progressive are ideal-typic categories; most advocates are neither purely traditionalist nor progressive in their views about community participation. In a number of instances and circumstances this is not contradictory. One can see, for example, community participation as a form of education that both affirms and clarifies social norms if there is a consensus that those norms are coherent and desirable. But if one suspects that the community's dominant way of thinking about crime and crime control is faulty, then one would wish to move beyond affirmation and clarification to seek change. As for crime, racial and sexual offenses in particular raise questions about dominant community views that might need to be challenged to successfully discourage offenders.[53] As for crime control, the "zero-tolerance" and "three-strikes" policies of some states raise questions about whether dominant community views about deterrence are coherent and desirable.

A number of more general theoretical fault lines concerning the meaning of community, the ultimate purpose of community-based justice, and the scope of these efforts separate traditionalists from progressives and help explain their interpretive differences over the meaning and purpose of community participation. Is community a fixed and timeless source of norms and standards, or is it constructed and dynamic, something that changes in response to new demands? Are communities, if they are to be considered communities, relatively homogeneous in their values and cultural practices, or must communities actively and self-consciously forge connections, given significant differences in values or cultural practices among community members? Is restorative justice merely the means for better crime control and response outcomes for victims, offenders, and communities, or would a truly restorative justice be part of a broader social movement for greater participation and greater justice in all domains of collective life?

Many of the characteristic images found in restorative justice literature and program descriptions seem to depend on the more traditionalist ways of

---

52. I follow Levrant et al., "Reconsidering Restorative Justice," in their judgment that political liberals and conservatives embrace restorative justice for different fundamental reasons. I expand on Levrant et al. in this chapter by noticing additional reasons and interpretive possibilities.

53. When Barbara Hudson asks restorative justice programs to "formulate strategies" to "change social attitudes from tolerance to disapproval" of racial and sexual violence, she is asking them to be more progressive, in my view. Hudson, "Restorative Justice: The Challenge of Sexual and Racial Violence," *Journal of Law and Society* 25 (1998): 247.

understanding restorative justice. Adorning a Vermont Reparative Probation program brochure, for example, is a tableau of an offender—clearly so because of his reversed baseball cap and visible tattoo—helping mend a fence while a farmer, presumably the property owner, helps. Here is a narrow purpose: crime response in the form of fixing what was broken (or community service for some other, less tangibly reciprocated offense) and a presumption of shared values and shared community conveyed through the image of collaborative work. Contrast that traditionalist picture with Christie's progressive verbal image of restorative justice as "a continuous discussion of what represents the law of the land."[54] These are not mutually exclusive images, of course, but they signal very different emphases and ideals.

The restorative justice reform movement, like other democratic professional efforts, may not have to take a particular stand on all the issues separating progressives and traditionalists. What is as striking as the interpretive differences, after all, is the agreement that lay participation is needed for reasons of efficacy, empowerment, and education. Yet we have lingered on this theoretical debate because it reveals that issues related to the meaning, purpose, and scope of lay involvement are likely to be continuously contentious for many democratic professionals in this and other domains.

Nevertheless, because democratic professionalism puts a premium on public awareness, rationality, and accountability regarding issues of power, authority, and public consequences of a given professional domain, it aligns more closely with progressive than traditionalist interpretations of lay involvement. Though professionals must foster environments of respect, they should also press and challenge laypeople to give reasons for their views, even those deeply held and hard to articulate. The practice-guiding interpretations of meaning, purpose, and scope of lay involvement and task sharing within any democratic professional effort ought to be adequate to the issues of power, authority, and public consequences of the professional domain considered.

Lay Participation and Civic Task Sharing in Practice: Vermont Reparative Probation

Begun in 1995, the Vermont reparative probation program currently extends throughout the state with sixty-two active community reparative boards. It is a

54. Christie, "Conflicts as Property," 8.

"best case" example for the purposes of examining democratic professionalism in practice because it is one of the most participatory restorative justice programs in the United States, in terms of the tasks professionals have been willing to share with lay citizens, numbers of citizens involved in the program, and the statewide distribution of reparative boards.

Following the organizational restructuring of the Department of Corrections, Vermont courts can follow two tracks and use four levels of sanctions in sentencing. The "risk management" track is for violent offenders and other felony offenders thought to be likely recidivists, and the "reparative programs" track is for nonviolent offenders. Common reparative offenses include some relatively serious crimes, such as burglary unoccupied, attempted grand larceny, driving to endanger, and DUI (first and repeated offense). Legal sanctions include, in order of increasing severity, probation, supervised community sentences, preapproved furlough, and incarceration. Reparative probation is part of the reparative programs track, and community boards typically use sanctions such as community service, victim reparation, and formal and informal apology.

After establishing guilt, judges sentence offenders directly to the reparative probation program with the requirement of completing the program. The offender has the right to refuse reparative probation, in which case the judge determines and imposes the conditions of the sentence. If the offender accepts reparative probation, then after sentencing, the court and reparative services unit—previously called a probation agency—conducts an orientation and intake session with the offender to explain the reparative probation program. This unit also gathers information about the crime, the offender's history, and the extent of damages or injuries caused and schedules a first meeting before a community board. A reparative team of correctional staff and volunteers prepares an information packet for the community board that includes the probation order, offense information (affidavit), criminal record check, and any victim information available. This team is also responsible for processing paperwork, identifying and contacting victims, monitoring offender compliance with community board decisions, and recruiting volunteers to serve on community boards. The sixty-two boards currently operating throughout the state include more than three hundred fifty citizen board members and handle around fourteen hundred cases a year.[55]

Reparative board meetings are technically public meetings and take place in informal rooms in public libraries, community centers, town halls, or police

---

55. Vermont Department of Corrections, "Facts and Figures" for 2004, http://www.doc.state.vt.us/.

stations. Though open to the public, attendance of parties other than those related to victim or offender is not too common. Typically, the board is composed of five or six citizens and assisted by a staff coordinator—a Department of Corrections staff member or volunteer who is responsible for taking the minutes of the meeting and for distributing information packets on offenders to board members. Boards have chairs who take some responsibility for ordering the schedule, but the direction and character of board–offender dialogue is something determined by all board members. Offenders are called up, one by one, to answer board-members' questions and determine the requirements for successful completion of the program or to check in with the board. If victims or other affected parties are in attendance—something that happens only in a minority of cases—they are invited to sit in with the board and interact with the offender. An average reparative board session with a single offender lasts between a half hour to an hour. Meetings are usually scheduled at the end of the workday.

Offender contact with reparative boards is typically concentrated in two to three meetings. In the first meeting, the offender is called up to the table where the board members have convened and is greeted by the members, who take care to introduce themselves. After the greeting, board members will ask questions about the offense to review what happened and more generally engage the offender in dialogue about the offense.[56] Though they have a good deal of authority in terms of both how to conduct the meeting and their discretion over the requirements asked of offenders, boards have five goals written in training materials as very broad guidelines:

1. Victims describe the impact of the offender's behavior.
2. Offenders make amends to victims and affected parties.
3. Offenders make amends to the community.
4. Offenders demonstrate healthy behaviors and learn ways to avoid reoffending.
5. The community offers reintegration.

56. For more on the theory and practice of offender-board dialogue in Vermont reparative boards, see David Karp, "Harm and Repair: Observing Restorative Justice in Vermont," *Justice Quarterly* 18 (2001): 727–57, and "The Offender/Community Encounter: Stakeholder Involvement in the Vermont Reparative Boards," in *What Is Community Justice? Case Studies of Restorative Justice and Community Supervision,* ed. Todd Clear and David Karp (Santa Monica: Sage, 2002), 61–86; Bazemore and Umbreit, "A Comparison of Four Restorative Justice Conferencing Models," 3–4; and Dzur and Wertheimer, "Forgiveness and Public Deliberation," 8–11.

If no victims are present or if no victim is identified for the offense, then the board moves on to the other goals. Sometimes, even if no victim is present at the board meeting, an offender is asked to perform restitution or write a letter of apology. Demonstrating healthy behavior and learning to avoid reoffending may be fulfilled by classes tailored to the offense. For example, a DUI offender might be asked by the board to attend a one-hour "Encare" session involving emergency room nurses who relate their experiences treating victims of drunk-driving accidents. Offenders may also be asked by the board to reflect more generally, for example, by writing an essay on the importance of law and the social consequences of offenses like the one they committed.

At the first meeting, the board deliberates, sometimes in private but frequently with the offender present, on the tasks it will require of the offender. They then allow the offender ninety days to complete the tasks, sometimes asking the offender to return after a month or two as a check on progress. At the end of the ninety-day period, offenders who have successfully completed their tasks are congratulated at a closure meeting. The board can return offenders to court for resentencing if they fail to complete their tasks.

Facing the Challenges in Professional Role Modification

Balancing Lay Participation in Criminal Justice with Impartiality, Proportionality, and Safeguards for Individual Rights

A number of critics of restorative justice have worried that devolving sentencing authority in programs like the one in Vermont will produce an uneven and unfair system of punishment.[57] Depending on whether the victim is punitive or forgiving and on the general norms of the particular restorative justice program, an offender in one case can receive a very different set of burdens than another even if the offense is the same. Critics worry that informal procedures such as those used by community reparative boards offer few protections against biased, partial sentencing decisions and may have great difficulty achieving standards of proportionality that fit the burden to the offense. Andrew Ashworth, for example, argues that devolution of responsibility to restorative justice forums

---

57. Andrew von Hirsch and A. J. Ashworth, "Not Not Just Deserts: A Response to Braithwaite and Pettit," *Oxford Journal of Legal Studies* 12 (1992): 83–98; see also von Hirsch, "Penal Theories," 659–82.

is a mistake since "it should remain the responsibility of the state towards its citizens to ensure that justice is administered by independent and impartial tribunals, and that there are proportionality limits which should not only constrain the measures agreed at restorative justice conferences etc. but also ensure some similarity in the treatment of equally situated offenders."[58]

Some restorative justice advocates have responded that mainstream criminal justice procedures are far from impartial and proportional and therefore cannot properly be used to judge informal proceedings like community reparative boards. They have pointed out that consent to a sentencing agreement is a critical feature of such restorative justice programs. And they have challenged impartiality and proportionality as "constructs" of retributive justice that place undue emphasis on outcomes rather than the process of justice.[59] Such responses are misguided. Democratic professionalism may involve trade-offs, but values as important as impartiality and proportionality ought not be traded off too early and needlessly. In the first case, though failures of impartiality and proportionality do occur in mainstream criminal justice, they are still problems to be treated as breaches of justice when brought to light. Second, "consent" is no magic bullet for legitimating any and all procedures and outcomes. An appeal to the normative value of consent must always be accompanied by an adequate description of the circumstances of consent. Under the coercive context of criminal justice, what is consented to must be examined very carefully. Third, impartiality and proportionality have a distinguished pedigree in most moral theory, not just retributive theories of criminal justice.

A better tactic for advocates of lay participation and task sharing in criminal justice is to accept rather than deconstruct the standards of impartiality and proportionality and show how more deliberative, less mechanical, and more communicative procedures such as community reparative forums can play more fairly than mainstream procedures. Restorative justice programs must be vigilant about consent and ensure that offenders know they can default back to traditional sentencing arrangements at any point in the process.

In practice, one way restorative justice professionals have managed the tensions between traditional values and lay participation is to avoid task sharing that could violate traditional values. This sort of division of labor is evidenced

---

58. Andrew Ashworth, "Responsibilities, Rights, and Restorative Justice," *British Journal of Criminology* 42 (2002): 591.

59. Allison Morris and Warren Young, "Reforming Criminal Justice: The Potential of Restorative Justice," in *Restorative Justice,* ed. Strang and Braithwaite, 21–22.

in two ways in restorative justice programs: tasks are shared according to the seriousness of the offense and the stage in the criminal process. Some restorative justice thinkers, but not all, acknowledge that lay involvement may be more appropriate for less serious offenses because those offenders are more likely to still have some ties to the community and thus more potential for rehabilitation and reintegration.[60] Cases involving more serious offenses are to be handled according to mainstream procedures, with criminal justice professionals playing their traditional roles.

Another common distinction is that restorative justice does not apply to the blame-fixing stage of the criminal justice process.[61] The importance placed on offenders taking responsibility for their actions makes applying it to people who deny they committed the acts at all more difficult. This implies another likely division of labor within restoratively oriented criminal justice systems. Professionals may still be needed to play their roles as much as they do currently when a fact-finding process is needed to determine guilt.

Vermont Reparative Probation exemplifies both types of division of labor and differentiates according to both the seriousness of the offense and the stage of the process. The line between what professionals do and what citizens do is quite sharp in Vermont. In a division of labor according to seriousness of offense, "high-risk," "high-severity" offenders receive formal social control from criminal justice professionals, while members of community panels provide something closer to informal social control for the rest. The Vermont program provides a particularly clear articulation of the justification for this division of labor: the Department of Corrections does what it does best when it deals only with high-risk, high-severity offenders—those people who need substantial rehabilitation or, in the worst case, need incarceration to avoid harming others. The cold machine of the criminal justice system is seen as less effective with first- or second-time offenders who have committed less-severe crimes.

> We realized that the corrections professional perspective that our job
> was Risk Management was serving only part of the market, and was

---

60. See Mark S. Umbreit, "Violent Offenders and Their Victims," in *Mediation and Criminal Justice: Victims, Offenders, and Community*, ed. M. Wright and Burt Galaway (Thousand Oaks, Calif.: Sage, 1989), 99–112; and Braithwaite, *Restorative Justice and Responsive Regulation*, 16, and *Crime, Shame, and Reintegration*, 55, 73.

61. David Karp and Todd Clear, "Community Justice: A Conceptual Framework," in *Criminal Justice 2000*, vol. 2 (Washington, D.C.: National Institute of Justice, 2000), 353–55. But see Braithwaite, *Restorative Justice and Responsive Regulation*, 25.

shortsighted as well. Yes, we were good at risk control and risk reduction, and we would be really successful if only we could get the right kind of offenders. It's just that the courts and the system and the legislature want us to have all of these other kinds of offenders too—offenders who commit nonviolent crimes, and who are not a real threat to do serious crime, but who do need something else, something we are not providing.[62]

Further, in efficiency terms, the motivation is to "free up scarce court and correctional resources to meet the more urgent priorities of determining justice and providing sanctions and services in cases involving more serious crimes."[63]

For those types of offenses deemed appropriate for restorative programs, the second division of labor widely accepted in restorative justice theory and practice is for professionals to dominate the blame-fixing stage but then defer to community members when it comes to determining sanctions. Restorative justice programs thus may have more effect on the criminal justice professionals conventionally involved in sanctioning than those involved in blame fixing.

As a postconviction sentencing program, Vermont Reparative Probation has relatively little impact on courtroom professionals. Prosecutors and defense attorneys play much the same roles as before, except that reparative probation may now be part of a negotiation process. Judges play their traditional role in blame fixing and sanctioning. Reparative probation is a new option, but one that has only a minor impact on the roles attorneys and judges perform. The change is much greater for corrections professionals, who give control to the community boards over determining and monitoring the terms and conditions of probation in a large number of cases. In Vermont, traditional courtroom professionals played an advisory role in the founding of the program but did not have much impact in the daily operations of community boards. In Salt Lake City, in contrast, the city prosecutor and a well-known defense attorney served as facilitators on their community board.

Another way restorative justice professionals can protect traditional core values is by training and monitoring the citizen volunteers involved in the program. Consider the core value of protecting the rights of offenders. The Vermont program relies entirely on indirect supervision through the selection and

62. Perry and Gorczyk, "Restructuring Corrections," 32.
63. Dooley, "Restorative Justice in Vermont," 33.

training of community volunteers and through written guidelines, giving the professionals a behind-the-scenes role. In Vermont, restorative justice professionals carry out the traditional task of making sure offenders are treated fairly through the choice and training of board members and through the production of semiformal guidelines that loosely direct board–offender interactions. In addition to guidelines that structure the topics addressed in the interaction, the Department of Corrections established criteria for the tasks mandated for the offender by the board: fairness, meaning that tasks should be "scheduled and assigned so as to consider the offender's basic responsibility to work and provide for family, and not unduly interfere with these responsibilities"; equity, meaning that tasks should be modulated to accord in severity with the offense committed and that they should be applied consistently to those who have committed the same offense; and relevance, meaning that tasks should be "based on the nature of the act itself" and "be closely associated to and right the specific harm caused."[64]

These guidelines are driven by the idea that the tasks are part of a learning process for the offender. Retributive, punitive, and offender-based perspectives are seen as in tension with the value of restoration, and it is the job of the restorative justice professional to correct or modify these perspectives either in preboard or follow-up training of board members. As Lynne Walther and John Perry write in a third-year review of the Vermont program, "Some Board members have exhibited punitive activity (at worst), and offender-based goals (at best), rather than restorative, inclusive values. We believe this behavior will change with the pressure of peer reviews and inservice training."[65]

Division of labor and behind-the-scenes monitoring of both traditional and restorative values are not without costs. Pushed too far, such efforts diminish the potential for efficacy, empowerment, and education on the part of lay participants, in particular, but also for the larger community more generally.

Managing Complexity: Facing New Roles and Leaving Old Ones

Division of labor is one way restorative justice professionals have both satisfied important traditional institutional norms and managed complex new roles. Still,

64. Vermont Department of Corrections, "Reparative Program Directive 424.04" (Waterbury, Vt.: Department of Corrections, 1997), 9.
65. Lynne Walther and John Perry, "The Vermont Reparative Probation Program," *icca Journal on Community Corrections* 8 (1997): 12.

the commitment to lay participation adds two significant new roles—recruitment and deprofessionalization—requiring continuous vigilance. Recruitment means engaging and coordinating community members, as well as attending to their representativeness. Deprofessionalization means that task sharing really occurs and that real community involvement, not just token participation, is present.

The ease or difficulty of recruiting community members varies. The initial selection of board members in Vermont was a very informal process. Department of Corrections staff asked community leaders to nominate people for the boards. Further recruitment has continued by word of mouth and some newspaper advertising and reporting. The rapid pace with which the number of Vermont's reparative boards has grown shows the commitment of the Department of Corrections but also suggests that recruitment is relatively easy there, perhaps reflecting Vermont's tradition of local participation in town meetings.

Facilitating community involvement also means making sure board members are representative of the larger community in which a given board is housed. Because of the informal recruitment process, especially in the early years, Vermont community boards probably slightly overrepresent people who have had some connection to the criminal justice system, such as retired case managers or previous volunteers. Board membership clearly favors those with the time and income security for community service. As boards have spread across the state, the Department of Corrections has become more interested in the diversity of boards and is currently making new outreach efforts. In a Department of Corrections directive, representativeness is defined as follows: A board "should be as diverse a group as is the community in the areas of economic status, gender, age, ethnic background, religious preference."[66] Ex-offenders, people who have been crime victims, those with a history of community service or who represent key community institutions, and people with a commitment to restorative justice principles are also seen as adding to the diversity of the board.

Once community members are recruited, deprofessionalizing requires a constant vigilance by restorative justice practitioners over their own tendencies to take over tasks that could be done by community members. Michael Dooley, former director of reparative programs in Vermont, notes, "At the outset there was resistance and concern on the part of traditional corrections staff to the notion of working with volunteers and doing correctional business through

66. Vermont Department of Corrections, "Reparative Program Directive," 11.

community boards. This way of doing business is, in fact, very foreign to a staff rooted in a traditional approach to delivering correctional services."[67] Ultimately, Vermont established a program with a clear division of labor, which gives community members considerable autonomy. Monitoring deprofessionalization may also require attention to professionalizing tendencies among board members themselves. Reprofessionalization has been of increasing concern in Vermont, where board members have now organized e-mail networks and annual conferences. Some boards have asked to be paid, not just for the money but also for the status a paid position conveys. In reaction to these developments, both the commissioner of corrections and the department's director of planning expressed in interviews an interest in discouraging "little judges" and in maintaining the informality of boards by "building inefficiency into the system," perhaps by making service on reparative boards paid but also mandatory and time limited.

None of these role changes appear to be overly challenging to reform-minded professionals involved in restorative justice. A tension may be present, however, in some of the rhetoric of the movement. Two common ideas in restorative justice advocacy are the cost-effectiveness of lay participation and the eagerness of the public to take back tasks that have been professionalized. Neither of these appears to be true. As with public journalism efforts to convene and listen to a representative sample of the community, these are not without significant costs in professional time and other resources. Further, both public journalism and restorative justice are top-down efforts. Restorative justice advocates presume to give back something the community wants—namely direct, hands-on control of criminal justice decision making. What I see in practice, however, is a different story. Though there was and is public support in Vermont for volunteer activity in criminal justice, it was not "heard" until members of the Department of Corrections decided to research specific ideas for getting the public involved. This is striking because even in a state with a long history of local self-government and participatory politics, citizen involvement was "seeded" in a top-down fashion by professionals. In no way did reparative probation as a program idea emerge from the bottom up, through social movement or party politics.

A restorative justice "true believer" may say that at the *outset* of restorative justice programs, professionals must take the lead in educating the community and finding political support for community involvement in hitherto professionally

67. Dooley, "Restorative Justice in Vermont," 35.

dominated institutions. Once that stage has passed, though, the community will take back what is deservedly theirs. I see it differently and expect a long-term future for democratic professionals within the criminal justice domain. Community involvement is something that may involve considerable long-term social change to accomplish. At a time when it is hard for even the most devoted local party activist to get 50 percent of a neighborhood to turn out to vote in a presidential election year—even given a stable party system with established political networks at the national, state, and local levels—I question whether "giving back" the criminal justice system is as easy as the rhetoric implies. Such broad social shifts in responsibility are more difficult, politically and socially, than restorative justice advocates may wish to admit.

Community Involvement for Community Change: Limits and Possibilities of Democratic Professional Forums in the Public Sphere

Restorative justice advocacy involves a critique of mainstream retributive and rehabilitative models of criminal justice and of state and professional dominance of criminal justice procedures. A connection is drawn between these critiques: If criminal justice were less state oriented and if the voices of laypeople such as victims, offenders, and community representatives were dominant instead of the voices of professionals and officials, then the system would be more just and more cost efficient. Though exploring the idea of "more just" is well beyond the scope of this chapter, for restorative justice reformers it means something like being accountable for what happens on behalf of public interests within the criminal justice domain.

What is exciting but also extremely fragile in restorative justice reform efforts is the fluid way that reformers seek to build this civic accountability and public cultural criticism even as community participation is fostered and respected. In practice, this means that alongside traditional evaluation indicators such as victim satisfaction and offender recidivism, some kind of measure of public education and civic accountability is needed to judge the successes and failures of restorative justice programs. Thinking of both the normative conception of public deliberation from Chapter 1 and the substantive values of restorative justice, two thresholds that engaged and participatory publics might reach regarding criminal justice seem particularly relevant: a rationality threshold in which citizens' views of punishment, sentencing, and the criminal justice process are tested against one another's views, challenged, and pressed for grounding in principles, reasons, and facts; and a responsibility threshold in which citizens come to recognize that what is done to offenders (and victims) in criminal justice proceedings is a matter of policy and therefore is ultimately their democratic responsibility.

These thresholds are difficult to cross even for the most participatory of programs. Although the amount of lay participation and the authority given over to board members is very high in the Vermont program, the restorative justice dialogue that is encouraged by the community board is narrowly focused on repairing the specific harm caused by the offender. Board members are guided to focus their attention on the impact of an offense on victims, as well as on what the offender and community can do to "make things right" and avoid future offending. Although the reparative board encounter could be used to discuss the rationality or desirability of the social and legal norms that grant the board authority, the harm-repair focus of the forum on the particular offense operates against such a tendency.[68]

Further reducing the impact of board deliberation on rationality and responsibility, most of the cases heard by reparative boards are offenses that would not receive incarceration under traditional court settings. Indeed, this is characteristic of restorative justice programs throughout the United States, with most having an even narrower scope than that of Vermont. "Most restorative justice practices," writes Kurki, "are targeting first-time, misdemeanor juvenile offenders."[69] Although reparative offenses in Vermont can include some relatively serious crimes, it is clear that the reparative net is catching fairly small fish. In one study that videotaped one meeting from nearly all the community reparative boards statewide, the cases heard included sixteen drunk-driving offenses, twelve thefts or frauds, eight underage-drinking offenses, five simple assaults, four furnishing alcohol to minors, four miscellaneous driving offenses, two harassments by telephone, and one controlled-substance possession.[70] If the restorative justice goal of diminishing or gaining accountability for punishment were at the forefront of the program, reparative probation would ideally handle more serious offenses—namely, those traditionally warranting incarceration. But increasing the scope of reparative probation would require policy changes, and policy changes require public support.

---

68. See Karp, "Harm and Repair."
69. Kurki, "Restorative and Community Justice in the United States," 290.
70. Karp, "Harm and Repair," 735.

Conclusion

The Vermont example shows that the democratic professionalism evidenced in restorative justice programs is a long-term process that may result in more widespread participation and dialogue about criminal justice in multiple public spheres, but it has a long way to go. To take root in a way that lives up to the goals of greater civic empowerment, education, and accountability, restorative justice efforts will probably have to take the form of a series of widely discussed policy reforms rather than remaining a matter of criminal justice administration. Here, perhaps, a ratcheting effect is possible. Microdeliberative forums such as community reparative boards, if publicized and politicized, may spark debate in state and local political campaigns and policy-making initiatives, which, in turn, may produce funding for more widespread civic participation and, potentially, the support needed for more robust restorative justice forums. Without public support, forums will not be able to have a meaningful impact on public rationality and responsibility.

Though the link between community boards as forums and broader public debate and decision has not been clearly established in restorative justice programs such as the one in Vermont, these experiments in democratic professionalism provide a new way of thinking about public deliberation. As shown in Chapter 1, deliberative democratic theory has encountered questions about how deliberation can translate into action and about how the "messy" dialogue among part-time political actors in the multiple public spheres of everyday life could influence the starched-shirt officials operating within formal democratic procedures. Community boards bridge these two spheres. Both formal and informal, they allow lay citizens to make decisions that have traditionally been considered official decisions. They are public, deliberative, but do not rest at the stage of deliberation. Their outcomes have concrete effects on people's lives.

The public deliberation of restorative justice is imperfect, of course, from the perspective of the ideal-typic account of deliberative democrats because it is somewhat coercive, allows inequality among participants, and may deviate from norms of rationality and respect. It is somewhat coercive since in some (but not all) restorative justice programs, offenders may suffer greater penalties if they do not participate.[71] In most programs, offenders are in an unequal, subordinate

71. Robert B. Coates, "Victim-Offender Reconciliation Programs in North America: An Assessment," in *Criminal Justice, Restitution, and Reconciliation* (Monsey, N.Y.: Criminal Justice Press, 1990), 128.

position to victims since the victim's voice is usually privileged and affirmed by the other participants. Public deliberation in restorative justice proceedings is likely to be unreasonable and disrespectful at times if victims or their supporters are allowed to express their emotions. Yet these differences in themselves are not troublesome. Restorative justice programs, like other democratic professional efforts, are likely to differ from the ideal-typic public deliberation of democratic theorists in ways that reflect nonideal motivational and practical realities of criminal justice and the other formal, informal, and hybrid domains of middle democracy: citizens come into a forum with passions not just reasons; they bear histories of conflict with others; they often feel that they have been treated unfairly; they hold stereotypes of classes, races, and regions; and they rationalize the pursuit of their own self-interests in collective decisions.[72] What matters is how restorative justice programs manage to minimize coercion, inequality, and the effects of emotional expression and approximate deliberative conditions of rationality and respect.

Even if broader public debate is slow to change as a result of community boards, it is fair to say they exemplify public deliberation in action. Democratic professionals in Vermont have done exactly what Tocqueville and Dewey theorized—insert lay citizens in the operation of government, even if only on a small scale, and share tasks of governing that aim to educate, empower, and further the accountability of citizens and better support the legitimacy of officials performing tasks that should not be shared.

---

72. While restorative justice is largely a body of work created by "critic practitioners"—people who have had a good deal of experience working in the criminal justice system—deliberative democratic theory is almost completely academic in origin. As argued in Chapter 1, more inquiry is needed into how the ideals of public deliberation function in nonideal circumstances—namely, the imperfect real world of politics, where trade-offs between values are often required and where it is not possible to satisfy all the standards of structure and conduct posed by agent- and system-level deliberative norms. For more on this point, see, for example, Frederick Schauer, "Talking as a Decision Procedure," in *Deliberative Politics: Essays on Democracy and Disagreement,* ed. Steven Macedo (New York: Oxford University Press, 1999), 22.

7

BIOETHICS

As late as 1966 physicians had a monopoly over medical ethics; less than a decade later, laypeople,
dominating a national commission, were setting the ethical standards.
Medical decision making had become everyone's business.

—DAVID ROTHMAN, *Strangers at the Bedside* (1991)

The last two decades have seen a rapid growth in the number and status of ethics consultants, or bioethicists, within the medical profession. Typically unlicensed in medicine, ethics consultants are laypeople who help address and resolve moral uncertainties and value conflicts related to patient care, professional relationships, institutional standards, and organizational purposes. In the course of one generation, they have become the moral ombudsmen of the medical profession.

As a case of democratic professionalism, the bioethics movement in medicine is instructive about the possibilities and potential pitfalls of the ideal in practice. On the one hand, it has firmly established the role of laypeople—namely, ethics consultants—into one of the most complex, fast-paced, and specialized professional domains. Bioethicists are walking admissions that the medical profession requires something other than technical proficiency and cost-effectiveness in order to function well. The fact that most American hospitals currently have ethics consultation services has to be seen as a success of the bioethics reform movement. The degree of task sharing between physician and ethics consultant that occurs now in nearly every hospital is evidence that professions with a high degree of specialized expertise and knowledge requirements can successfully integrate lay participation.

On the other hand, institutional and organizational success has been accompanied by an inward turn and reprofessionalization of the movement. Though they are sharing tasks with medical professionals, gaining knowledge and experience within the hospital and clinic, ethics consultants have lost their lay connection with outside currents of community concern and have become specialists, experts, professionals in their own right. The American Society for Bioethics and Humanities, a well-respected professional body, holds yearly conferences; numerous academic centers and training programs promise to provide specialist training in ethics consultation. Even given its lay status within the professional domain of medicine, the bioethics movement may have less contact with the general public than traditional academic disciplines. Its institutional success and patterns of self-definition have short-circuited its broader potential as a democratic professional movement.

This chapter begins by briefly sketching the history of the movement and describing contemporary institutional sites of bioethics practice. As with the other two cases, I will then discuss the characteristics of this lay role within the professional domain and examine both the tensions involved in the role and how bioethicists have sought to resolve them. Because bioethics is a mature democratic professional movement that is struggling with its identity as both a lay movement bringing important social interests and values into the medical profession and an established institutional practice and role, this chapter focuses on some of these challenges. I pay close attention to critical reflections from medical sociologists and anthropologists who challenge mainstream bioethics methods and practice. The tensions in the role and the related criticisms have prompted some bioethicists to reconstruct their institutional practice in ways that reconnect to nonspecialist members of the larger public. Bioethics practices more in keeping with democratic professionalism come to prominence once the role of moral adviser in a major social institution is recognized as something that no single individual or small group can perform.

Bioethics: A Social Movement Making the Long March
Through the Institutions at Double Time

Bioethics focuses on the ethical issues faced by the health sciences, such as the implications for human well-being of innovations in health care and the use of human subjects in medical research. The term "bioethics" signals both affiliation with and departure from the ancient discipline of medical ethics. Traditional medical ethics, often associated with Hippocrates, centers on the internal problems of medical practice such as the proper relations between doctor and patient and the professional obligations of doctors.[1] Traditional medical ethics represents the interests and dilemmas of medical practice and has typically been the purview of physicians.[2] Ethical codes of conduct are good examples of the traditional medical ethics approach; they govern quality of care and no doubt benefit patients, but they also serve professional interests in status attainment and monopoly of expert authority.

Bioethics, like traditional medical ethics, is concerned with quality of care, relations between doctor and patient, and other internal professional issues of interest to health care workers. But it is also concerned with external issues important to patients and the larger society outside the medical profession. If traditional medical ethics is a form of self-critique and self-control, bioethics introduces a degree of public critique and control. Bioethics represents interests in health care outside the practice of medicine. Reflecting this role, many bioethicists have had theological or philosophical training rather than medical training. The methodology and ethical questions of contemporary analytical philosophy have profoundly shaped bioethical discourse in the last quarter century.

The Birth of Bioethics

Most historians place the birth of the distinct practices and questions that make up bioethics in the long decade of the American 1960s, "in an era of affluence and social utopianism, in a culture that was experimenting with an expansive array of newly found rights and unprecedented opportunities for personal freedom."[3] Two broad spheres of interest engaged scholars from outside medicine, politicians, and the general public. The first was the topic of human-subject research. In 1966, Henry Beecher, a Harvard Medical School professor, published a whistle-blowing article in the *New England Journal of Medicine*. Beecher criticized as unethical the research design and practice of a number of medical studies that had appeared in professional journals. In addition, the four-decade-long Tuskegee syphilis experiments, begun in 1932 and brought to public attention by a newspaper exposé in 1972, dramatically reinforced the need for rules derived outside biomedical research circles. In response to Tuskegee, the widespread

---

1. Helga Kuhse and Peter Singer, "What Is Bioethics? A Historical Introduction," in *A Companion to Bioethics,* ed. Kuhse and Singer (Cambridge: Blackwell, 1998), 4.

2. David J. Rothman, *Strangers at the Bedside: A History of How Law and Bioethics Transformed Medical Decision Making* (New York: Basic Books, 1991), 103.

3. Daniel Callahan, "Religion and the Secularization of Bioethics," in "Theology, Religious Traditions, and Bioethics," special supplement, *Hastings Center Report* 20, no. 4 (1990): 2.

controversy surrounding Beecher's findings, and other related events, Congress established the National Commission for the Protection of Human Subjects of Biomedical and Behavior Research to draw up human-subject guidelines.[4] The significance of this commission for the growth of bioethics was that it drew on experts from outside the medical profession and engaged public debate on these issues. As Albert Jonsen writes, "Perhaps more than any other impetus, [the commission's] work brought into being a discipline of 'bioethics,' with a literature filled with concepts such as autonomy of patients, standards for informed and proxy consent, and the equilibration of risks and benefits."[5]

A second sphere of interest that fixed public and interdisciplinary scholarly attention on the medical domain in this period had to do with the difficult social and individual dilemmas posed by new technologies, especially life-prolonging technologies. These technologies brought life-and-death decisions and micro-allocative decisions—those involving the distribution of scarce technologies and treatments within hospitals and clinics—to the public's attention. Many consider 1962 to be the birth year of bioethics because of Shana Alexander's *Life* magazine story, "They Decide Who Lives, Who Dies," which described the operation of a selection committee at Swedish Hospital in Seattle. The "God Committee" had developed criteria for the allocation of hemodialysis technology, a scarce medical resource needed by people suffering from terminal kidney disease and only recently made possible by medical innovation. Another critical year was 1976, when the New Jersey Supreme Court decided *In the Matter of Karen Ann Quinlan,* in which physician and family struggled for authority of medical decision in the case of a persistently unconscious patient. Events such as these revealed to an increasingly interested public the insufficiency of internal professional norms to adequately govern medical practice. Microallocative decisions, such as those made by the "God Committee," and clinical life-support decisions, such as those in *Quinlan,* could no longer be seen as medical decisions or even medical-ethical decisions solely within the purview of physicians. Partly because of the level and value orientation of social engagement in this period and partly because of their dramatic character, these came to be seen as public issues, decisions to which society as a whole had something to contribute.[6]

4. Rothman, *Strangers at the Bedside,* 182–89.

5. Albert Jonsen, "The Birth of Bioethics," special supplement, *Hastings Center Report* 23, no. 6 (1993): 2.

6. In accounting for the growth of bioethics, I follow Renee Fox's explanatory emphasis on both biomedical technological developments and social movement activity that called for reform in a number of social domains in American life. Fox argues that "the florescence of bioethics in the United States

The development of new technologies in the postwar era posed serious challenges to the medical profession. Though new technologies meant a reinforcement of specialized medical authority, as physicians were able to claim promising new skills, they also raised doubts about whether physicians had adequately grasped the ethical significance of their new abilities. Just as "the professions take their shape from a series of socially defined problems of order which their knowledge permits them to control," "new skills present a problem of professional control to be handled . . . by renewed ethical analysis and commitment." By welcoming in bioethicists who were not professionally located in the field of medicine, the medical profession would pay the price of public scrutiny, but the gain would be the maintenance of a public face of "disinterested service" and the "extra-professional status such service commands."[7]

The postwar era saw the conjunction of an increasingly sophisticated science and practice of medicine and a shattering of traditional social trustee medical authority. Technical sophistication, professional specialization and subspecialization, and increasingly corporate hospital management all made medical practice more expert and professional in its own terms, yet these developments also increased the social distance between hospitals, clinics, and doctors on the one side and their patients and society at large on the other. David Rothman calls the result of these postwar developments the production of the "doctor as stranger." Not only did the hospital as a neighborhood institution begin to vanish and become replaced by more commercial entities less tied to ethnic and religious groups, but the picture of the doctors who made house calls and were devoted to the all-purpose care of their patients also became replaced by the image of trained specialists who spent very little time even speaking with patients—who now could not be said to be under the specific care of anyone in particular. By the early 1960s, home visits were less than 1 percent of doctor-patient contacts, and only 20 percent of doctors identified themselves as general practitioners. Rothman writes that the social distance between doctor and patient outside the hospital was reproduced inside as well: "[P]atients had no way of anticipating whether they would require the services of a cardiologist or neurologist, and thus had no way of knowing the physician across the desk in a time of crisis. . . . [T]he odds were that as the stakes in illness mounted and

---

may be as much an expression of metamedical, collective conscience issues with which American society is grappling, as it is a consequence of spectacular developments in medicine and biology" ("Advanced Medical Technology—Social and Ethical Implications," *Annual Review of Sociology* 2 [1976]: 231–68).

7. Andrew Abbott, "Professional Ethics," *American Journal of Sociology* 88 (1983): 878.

decisions became more critical, the patient was more likely to be in a strange setting surrounded by strangers."[8]

If bioethics was born as a social-critical reaction to these developments, it grew up in a regulatory environment. The recognition of patients' authority to control their own treatment and the larger social significance of microallocative and clinical dilemmas gave rise to a new public role for bioethicists and explained why an increasingly rights-conscious and medical technology–skeptical American public accepted bioethics as a critical discourse. But it became clear, in the words of Daniel Callahan, a pioneer in the field, "that the field was not going to be dedicated to whistle-blowing—bioethics has not turned out many Ralph Naders."[9] Rather than being a strong voice of critique, bioethics developed as a form of "regulatory ethics," something that allowed ethicists a more powerful internal role in organized medicine.

As it happened, the price of public scrutiny levied by bioethicists turned out to be rather small change. Medicine did not have to put up with whistle-blowers but with ethicists who proved to be, in Callahan's words, a "friendly force within medicine."[10] Medical sociologists and historians often portray the regulatory bearing of bioethicists as the result of institutional capture and neutralization by organized medicine interested in absorbing a potentially disempowering discourse. Charles Bosk argues, for example, that "bioethics was a contemporaneous alternative to a more forceful challenge to medicine spearheaded by consumer and patient activists. This later challenge was more confrontational in tone, more insistent on structural change, and more focused on the politics of health care than was the bioethics movement. By assimilating bioethics, organized medicine was able to defang this other, broader challenge."[11] Yet there are less dramatic reasons for the regulatory shape bioethics took, reasons that bioethics practitioners themselves are more likely to stress. It is one thing to make a forceful critique of the medical profession when making policy demands on the state; it is another to perform this role in hospitals while working side by side

---

8. Rothman, *Strangers at the Bedside,* 128–29.

9. Daniel Callahan, "Why America Accepted Bioethics," in "The Birth of Bioethics," special supplement, *Hastings Center Report* 23 (1993): 8.

10. Callahan, "Why America Accepted Bioethics," 8.

11. Bosk targets academic philosophy as one reason bioethics, once institutionalized, lost its social critical edge: "the conceptual flexibility of the philosopher's principles served the physician seeking legitimation for a course of action. Action and principles needed only be described in ways that emphasized their fit. The more general the principle, the easier the task" ("Professional Ethicist Available: Logical, Secular, Friendly," *Daedalus* 128 [1999]: 60, 64).

with health care workers desperate to make good clinical decisions with imperfect information about patient needs.[12]

Institutional Settings

The double role of bioethicists—part external watchdog over increasingly complex and morally confusing practices and part internal defense against threats to the legitimacy and status of medicine—has been difficult to manage due to the dramatic growth of bioethics both in scholarly writings on medical topics and in the presence of people trained in applied ethics in hospital settings and on oversight committees. The more responsibilities ethicists have come to shoulder, the more questions emerge about just what it is they are doing. Currently, bioethicists have a range of institutional locations for their work, from university ethics centers to the editorial pages of newspapers, but we can distinguish three main sites where these laypeople contribute to authoritative decisions regarding medical practice.

One site is the expert commission put together for the purpose of advising policy makers. An early and influential commission that heralded the transition from medical ethics to bioethics was the National Commission for the Protection of Human Subjects of Biomedical and Behavioral Research. The result of increased awareness of the moral complications of research using human subjects and, in particular, the controversies surrounding Tuskegee, an immediate cause of the National Commission was the issue of using live fetuses for medical research. Active from 1974 to 1978, the commission was composed of eleven members: three physicians, three lawyers, two biomedical researchers, two ethicists, and one member of the public. According to Senator Edward Kennedy, chair of the Labor and Public Welfare Committee and sponsor of the legislation supporting the commission, its goal was to "focus the most creative minds in the nation on complex moral, ethical and religious problems and [to] help clarify them both for society as a whole and for the individual investigator."[13]

Eager to share the daunting responsibilities of moral expert, the commission called for essays on the general topic of moral principles as well as the more

---

12. See Arthur Caplan, "Can Applied Ethics Be Effective in Health Care and Should It Strive to Be?" *Ethics* 93 (1983): 311–19; and Jonathan D. Moreno, "Ethics Consultation as Moral Engagement," *Bioethics* 5 (1991): 44–56.

13. Albert Jonsen, *The Birth of Bioethics* (New York: Oxford University Press, 1998), 99.

specific topic of research ethics, all but one of which were written by philosophers.[14] After an "ethical-principles" retreat and debate, philosopher Stephen Toulmin drafted a report of the debate's results that became known as the *Belmont Report*. The report, endorsed by the commission and published in the Federal Register, significantly influenced the rise of bioethics. As Jonsen notes, the report's "principles found their way into the general literature of the field, and, in the process, grew from the principles underlying the conduct of research into the basic principles of bioethics."[15] What is significant about the commission and the *Belmont Report* is the pattern set for later commissions, which suggested that the moral issues generated by a new technology or micro- and macroallocation dilemmas could be adequately defined by individuals trained in the academic discussion of ethics. Since the publication of the *Belmont Report,* there have been more than a dozen national commissions and a number of state commissions; most have placed seats at the table for bioethicists.[16]

A second institutional site of bioethical work is the Institutional Review Board (IRB). Federal law requires all institutions accepting research support funds from the government to maintain an IRB. Federal guidelines state that an IRB must have a minimum of seven members, which must include a member of the community, a scientist, a nurse, and a physician. The tasks of IRBs are less contemplative and analytical than those of bioethics commissions. Generally speaking, IRBs check proposed research studies to see if they conform to standards of ethics, human safety, and professional conduct.[17] More particularly, IRBs review—in a forward- rather than backward-looking mode—the adequacy and completeness of consent forms and gauge risks and benefits of proposed research. Given the tasks of IRBs, the responsibilities of ethicists serving on them are narrowly focused on the research protocols of particular research proposals. Still, IRBs provide one avenue into the medical domain for those concerned with ethical issues. More important, service on IRBs has sharpened the applied ethics skills of those academic philosophers who have served and familiarized them with the language of medicine.

IRBs paved the way for a third institutional site of bioethics, the Institutional

14. Jonsen, *The Birth of Bioethics,* 102.

15. Jonsen, *The Birth of Bioethics,* 104.

16. Susan Cartier Poland, "Bioethics Commissions: Town Meetings with a 'Blue, Blue Ribbon,'" *Kennedy Institute of Ethics Journal* 8 (1998): 91–109.

17. Charles L. Bosk and Joel Frader, "Institutional Ethics Committees: Sociological Oxymoron, Empirical Black Box," in *Bioethics and Society: Constructing the Ethical Enterprise,* ed. Raymond G. De Vries and Janardan Subedi (Upper Saddle River, N.J.: Prentice Hall, 1998), 95.

Ethics Committee (IEC). The idea that an internal committee could help patients and physicians navigate through difficult medical decisions emerged informally in hospitals across the United States starting in the 1970s. Unlike IRBS, IECS are not the product of federal mandates and they have a far broader and less well-defined scope of authority. IECS have become part of the contemporary hospital landscape as the result of the medical establishment's internal needs. As Diane E. Hoffmann writes: "The motivation for establishing these committees has been mainly internal: nurses, social workers, and physicians initiated the committees as a better way to deal with cases that involved the withholding or withdrawal of life-sustaining treatment."[18] An early advocate of IECS in the United States was Karen Teel, a physician who wrote an article on the difficult legal and ethical issues surrounding denial of treatment to severely impaired newborns.[19] She argued that IECS could bear some of the burden of morally challenging medical decisions, thus freeing physicians to act and keeping such cases from becoming legal disputes. Teel's argument launched the rapid growth of IECS when the New Jersey Supreme Court endorsed it in its *Quinlan* decision. Like Teel, the court believed IECS had an important role in keeping cases concerning the withdrawal of treatment out of the legal system.

In the 1980s, state and professional organizations followed the New Jersey Supreme Court's vote of confidence in IECS. In 1983, the President's Commission for the Study of Ethical Problems in Medicine and Biomedical and Behavioral Research recommended that health care institutions explore the use of ethics committees for decisions regarding incapacitated patients. In 1990, Maryland mandated IECS while New Jersey mandated that either IECS or prognosis committees be established. Though the federal government has not issued a mandate through statute or regulation, professional organizations—perhaps in a preemptive move to avoid such a federal mandate—have stepped in. In 1992, the Joint Commission on the Accreditation of Healthcare Organizations began to require a "mechanism(s) for the consideration of ethical issues in the care of patients and to provide education to caregivers and patients on ethical issues in health care" as a condition for accreditation.[20] Most hospitals now have ethics committees or ethics consultants in operation.[21]

18. Diane E. Hoffmann, "Evaluating Ethics Committees: A View from the Outside," *Milbank Quarterly* 71 (1993): 677.

19. Karen Teel, "The Physician's Dilemma: A Doctor's View: What the Law Should Be," *Baylor Law Review* 27 (1975): 8–9.

20. Elizabeth Heitman, "Institutional Ethics Committees: Local Perspectives on Ethical Issues in

IECs perform three main tasks for health care organizations: staff education, internal policy advice, and case review. Staff education concerns "the institution's policies and relevant law on such issues as DNR [do not resuscitate] orders, advance directives, withholding and withdrawing treatment, and surrogate decision making" as well as the process for contacting the institution's IEC for consultation. Policy tasks performed by IECs include formulating institutional guidelines to resolve dilemmas in common conflict areas. The policy advice most often needed is the definition of guidelines for withdrawing or withholding resuscitation and life support.[22] The most common and also most controversial task performed by IECs is case review. Case review, or clinical-ethical consultation, is the committee's intervention in a clinical decision at the behest of patients or attending physicians. This task is controversial precisely because it highlights just how difficult the bioethicist's role is to maintain within health care organizations. Some physicians have questioned IECs—and nonphysician ethics consultation in general—because they dispute the qualifications of bioethicists with no formal medical training, while other physicians have all too readily embraced IECs and ethics consultants as an easy way to turf difficult decisions.[23]

The Democratic Professional Character of Bioethics

Like the public journalism and restorative justice movements, the bioethics movement is a response to severe pressures faced by a profession. New technology and developments in the science, practice, and management of medicine led to improvements in both the sheer skill and expertise as well as an increase in the social distance between profession and patient. Also contributing was a cultural environment in which key medical issues related to when life and death begins and how scarce life-saving technology can be distributed became seen as personal and political and certainly not merely professional. Like these other movements, bioethics is a response to the decline of professional authority based on traditional social trustee grounds of expertise. Jonathan Moreno writes:

Medicine," in *Society's Choices,* ed. Ruth Ellen Bulger, Elizabeth Meyer Bobby, and Harvey V. Fineberg (Washington, D.C.: National Academy Press, 1995), 410.

21. Jonathan Moreno, "Ethics Committees and Ethics Consultants," in *A Companion to Bioethics,* ed. Kuhse and Singer, 47.

22. Heitman, "Institutional Ethics Committees," 414.

23. Moreno, "Ethics Committees and Ethics Consultants," 48.

> [B]ioethics functions partly as a social reform movement, especially in so far as it has participated in the revolution in the way most people think of doctor-patient relations. Surely no profession has undergone more change in public attitudes in a shorter time than has medicine, and no profession's values have undergone more relentless scrutiny— in spite of the fact that medicine is also the profession that has historically been the most jealous of its prerogatives. Barely thirty years old, the lifetime of bioethics is also the period in which the official values of "paternalistic" medicine have been shattered.[24]

Increased sensitivity to the treatment of patients and research subjects met increased skepticism about professional authority, and the bioethics movement was formed. From the medical profession's perspective, participation of lay bioethicists within hospitals and clinics is a way of rebuilding frayed relations of trust with concerned patients inside and the community outside.

Moving from the cases of public journalism to restorative justice to bioethics, the role of lay participants has become increasingly formalized. In public journalism, public listening and forum events are episodic. Though the impact of lay participants on what is covered as news and how it is framed may be great, there is no tendency to grant authority over even a specific set of stories to community members in a regular and systematic way. Restorative justice programs, by contrast, give over a degree of authority in a regular and systematic fashion for a specific set of tasks. Especially in a program such as Vermont Reparative Probation, community participation has a fixed, if somewhat limited, role. In the case of bioethics, however, the division of labor between medical professional and layperson grants the ethics consultant a large and increasingly professionalized role, the dimensions and expectations of which are in flux.

Bioethicists are nonprofessionals who have taken charge, so to speak, of monitoring the normative dimensions of the medical practice. In many respects, this is a remarkable development. "As late as 1966," David Rothman writes, "physicians had a monopoly over medical ethics; less than a decade later, laypeople, dominating a national commission, were setting the ethical standards. Medical decision making had become everyone's business."[25] Yet, as a case of democratic professionalism, the success of bioethics is equally instructive about what might be called the democratic costs of task sharing.

24. Moreno, "Ethics Committees and Ethics Consultants," 48.
25. Rothman, *Strangers at the Bedside,* 168.

In what follows, I will examine more closely the difficulties involved in this kind of professional task sharing, which appear in the almost impossible job descriptions that bioethicists have written. They also surface in the criticisms levied against mainstream bioethics theory and practice. Because ethics consultation has become so successfully rooted in the medical domain, I will focus less in this chapter on why and how such lay participation became legitimated and will attend more to the institutional challenges involved in maintaining the lay character of the bioethics movement—something that has been much less successful.

The Expansive Roles of Ethics Consultation

Ethics consulting on committees, or in the clinical setting with hospital staff and patients, appears to be the least public of the roles currently played by bioethicists. Seen more closely, however, ethics consultation reflects conflicts of interest, asymmetries of power, and difficulties of interpretation and representation that are inherently political. The tensions we see in ethics consultation reflect the democratic professional character of the bioethics movement as it has successfully altered medical practices and institutions.

A Liminal Role: Betwixt and Between Doctors and Patients

"Liminality" is a better word than "marginality" to describe both the positive and negative features of a fluid and structurally ambiguous role. Marginality implies powerlessness and lack of status, yet bioethics consultants have considerable informal power and legitimately posses a number of status markers—institutional affiliation, titles, white coats and beepers, among others. Liminality better conveys the fluidity and ambiguity of social roles. Anthropologist Victor Turner theorized liminality as an "interstructural situation" marked by a lack of fixed social rules or obligations that could guide behavior, a certain structural invisibility or anonymity in comparison to those outside the liminal state, and a curious unity of opposite symbols attached to the liminal state: "This coincidence of opposite processes and notions in a single representative characterizes the peculiar unity of the liminal: that which is neither this nor that, and yet is both."[26]

---

26. Victor W. Turner, "Betwixt and Between: The Liminal Period in Rites de Passage," in *Symposium on New Approaches to the Study of Religion: Proceedings of the 1964 Annual Spring Meeting of the American Ethnological Society*, ed. June Helm (Seattle, Wash.: American Ethnological Society, 1964), 7.

Liminality marks a number of dimensions of bioethics consultation: consultants are inside and outside the medical system, their judgments oscillate between carrying formal and informal authority, and their allegiances are pulled from the private realm of patient need to the public realm of social meaning. Role complexities such as these are likely to be faced in any democratic professional relationship forged in complex organizations.

Table 4. The liminality of bioethics consultation

Inside	Outside
Role of colleague: To uphold medical values and help health care team resolve problems	Role of whistle-blower: To guard against neglect of medical and other values by health care team
Formal	*Informal*
Role of ethical authority: To offer authoritative, impartial judgment	Role of mediator: To offer flexible, creative mediation
Private	*Public*
Role of intimate: To recognize the private, individual significance of decision	Role of critic: To recognize the cultural, social significance of decision

The inside/outside, interstructural location of consultants has been central to the growth of bioethics as it achieved institutional attachments. As noted earlier, bioethics has grown in institutional strength as a result of the legitimacy needs of the medical system and profession, yet the movement provides legitimacy because bioethicists are not part of the system and profession. The tensions between the internal and external functions of bioethicists appear in the conflicting demands to be a good colleague—and to avoid being a "moral policeman" in the hospital—and to be a whistle-blower when health care staff members are negligent. As Moreno and others have noted, bioethicists "are expected to have insightful and sometimes even unsettling things to say about the way doctors relate to patients. . . . But if the ethicists were only critics they would not be welcome for long in health care institutions, but would be derided as inhabitants of an 'ivory tower' with nothing helpful to contribute."[27] The tension between these demands is seen by ethics consultants as inherent to their interstructural location—simply part of the job that they are expected to manage.[28]

27. Moreno, "Ethics Consultation as Moral Engagement," 51.
28. See Joel E. Frader, "Political and Interpersonal Aspects of Ethics Consultation," *Theoretical Medicine* 13 (1992): 31–44; and John La Puma and David L. Schiedermayer, "Ethics Consultation: Skills, Roles, and Training," *Annals of Internal Medicine* 114 (1991): 155–60.

Another liminal characteristic of ethics consultation is the formal/informal nature of its authority. There is little doubt that ethics consultants make a difference in the cases they are called to judge. Empirical studies show that ethics consultations do have an impact on physicians in their choice of patient management plans and that physicians often defer to the specific judgments that ethics consultants are called to make—usually on the justification for providing or withholding life-support therapies.[29] However, no formal authority behind ethics consultation exists to legally bind the physician to following the consultant's advice. This informal status is seen as a helpful alternative to formal, judicial decisions, which are "too slow for clinical decisions" and too adversarial—polarizing rather than reconciling the divergent views of hospital staff, physicians, patients, and families. At the same time, however, the lack of formal status raises worries about ease of manipulation through job description. When ethics consultants are used in hospitals to merely confirm medical judgments, support hospital staff psychologically or emotionally, and reduce legal liability, their judgments cannot be seen as impartial or helpful to all parties.[30] The fluidity of ethics consultation allows bioethicists to mediate conflicts between patients, hospital staff, families, and communities, but it also raises the possibility that their authority will somehow be compromised by one of these interests.

A final liminal characteristic has to do with the public/private allegiances of ethical consultation. Bioethics is to be patient centered, to interpret accurately and represent faithfully the meanings and intentions of patients in critical situations. Bioethics is to appreciate the specific medical goals of healing particular patient problems. These patient and medical allegiances focus consultants' attention to a realm of immediate, private urgency. Yet, bioethicists must also recognize that private problems may indicate something of more than personal or medical importance. The public/private tension surfaces in the conflicting demands to resist the "ethicization" of issues that have social or political significance, on the one hand, and to resist the "politicization" of intimate choices, on the other. Bette-Jane Crigger captures the difficulty of public/private allegiances when she recognizes that "meanings and values come painfully to the fore" in the medical domain: "Without wanting to, or being very comfortable doing it, we as a society have found that we must ask what is right to do rather

29. Henry S. Perkins and Bunnie S. Saathoff, "Impact of Medical Ethics Consultations on Physicians: An Exploratory Study," *American Journal of Medicine* 85 (1988): 761–65.
30. Bernard Lo, "Promises and Pitfalls of Ethics Committees," *New England Journal of Medicine* 317 (1987): 46–50.

than what can be done." At the same time, however, Crigger recognizes the "intimate and private" nature of health care decisions, "that it is widely preferred such decisions not take place in the full glare of public scrutiny" in part because "they are decisions about intrusions into individuals' *bodies*."[31] Medical decisions represent social meanings—the very concern for individual health and well-being that puts the consultant into the position of watchdog over the medical profession. Yet they also represent private meanings—the very meanings that the non-physician is thought to be able to represent better than courts or physicians and perhaps even families.

In these ways, the position of ethics consultant is indeed a "coincidence of opposite processes and notions in a single representative"; yet, the role has—as Turner suggested of liminal states—a "peculiar unity: that which is neither this nor that, and yet is both."[32] Recognition of liminality dashes any hope that issues of power, allegiance, and representation can be easily settled—as if the bioethicist was simply faced with the choice of being part of the powerful medical system or being the institutionally embattled advocate of patient or public needs. Liminality is a function of a complicated field of demands that press the ethical consultant to be neither this, that, or both. More striking in this case than in restorative justice or public journalism, liminality is an issue for all laypeople serving in complex, hierarchical domains, sharing some tasks and some authority but not other dimensions of professional roles. The fluidity of the bioethicist role signals that it is not bureaucratized, which, though making organizational life difficult for the layperson, has some benefits from the perspective of democratic professionalism.

An Overloaded Role: Facing a Multiplicity of Expectations

The term "overload" reflects the range of normative expectations and lack of guidance in meeting such expectations.[33] The normative expectations of concern

31. Bette-Jane Crigger, "Negotiating the Moral Order: Paradoxes of Ethics Consultation," *Kennedy Institute of Ethics Journal* 5 (1995): 93.

32. Turner, "Betwixt and Between," 7.

33. At around the time of bioethics' birth, Talcott Parsons recognized the general problem of overload in the complex society of the United States, which was undergoing major changes while adhering to a strong and general value system: "[T]he more complex the society, the greater the difficulty of defining the requisite norms, a difficulty which is greatly compounded by rapid change. . . . The individual is left with a great deal of responsibility, not only for achieving within the institutionalized normative order, but for his own interpretation of its meaning and of his obligations in and to it" ("Youth in the Context of American Society," *Daedalus* 91 [1962]: 275).

are features of the ethics consultant role that flow, in part, from the liminality of ethics consultation but demand separate conceptual treatment. The expectations of pluralistic sensitivity, macro- (social, political, and economic) and microlevel (personal, familial) attentiveness, and technical competence, though closely linked to the interstructural and fluid nature of the ethics consultant role, would persist in some form were that role to be more institutionally fixed. Like liminality, overload reflects the difficulty in setting boundaries for the new role emerging from democratic professionalism in the medical domain. It also, however, reflects a failure to see that the demands placed on the ethics consultant ought to be shared more broadly, made more a part of public responsibility and accountability.

Table 5. Normative overload in bioethics consultation

Pluralistic sensitivity	*Macrolevel attentiveness*
Normative expectation: Cultural, religious, secular differences in values must be translated and mediated	Normative expectation: Social, economic, political features of medical decision must be given place in clinical ethics judgment
Microlevel attentiveness	*Technical competence*
Normative expectation: Personal, familial features of medical decision must be given place in clinical ethics judgment	Normative expectation: Practical familiarity with biomedical and ethical knowledge needed for clinical ethics judgment

A primary normative expectation is sensitivity to the plurality of legitimate moral positions on health care issues. The ethics consultant is expected to translate and mediate disagreements on treatment that stem from cultural, religious, and secular differences in values. This expectation is sometimes neutrally expressed as a need for "sound interpersonal skills" and "conflict resolution skills" in contexts where "professional staff and patients . . . are not always speaking the same language and are clearly looking . . . at these [ethics consultation] interactions with radically different interpretations of their meaning."[34] Pluralistic sensitivity is also more substantively expressed as a need for "reciprocal participatory engagement across different worlds of experience" to discover "the meanings and relationships in distinctive local worlds."[35]

34. Moreno, "Ethics Consultation as Moral Engagement," 55; and John A. McClung, Russell S. Kamer, Margaret DeLuca, and Harlan J. Barber, "Evaluation of a Medical Ethics Consultation Service: Opinions of Patients and Health Care Providers," *American Journal of Medicine* 100 (1996): 460.
35. Arthur Kleinman, "Anthropology of Bioethics," in *Writing at the Margin: Discourse Between Anthropology and Medicine* (Berkeley and Los Angeles: University of California Press, 1995), 54, 67.

Related to the public/private dimension of bioethics practice but not reducible to it, the expectations of macro- and microlevel attentiveness direct the ethics consultant to respect the personal and intimate world of patients yet to not forget the public and systemic aspects of health care decisions. Microlevel expectations are often expressed in the demand to pay attention to the particularity of patients. More than simply respecting patient autonomy, this means recognizing the debilitating pressures of the specific condition experienced by an individual patient and the sometimes idiosyncratic needs of a patient. The microlevel expectation is expressed in the following: "Busy physicians, even those with an interest in ethics, may tend to marginalize patients' personal values and histories, with these data falling to the side, especially when a patient is critically ill. The ethics consultant has the special training and professional charge to help gather the relevant data and restore a central ethical focus to a given case."[36]

Macrolevel expectations, by contrast, involve seeing patients not as the particular people they are but as an instance of larger systemic problems. The infant in the neonatal intensive care unit (NICU) may be more than a suffering person; he may be representative of conditions of poverty and limited access to social services. Renee Fox is famous for her argument that bioethicists have been less than attentive to macrolevel issues:

> [R]elatively little attention has been paid to the fact that a disproportionately high number of extremely premature infants of very low birth weight, with severe congenital abnormalities, cared for in NICUS are babies born to poor, disadvantaged mothers, many of whom are single teenagers and also non white. Bioethics has been disinclined to regard the deprived conditions out of which such infants and mothers come as falling within its purview.[37]

The elderly woman who explains her resistance to surgery by saying that she has lived long enough and that medical care ought to be distributed to the young rather than the old may be articulating firmly held beliefs that have defined her as the particular individual she is; yet, at the same time, she may also be representative of the unjust treatment of the elderly in a youth-oriented

36. John La Puma, "Consultations in Clinical Ethics—Issues and Questions in 27 Cases," *Western Journal of Medicine* 146 (1987): 636.

37. Renee C. Fox, "The Evolution of American Bioethics: A Sociological Perspective," in *Social Science Perspectives on Medical Ethics,* ed. George Weisz (Dordrecht: Kluwer, 1990), 208.

society.[38] These are just two of the many cases in which the ethics consultant is expected to be attentive to microlevel details of personal idiosyncrasy as well as macrolevel issues represented by individual patients' decisions and conditions.

A final expectation is a form of technical competence that combines clinical ability with moral reasoning skills. Though there is some controversy about how much clinical ability ethics consultants should have, many believe that clinical knowledge can help consultants determine a range of options and can help clear away medical issues so that value questions can emerge more perspicuously. This expectation of clinical competence can be rather neutrally put as the need to understand a patient's "history, personal situation, and medical illness sufficiently well to help in managing the illness."[39] But it is evident from examples given by even those who think nonphysicians are capable of consulting that clinical competence is quite a substantive expectation. For example, Joel Frader, who is sympathetic to the idea of nonphysicians offering clinical-ethical consultation, writes as follows:

> [T]wo clinicians may struggle over discontinuing life support provided a critically ill patient. The difficulty might involve uncertainty over the clinical finding of flaccidity. One clinician might claim that residual (pharmacologic) neuromuscular blockade clouds the interpretation of the examination. The experienced ethicist might remind the doctors that a simple clinical tool, a twitch monitor, could provide an answer about the integrity of the neuromuscular pathways in a few moments.[40]

In addition to clinical competence, the ethics consultant must possess the moral reasoning skills that individuate their judgments from those of other clinical consultants—though, again, there is some controversy over just what sort of moral reasoning skills a consultant must have. Recent critiques of bioethics focus on the adequacy of analytic philosophy and applied ethics methods for consultants, but their criticisms—and proposed solutions—reflect the deeper tensions of liminality and overload. The liminality and overload issues faced by bioethicists suggest that their role has taken on too many responsibilities and has sought to reprofessionalize, albeit for laypeople, certain tasks that must be shared more broadly.

38. Crigger, "Negotiating the Moral Order," 100–102.

39. John La Puma and Stephen Toulmin, "Ethics Consultants and Ethics Committees," *Archives of Internal Medicine* 149 (1989): 1110.

40. Frader, "Political and Interpersonal Aspects of Ethics Consultation," 36.

Contested Methods and Practices: Critiques of Bioethics

The liminality of the role and its overload of normative expectations have made bioethicists vulnerable to critique, even as their numbers and status have increased. Immanent critiques, mostly written and endorsed by bioethicists trained in philosophy, call into question the prevailing analytical and applied ethics methodology of bioethics—often summed up in the catchword "principlism." Other, more radical critiques—what I call the skeptical and bioethnographic critiques—have been written and endorsed by social scientists trained in sociology and anthropology. These do more than criticize the dominant method; they point to the tensions in the ethics consultant's liminal role and seek to reconstruct bioethics method and practice to relieve them. I will argue that contemporary critiques of bioethics lead to a kind of democratic soul-searching, a reconceptualization of the consultant's role that is closer to the spirit of democratic professionalism than current mainstream thought and practice.

Immanent Critiques

As bioethicists entered the hospital setting as ethics consultants, they confronted difficult decisions that challenged a certain paradigmatic approach to applying ethics to practical cases. Called "principlism" by its critics, this approach is closely related to the analytical tradition in philosophy that influenced the ethics representatives on the early bioethics commissions. This tradition emphasizes the clarification of principles thought to be shared by all reasonable people for the purpose of deriving practical guides for action.[41] The *Belmont Report* defined three such principles, respect for persons, beneficence, and justice. Later, and even more influentially, Beauchamp and Childress's *Principles of Biomedical Ethics* reconstructed the earlier list to arrive at the principles of autonomy, beneficence, nonmaleficence, and justice.[42]

Principlism has had two broad positive effects on bioethics. The appeal to norms transcending the traditional maxims of medical ethics was an important break with the internal morality of medicine. Principles supplied just such an external critical view needed in the face of increasingly complex, innovative, and bureaucratized medical practice. Henk ten Have puts this point well:

41. See James F. Childress, "A Principle-Based Approach," in *A Companion to Bioethics,* ed. Kuhse and Singer, 61.

42. Jonsen, though a critic in some respects, calls this work "magisterial in the field" of bioethics (*The Birth of Bioethics,* 104). Barry Hoffmaster calls it the "Bible" of bioethics ("The Theory and Practice of Applied Ethics," *Dialogue* 30 [1991]: 219).

[P]rofessionalization and institutionalization of medical ethics received an enormous stimulus because both the adequacy and the relevance of medicine's internal morality were called into question. In response, professional ethicists have placed more and more emphasis on the role of external morality: the principles, norms, and rules operative in society that may bear on medicine and are frequently codified in law.[43]

Second, for scholars interested in ethics and medicine, the *Belmont Report* and *Principles of Biomedical Ethics* represented an imaginary consensus on general rules, a common starting point for interpretation and reconstruction. Bioethics is hard to classify as a traditional academic discipline, even an interdisciplinary discipline, but it is certainly a discourse with common language, method, and style of writing. To speak with one another, to collaborate, to critique productively, bioethicists required such an imaginary consensus.[44]

Though still dominant, principlism has met significant internal challenges in the last decade. Virtue thinkers, feminist theorists of care, and casuists wish to ground an overly abstract and formal mainstream approach in the reality of medical practice. According to the virtue and caring critiques, autonomy serves in the principlist approach as a dominant value that neglects important roles and relationships between doctor and patient, patient and family, family and community. To helpfully intervene in clinical decisions, bioethicists ought to recognize these relationships along with the unique roles and shared sentiments of doctor and patients. For casuists, principles are too broad to resolve ethical problems arising from clinical issues. Ethical problems faced by consultants are not conflicts of values resolvable by appeal to overarching principles. Instead, they "typically arise because the details of the particular situations that confront [physicians] either embody conflicts between two or more coexisting demands, about whose moral 'value' we basically agree; or else arise at the margin of application of ideas . . . about which there would have been no problem, if the case in question had been paradigmatic—central, and free from ambiguity."[45] Appeal to principles fails in case review because doctors already agree on principles such

43. Henk ten Have, "Principlism: A Western European Appraisal," in *A Matter of Principles? Ferment in U.S. Bioethics,* ed. E. R. DuBose, R. P. Hamel, and L. J. O'Connell (Valley Forge, Pa.: Trinity Press, 1994), 104.

44. On this point, see Fox, "The Evolution of American Bioethics"; Jonsen, *Birth of Bioethics*; and Rothman, *Strangers at the Bedside.*

45. Stephen Toulmin, "Casuistry and Clinical Ethics," in *A Matter of Principles*, ed. E. R. DuBose et al., 314.

as autonomy, beneficence, nonmaleficence, and justice yet still are faced with hard practical choices in cases where such principles conflict or are only ambiguously related to the problem at hand. In response, casuists recommend reflecting on the particular concrete knowledge gained in everyday experience in the hospital or clinic in order to develop paradigmatic guiding cases of successful resolution to common ethical dilemmas.

Such immanent critiques reflect the tensions inherent in occupying the liminal place both inside and outside the medical system. Bioethicists are where they are in the clinical setting precisely because they bring in perspectives thought to be relevant to medicine yet sidelined in medical training and practice. So it would be a mistake to bring bioethics back too close to the very norms that prompted the call for something different from medical ethics. Yet whether virtue based, caring oriented, or casuistic, the goal of immanent critique is not to reject the outsider role but to discover a more organic combination of insider representative of medical norms and outsider advocate of social norms that transcend the medical domain. These critiques do not wish to challenge or undermine the liminal role of the bioethicist as institutional mediator between patient and hospital, public and profession. The bioethicist is still to help patient and staff arrive at good decisions in the face of financial and temporal pressures. The change is not in role but in method: bioethics consulting is to be done with greater sensitivity to the duties of doctors, the relationships involved, and paradigmatic cases.

Yet, what immanent critics treat as a problem of method is much more complex. The incremental changes to the role of ethics consultant do little to fix the structural position on one or the other side of the inside/outside, public/private, formal/informal poles. Nor do they relieve any of the normative expectations on the consultant; if anything, they add new foci and competencies to these expectations. The root issues posed by the liminal and overloaded condition of ethics consultants have not been diagnosed adequately by immanent critics.

Skeptical Critiques

Other critics are more far-reaching and question the role of bioethics expert itself, not merely the method of principlism used in the role. The most radical critiques are skeptical arguments about the possibility of moral expertise and the desirability of moral experts. When critics such as Cheryl Noble argue that "moral problems are everybody's business," they raise a cluster of related skeptical questions about methods of moral analysis, the particular suitability of philosophy in the context of medicine, and the role of experts in democracies. The methods of moral analysis common in bioethics presume that one can divorce moral issues from a complex social and historical context, deliberate about them using general theoretical models or principles as guides, then return back to the decision context to produce a better outcome. "To be amenable to these techniques, moral problems must be abstracted from their social settings so that they appear purely moral. In fact, were moral questions more richly defined and conceived, the professional inability of philosophy to deal with them would be glaringly obvious."[46] Skeptics argue that in practice, philosophers are cursed by their own tools and are able to answer only such abstracted questions rather than those that patients and hospital staff need answered.

Philosophy is a doubtful aid to clinical decision making, argue skeptics, because its method and approach differ greatly from those of medicine. Ruth Shalit claims that bioethics "is not medicine, which is to say it is not science, which is to say it is to a very large degree whatever anyone wants it to be." Of all the disciplines that could be helpful in sorting out complex clinical dilemmas, philosophy may be a poor choice: "The philosopher's recommendation depends on a set of criteria that is not agreed upon, but varies from culture to culture and, more and more, from individual to individual. One man's categorical imperative is another man's heresy."[47] This skeptical point about philosophers' qualifications to make clinical judgments is buttressed by survey evidence that bioethics consultants give a wide variety of responses to the same clinical problem.[48] The question of how bioethicists might be certified—whether there is a coherent body of scholarship they should master and a discrete set of analytical skills they should possess—raises vexing debates among philosophers.[49]

Even if bioethicists were capable of adequately answering the right clinical questions and did so in a way that showed a higher level of agreement, skeptics argue, the role of moral expert is in tension with the democratic belief that moral problems are everybody's business. This addresses the public and outsider

46. Cheryl N. Noble, "Ethics and Experts," *Hastings Center Report* 12, no. 3 (1982): 7.

47. Ruth Shalit, "When We Were Philosopher Kings: The Rise of the Medical Ethicist," *New Republic*, April 28, 1997, 24.

48. Ellen Fox and Carol B. Stocking, "Ethics Consultants' Recommendations for Life-Prolonging Treatment of Patients in a Persistent Vegetative State," *Journal of the American Medical Association* 270 (1993): 2578–82.

49. Larry R. Churchill, "Are We Professionals? A Critical Look at the Social Role of Bioethicists," *Daedalus* 128 (1999): 253–74.

features of bioethicists' liminal role: if ethicists are to represent the public's interests in medicine, they cannot do this simply by virtue of their philosophical
training. By making moral problems of medicine their business, bioethicists take
a degree of moral responsibility away from ordinary citizens—a delegation of
authority to moral experts that may be undesirable. "If you take democracy seriously, then the basic rule is that every philosopher is simply a citizen, and every
citizen a philosopher, capable of making decisions that reflect his or her con-
scientiously held beliefs."[50]

The skeptical critique of bioethics is a dramatic challenge to the role of the
bioethics consultant. It implies that the role might be better filled by members
of other disciplines or by nonacademic members of the public. For the purpose
of improving medical decisions, skeptics prefer a moral sensitivity to a particular
patient's beliefs, relationships, and social context rather than analytical ability
and knowledge of theoretical models. To open up hospitals to public scrutiny,
skeptics prefer people who "understand the economic, psychological, and social
pushes on moral thinking" rather than those trained in "techniques of logical
and conceptual analysis." As Noble writes, "I cannot see how philosophers' training makes them more valuable to the medical world than innumerable other
potential candidates and I can see some ways in which it makes them less."[51]

Like immanent critics, though, skeptics do little to gel the fluid role of bioethicist. On the surface, skeptics appear to favor a more outsider, public, and
formal role. Yet they do not explain how the needs for collegiality, for guarding
intimate choices, and for rapid, creative advice can be met. Apart from relaxing the expectation for philosophical training, the skeptical critique does nothing to relieve the other normative burdens of pluralistic sensitivity, macro- and
microlevel attentiveness, and technical competence. Skeptics exacerbate overload problems by underestimating the needed competencies of consultants.

Bioethnography Critiques

A more nuanced, though still radical, challenge to bioethics can be termed
the "bioethnography critique." Like immanent critics, bioethnographers reject
principlism as a paradigm for thinking about medical dilemmas and endorse a
more context-oriented method. Like skeptics, bioethnographers have misgivings

50. Shalit, "When We Were Philosopher Kings," 24.
51. Noble, "Ethics and Experts," 15.

about the current role of bioethicists. Yet unlike skeptics, bioethnographers articulate specific means for positively transforming that role. Skeptics point to the inadequacy of principlism and philosophers at managing liminality and meeting normative expectations, yet they do not suggest any replacement method or modified role. Bioethnographers agree with skeptics about the inadequacy of current methods and role description, but they are more constructive about alternatives.

The bioethnographic critique originates in the concerns of members of social science disciplines, such as sociology and anthropology, that bioethicists require a more developed empirical method to meet their normative expectations and must somehow resist the internal and formal aspects of their current liminal role. Like skeptics, bioethnographers believe that moral choices are difficult to decide or advise in abstraction from the context and life experience of the person who must make the decision.[52] Bioethnographers, however, do not join skeptics in rejecting the idea that there are better and worse methods for helping others with moral decisions. For Barry Hoffmaster and others, bioethics needs "a different brand of moral theory, one that is more closely allied with and faithful to real-life moral phenomena. Ethnography has a vital role to play in developing a more empirically grounded theory of morality."[53] Ethnography means two things here: an inquiry into the life, relationships, and beliefs of patients needing consultation, and an inquiry into the very construction of ethical choices in the medical domain. Together, these focus bioethnography on the normative expectations of pluralistic sensitivity and micro- and macrolevel attentiveness.

Larry Churchill questions whether a principlist bioethics is capable of serving the needs of or even communicating with patients who hold religious, local, and context-bound perspectives. How can a bioethicist trained to be impartial and schooled in rational principles address patients who use terms such as "sacrifice," "atonement," and "doing the Lord's work?" All patients require attentiveness to their particularity, a point Churchill raises by posing a simple question: if my spouse were facing a clinical ethics decision as a patient, what sort of competencies would I like to see in our counseling bioethicist? Someone with ethical training seems less important at such a moment than "allies who would support me, listen to my rambling narratives about my spouse, help me remember

52. Hoffmaster, "The Theory and Practice of Applied Ethics," 229.
53. Barry Hoffmaster, "Can Ethnography Save the Life of Medical Ethics?" *Social Science and Medicine* 35 (1992): 1425.

what is important to her, and decipher the meanings of the choices before me." To adequately address such cases requiring pluralistic sensitivity and microlevel attentiveness, bioethics as a method cannot be seen as "the mastery of some standard or normative way to decide" but rather the ability "to locate persons and their moral reasoning in the full and appropriate context, thereby displaying more clearly their meanings."[54]

As for the macro level, bioethnographers believe bioethicists currently fail to attend to such issues in part because of their principlist method and in part because of their role bias for colleagueship (insider rather than outsider status) and attention to issues of personal autonomy (private rather than public meanings). They argue that because bioethicists have been captured by the internal pressures and rewards of conformity to the medical way of decision making, they neglect macrolevel concerns. The strong form of the captured thesis maintains that bioethics has its analytic, morally individualist, and principle-oriented shape because of its institutional location in health care organizations. Charles Rosenberg, for example, holds such a strong thesis:

> As a condition of its acceptance, bioethics has taken up residence in the belly of the medical whale; although thinking of itself as still autonomous, the bioethical enterprise has developed a complex and symbiotic relationship with this host organism. Bioethics is no longer (if it ever was) a free-floating, oppositional, and socially critical reform movement: it is embodied in chairs and centers, in an abundant technical literature, in institutional review boards and consent forms, in presidential commissions and research protocols. It can, that is, be seen as a mediating element in a complex and highly bureaucratic system that must, nevertheless, manage ceaseless technical change. It is not an accident that the bioethical enterprise has routinely linked bureaucracy—committees, institutional regulations, and finely tuned language—with claims to moral stature.[55]

The claim to act as moral experts in the medical domain is made possible by the endorsement of just those practitioners and medical policy makers whose acts are to be held under scrutiny. As H. Tristram Engelhardt points out:

54. Churchill, "Are We Professionals," 264.
55. Charles Rosenberg, "Meanings, Policies, and Medicine: On the Bioethical Enterprise and History," *Daedalus* 128 (1999): 38.

Government has turned to bioethicists not just to determine what health-care policies can be justified, but also in order to provide a rationale for the policies governments wanted to pursue. . . . Bioethics, even if it cannot, in fact deliver a canonical, secular, content-full moral understanding, can still be recruited to aid those who wish to have power, and as a consequence it can provide the opportunity for bioethicists to share in power.[56]

The weaker form of the captured thesis holds that more mundane constraints of institutional vocabulary and colleague relations prevent bioethics from being more critical of the construction of moral dilemmas. Being in the belly of the medical whale, to use Charles Rosenberg's terms, means significant vulnerability to the dominant concepts, language, and social practices of health care workers.[57] Medical sociologist Patricia Flynn argues that ethics committee deliberations are marked by "habitual thought configurations," "habits of thought which involve the use of . . . the biomedical model" and which "are a part of the thought and discourse of physicians, nurses, social workers, psychologists, others in the health care industry, and increasingly patients and their families who are defined largely if not exclusively in relation to medicine." Bioethics does have a distinctive theoretical vocabulary and method of reaching decisions, but clinical ethics decisions are "medicine's game," "ultimately biomedicine defines the terms of the work of bioethics."[58] Bioethicists find themselves enmeshed not just in the concepts and language of medicine but also in the social networks of health care organizations: "It is only natural to want to respond helpfully to those with whom one works routinely, who are in positions of evaluation and remuneration. It is the natural character of this desire to be helpful that blunts the recognition of being captured by institutional agendas."[59]

Bioethnographers challenge the mainstream, principlist settlement on the role and expectations of ethics consultation: the bioethicist as one who helps a patient or clinician toward the right decision through the use of reason. For bioethnographers, this mainstream settlement unjustifiably favors the inside, private,

---

56. H. Tristram Engelhardt, "Bioethics and the Philosophy of Medicine Reconsidered," *Philosophy and Medicine* 50 (1997): 99.

57. See Bosk, "Professional Ethicist Available," 57.

58. Patricia Flynn, "The Disciplinary Emergence of Bioethics and Bioethics Committees: Moral Ordering and Its Legitimation," *Sociological Focus* 24 (1991): 151. Sociologists frequently hold *both* strong and weak forms of the captured thesis.

59. Churchill, "Are We Professionals," 257.

and formal sides of the ethics consultant role and naively sees philosophical analysis as the key to meeting normative expectations for clinical-ethical judgment. Instead, they offer a different settlement: the bioethicist as ethnographer and social critic. This reconstruction emphasizes the outside, public, and informal qualities of ethics consultation and proposes a more empirical and engaged method of judgment. Methods of ethnography such as participant observation and close reading and interpretation of informants' narratives help provide a "thick description" of ethical context.[60] Unlike mainstream methods of bioethics, ethnography presumes potential translation difficulties between the beliefs and values of patients, health care workers, and ethicists. To help people negotiate between these worlds the ethnographer must first describe them. According to Rita Charon, bioethnography renders a picture of ethics consultation as medical anthropology:

> The work of a social anthropologist in, say, the highlands of central Morocco is not unlike the work of the hospital ethicist in, say, the crash room of the neonatal intensive care unit. Like Geertz's ethnographer who accepts the task of making sense of conceptual structures "at once strange, irregular, and inexplicit . . . which he must contrive somehow first to grasp and then to render," the ethicist must somehow see clearly the moral dilemmas facing the patient and must engage in the grasping and the rendering, or the recognizing and the formulating, that require both the information and the story.[61]

What is sought, initially, is a closer understanding of the "lived world of the patient," the "individual particularities" of bioethical problems.[62] To be useful, the ethnographer must seek, second, a closer understanding of the context of moral choice making. Bioethical dilemmas are not simply clashes between different values; they are the product of social relations within the medical domain and between it and external forces. This second goal of ethnography is to "describe

60. "Thick description" is Clifford Geertz's term for social inquiry that is both closely grounded in the data of fieldwork and imaginative in interpreting the connections and meanings found in the data. It attempts "to bring us into touch with the lives of strangers" (*The Interpretation of Cultures* [New York: Basic Books, 1973], 16).

61. Rita Charon, "Narrative Contributions to Medical Ethics," in *A Matter of Principles,* ed. E. R. DuBose et al., 269.

62. Flynn, "The Disciplinary Emergence of Bioethics and Bioethics Committees," 154; and Hoffmaster, "Can Ethnography Save the Life of Medical Ethics," 1427.

as thickly as possible how ethical problems are ignored, unattended, recognized, managed, and resolved in medical settings."[63]

Like skeptics, bioethnographers suspect that ethics consultants are currently biased toward microlevel attentiveness and ethicize what are really political problems. Why is this a matter of ethical decision rather than an individual or social or political decision? What interests are served or thwarted by conceiving of this dilemma as an ethical one to be resolved in house? The thick description of the context of moral choices leads naturally to the role of social critic: bioethnography does not tell us how and whether problems are properly resolved but how problems are structured in the first place. The goal is to show "how problems in the workplace of the hospital come to be seen as ethical, and then what this labeling accomplishes in terms of conflict management."[64] The "real practice of moral decision-making" is particularistic and enmeshed in relations of power.[65] As social critic, the bioethnographer is sensitive to the subtle means of capturing ethical discourse and presumes as a methodological starting point that "ethical problems are caused by social structures, not cognitive errors."[66]

An initial worry about the bioethnography method is the problem that description is very different from judgment. Clinical ethicists can admit that ethnography is important and that in the best of all possible worlds it would be nice to know more about patients' particular moral universes and the context of power in which choice making occurs. Yet facts alone, even thick descriptions, will not produce good judgments since these are two different modes of thought. As Daniel Callahan argues, "[S]ocial science knowledge cannot in the end be decisive for the making of moral judgments." This is not just an argument from expedience that because clinical ethicists need to make judgments in a fast-paced environment there is no time for thick description. It is an age-old fact/value argument about the division of labor between those who carry the empirical burdens and those who toil the normative fields: moral choices require information, but they also involve values and mores that escape descriptive analysis. For Callahan, "[T]here may never be a full meeting of minds between those who see their work as developing sound moral judgments about right and wrong, good and bad, and those who see their vocation as providing

63. Bosk, "Professional Ethicist Available," 64.
64. Bosk, "Professional Ethicist Available," 65.
65. Hoffmaster, "The Theory and Practice of Applied Ethics," 219.
66. Daniel F. Chambliss, "Is Bioethics Irrelevant?" *Contemporary Sociology* 22 (1993): 650.

informed descriptions and explanations of actual practices and mores. Each may need the other but it is not yet fully clear just how they need each other."[67]

Bioethnographers recognize the force of this critique but can respond that ethnography and ethics are only contingently at odds. Reconstructed as more descriptive and more attuned to particular lives, the methods of ethics and ethnography can complement and make use of each other. The key is to hone the aspects of the ethnographic method that can contribute to clinical decision making. In other words, this is to "do moral ethnography and thereby to make more productive contributions to practical ethics; and to develop the moral theory implicit in ethnographic studies."[68] Concerned about the inability of current ethnographic method to direct clinical-ethics decisions, Arthur Kleinman offers the following four-stage model.

> *Self-reflexivity:* The bioethnographer is careful to disclose "her own moral positioning" on the particular issue facing the ethics committee.
> *Thick description:* The bioethnographer determines what "is locally at stake" for people directly affected by a decision, how they themselves perceive moral issues.
> *Deliberation:* The bioethnographer "triangulates across these different forms of knowledge to set out a framework for understanding how the intersection of moral processes and ethical discourse in this particular world defines the local human conditions of health equity and the local human consequences of health rights and responsibilities."
> *Debate:* The framework developed in deliberation "then becomes the grounds for community-wide conversation between stakeholders (e.g., laypersons and professionals), out of which will emerge an agenda for practical action."[69]

Under Kleinman's model, bioethnography becomes a mode of facilitating a better informed decision-making process in which the bioethicist plays a descriptive and social-critical role.

This is a promising answer to doubts about the compatibility of description and judgment, but it raises serious questions. One question is whether the

---

67. Daniel Callahan, "The Hastings Center and the Early Years of Bioethics," *Kennedy Institute of Ethics Journal* 9 (1999): 64, 65.

68. Hoffmaster, "Can Ethnography Save the Life of Medical Ethics," 1429.

69. Arthur Kleinman, "Moral Experience and Ethical Reflection: Can Ethnography Reconcile Them? A Quandary for 'The New Bioethics,'" *Daedalus* 128 (1999): 92.

external, public role of social critic is now overshadowing the internal, institutional role of clinical ethicist. Bioethnographers are rightly worried about ethicists being captured by the language and practice of medicine, yet they do not see the costs of their position of resistance. If the strong captured thesis is true—that clinical ethicists have a place in medical discourse only because they do not threaten established relations of power in health care organizations—then it seems appropriate to shift emphasis to the social-critical role. But if the weak captured thesis is true, then it may be more appropriate to balance institutional and public roles. This is a very old political problem that may never be resolved, but there is value in fighting from the inside rather than from the outside. The key to insider struggles is not to develop a counter-language, a new set of terms opposed to mainstream practice, but to be vigilant to the ways the biomedical model and hospital practices devalue other ways of knowing and speaking.

Even if the strong captured thesis is true, there are many ways to be a social critic. Thick description is one way, but so is the use of abstract concepts of rights, principles of autonomy and equality. The problem is not the analytical method of philosophy; it is how that analysis is used in institutional settings.[70] What grants the bioethnographic model its social critical force is not the method of thick description but the independent and detachable feature of facilitating public debate. Yet, that aspect could be joined to an analytic, principle-oriented discourse as well.

Ethnography may be an unpromising method to choose for providing context to moral decision making. The model of fieldwork in other cultures is daunting and places a great burden on a clinical-ethicist practicing in the United States. It is one thing to expect an anthropologically trained scholar to develop, over time, a thick description of a particular culture through series of interviews and cultivation of informants. It is another to expect someone, even someone trained in anthropological theory and method, to develop thick descriptions of the wide array of traditional, secular, progressive, religious, and ethnic cultures that make up contemporary pluralist society in the United States. The knowledge-gathering difficulty of that task is exacerbated by the time constraints placed on clinical consultation. Further, substituting ethnography for bioethics is not replacing a controversial with a neutral method. If there is current doubt about what

---

70. See, for example, Allen Buchanan's argument that counter to Marxist doubts about the critical value of analytical political theory, Rawls's principle-oriented theory of justice can be used in quite radical ways (*Marx and Justice: The Radical Critique of Liberalism* [Totowa, N.J.: Rowman and Littlefield, 1982]).

capabilities are needed in a bioethicist, there may be even more doubt in the field of anthropology about what makes a good ethnographer. James Clifford, a prominent critic of ethnographic method, has pointed to the ways the seemingly impartial and scientific elements of fieldwork actually enhance the power of the ethnographer to define the context as they see it. Far from relating an objective, "thick" description of a social context, ethnographers often give us the world as seen by their particular Western, secular, and professional standpoint. Clifford makes this point as follows:

> Henceforth neither the experience nor the interpretive activity of the scientific researcher can be considered innocent. It becomes necessary to conceive of ethnography not as the experience and interpretation of a circumscribed "other" reality, but rather as a constructive negotiation involving at least two, and usually more, conscious, politically significant subjects. Paradigms of experience and interpretation are yielding to discursive paradigms of dialogue and polyphony.[71]

Whether or not Clifford's critique is accepted whole, it weakens the case for ethnographic method as a resolution to problems of power.[72]

Though they articulate a compelling alternative view of what should typify bioethics practice, bioethnographers do not relieve some of the very tensions that caused their dissatisfaction with principlism. Thick description affirms the importance of pluralistic sensitivity and micro- and macrolevel attentiveness, but it offers little guidance on how to meet all these expectations in the time-sensitive context of the clinic. As for role characteristics, though bioethnographers favor outsider, informal, and public aspects, they do not reject the other poles. They assume without much argument that colleagueship, decision-making authority, and intimacy are qualities of lesser importance or that somehow naturally accompany the method of thick description.

Considered closely, bioethnography pushes toward an even more radical transformation of bioethics that privileges the democratic professional tendencies already present in the movement while downgrading features less consistent with democratic professionalism. With his demand for deliberation and debate,

71. James Clifford, "On Ethnographic Authority," in *The Predicament of Culture: Twentieth-Century Ethnography, Literature, and Art* (Cambridge, Mass.: Harvard University Press, 1988), 41.

72. For more on the problem of power in ethnographic representation, see Thomas McCarthy, "Doing the Right Thing in Cross-Cultural Representation," *Ethics* 102 (1992): 635–49.

Kleinman raises the possibility that the tensions and expectations of ethics consultants cannot be managed by one person, even one with a more empirical and engaged method than principlism. The possibility that ethics consultation is a process not a role, a social rather than individual responsibility, may the most promising solution to liminality and overload.

Reclaiming Bioethics as Democratic Professionalism

Some practitioners have argued even more explicitly than Kleinman that bioethicists should promote a more publicly involved decision-making process that is open, tolerant, and egalitarian. Rather than serve as an advocate of a particular choice, or even as the source of the best description of how "stakeholders" see their moral worlds, the bioethicist is to be a guardian of reflective spaces within the hospital. Such a role is closer to the ideal of democratic professionalism than what is advocated and practiced by either mainstream bioethicists or their critics. As Margaret Urban Walker puts this idea, ethics consultation is "a kind of interaction that invites and enables something to happen, something that renders authority more self-conscious and responsibility clearer. It is also about maintaining a certain kind of reflective space (literal and figurative) within an institution, within its culture and its daily life." In this view, bioethicists "are architects of moral space within the health care setting, as well as mediators in the conversations taking place within that space."[73]

The internal, institutional role of bioethicists would be closer to the democratic professional character of the movement than current mainstream theory and practice. Neither decision guide nor thick describer, the bioethicist is to be facilitator of dialogue and mediator among the different interests and languages present in clinical dilemmas. Their primary goal would now be the functioning of a deliberative process, one in which they play an important but not a dominant part. Facilitation means responsibility for creating and maintaining "moral-reflective spaces": regularly scheduled meetings open to parties affected by clinical decisions. "These will be actual spaces—places and times—where there are regular discussions, consultations, conferences, lectures, meetings, rounds, and so on, that animate and propel the moral life of that institution and link it

---

73. Margaret Urban Walker, "Keeping Moral Space Open: New Images of Ethics Consulting," *Hastings Center Report* 23, no. 2 (1993): 33.

to the larger communities of moral discourse in which it nests and to which it must account." Mediation means responsibility for dialogue that is respectful to all parties involved, discussions in which decisions are the result of "stakes being clearly assessed, parties becoming clear of their own and others' legitimate positions, compromises being achieved that will stand up satisfactorily to later review because of the care with which they were constructed."[74]

Walker identifies three broad skills helpful for these new roles. One is philosophers' traditional analytical ability to clarify critical concepts and values at stake in a discussion. This skill is needed to "keep track of where the discussion has (and has not) been going." Another is the less traditional ability of understanding how the larger community outside the health care organization thinks about clinical dilemmas. This is not the thick description of moral culture bioethnographers seek, but something less formal, a "very wide (and critical) conversance with the actual terms, usually diverse and not tightly systematized, of moral assessment in the society the institution takes as its community." A third skill is a critical awareness of particular power relations within the health care organization and between it and the community. The bioethicist must be sensitive "to configurations of authority and dynamics of relationship that can either help structure that space or deform it."[75]

An advantage of this way of reconstructing bioethical practice is that its democratic aspects closely relate to the reality of IEC and clinical consultant work. Bioethics in practice is often committee and consultation work done with others from different areas of the health care organization. The internal, institutional responsibilities of IECs include quite mundane tasks such as clarifying procedural rules and navigating legal and professional guidelines. Such work privileges just the facilitative and mediating skills stressed in the deliberative model. Even in the context of case review it may be more realistic to see the bioethicist as a mediator or facilitator of dialogue rather than a source of comfort and consolation to patients. Following Churchill's argument, we can see why patients usually resolve ethical crises by turning to friends and compassionate supporters, not hospital staff—even the best intentioned. As for external and public responsibilities, the democratic professional model again reflects a more realistic view. Rather than taking up the stance of social critic—something that would make internal, institutional facilitation and mediation more strained—

74. Walker, "Keeping Moral Space Open," 38, 40.
75. Walker, "Keeping Moral Space Open," 39.

the bioethicist fosters the flow of information between the health care organization and the public in which it is situated.

Additionally, unlike immanent critiques such as virtue ethics, feminist theories of care, and casuistry, the democratic professional ethicist is not to be a proxy decision maker but a guardian of a process that allows people to make their own decisions. Such a position relieves the methodological and democratic worries of skeptics while escaping their immobilizing implications. Even granting that "moral problems are everybody's business," majority opinion should still be held accountable to the standards of reasonable reflection. An important kind of knowledge that furthers public deliberation is useful for moral decision making. The democratic professional model also satisfies the bioethnographic demand for context by letting actors describe themselves while relieving the clinical ethicist of the knowledge-gathering burdens of thick description. This is just what prominent anthropological critics of ethnographic authority call for when they recommend "polyvocality" and collaborative narratives.[76]

To be a plausible model, though, a few ambiguities must be cleared up. Being a facilitator and mediator must mean more than simply ensuring that ethics consultants function according to minimal democratic procedures, with all voices affected by a decision present and fairly counted. Legitimate moral decisions are the product of quite stringent procedures that direct participants to reflect on their positions, not simply voice them. Applying the norms of public deliberation to the context of ethics consultation, Amy Gutmann and Dennis Thompson articulate four goals of deliberation as responsibilities of ethics consultants.

Legitimacy: If decisions are to be truly accepted by affected parties, all their reasons must be included and all their voices taken seriously in committee deliberation.

Publicity: Decisions are to be the product of "we-thinking," not merely the aggregation of individually held positions.

Respect: Participants in deliberation should try to see the merit in others' perspectives and seek an "economy of moral disagreement" that minimizes rejection of others' positions.

Self-correction: Committee deliberation is to contribute to a growth in knowledge in moral decision making about medical issues.[77]

76. See Clifford, "On Ethnographic Authority," 41.
77. Amy Gutmann and Dennis F. Thompson, "Deliberating About Bioethics," *Hastings Center Report* 27, no. 3 (1997): 38–41.

Merely facilitating and mediating discourse is insufficient; the bioethicist must further discourse that helps people reach decisions that meet their considered and durable approval.

The interest in legitimacy means that bioethicists may sometimes need to be critical of their medically trained and institutionally situated teammates. Clinical ethicists are to be more sensitive to issues of inclusion than they presently seem to be. From the standpoint of legitimacy, it matters, for example, that ethics consultants are currently called in more frequently by health care workers than patients.[78] Clinical ethicists are also to be more careful about issues of power. For the sake of legitimacy, it matters that IECs are usually funded by health care organizations and administered as part of their organizational structure.[79] These are technical issues because procedural solutions are available to solve such problems (e.g., ethicists responsible for meeting legitimacy requirements might be elected by the larger community and funded publicly through resources solicited from national or regional professional associations), but they show that the role of social critic emphasized by bioethnographers may sometimes be required by the legitimacy goals of the democratic professional model.

"Architect," "guardian," "facilitator," and "mediator" are terms that express a range of possible responsibilities that in theory should shift some of the normative expectations of bioethics consultation to the process and other parties involved. Yet, they are also terms that express the fact that the bioethicist must make substantive judgments about the legitimacy, publicity, and respectfulness of the process and the conversations it permits. In contexts marked by legitimacy problems, for example, the normative responsibilities of bioethicists will not be light, though they will, ideally, be shared by other parties inside and outside the medical domain. Further, in some contexts, the bioethicist might need to be a participant in conversations rather than remain a referee. In cases where the cognitive status of patients and the nature of their choices for treatment are unclear or where the reasons and self-descriptions offered by parties in bioethics conversations appear incoherent, mistaken, or the product of some form of external pressure, then the bioethicist may need to give voice to arguments not already in play. Recognizing this range of possible responsibilities, of course, means the democratic professional model escapes only by degrees the problems of liminality and overload.

78. James A. Tulsky and Bernard Lo, "Ethics Consultation: Time to Focus on Patients," *American Journal of Medicine* 92 (1992): 343–45.

79. For more on both these problems, see Bosk and Frader, "Institutional Ethics Committees."

Another ambiguity concerns just how, under the democratic professional ideal, the bioethicist becomes a relay of public discourse, communicating hospital guidelines and decisions outward and public reactions inward. Bruce Jennings imagines bioethicists sharing the responsibility of building reflective moral spaces for public debate outside of health care organizations: bioethicists "not only help design the democratic forum opportunities where this civic conversation can take place, they must participate in it as well."[80] Call this the "direct" account of public responsibility. At the other end of the spectrum of responsibility, Walker endorses a more "representative" account in which bioethicists represent the "reflective social dialogue" in the community. They are symbolic of health care organizations' agreement to "a visible and authorized process of communal moral negotiation as part of its life."[81] Neither of these attempts escapes difficulty. The direct account places heavy burdens on ethicists, while the representative version relieves them all too easily. As seen with the public journalism and restorative justice movements, facilitating public deliberation that actually functions in a legitimate, respectful, public, and self-correcting way is difficult, time consuming, and dependent on the collaboration of many social and political institutions. Symbolically representing the public voice is less demanding but also less capable of generating the sort of legitimacy desired. Something between these two models of public responsibility is more suitable for the goals and capabilities of bioethicists.

Considerable precedent exists in both mainstream bioethics theory and practice for a more active community role. An influential report, *Deciding to Forgo Life-Sustaining Treatment,* published by the widely respected President's Commission for the Study of Ethical Problems in Medicine in 1983, called on IECs to "serve as a focus for community discussion and education."[82] In practice, public engagement—in the forms of volunteer membership of committees and community outreach activities, among others—is not uncommon in all the institutional sites of bioethics, though empirical evidence clearly indicates that it is currently marginalized.[83]

---

80. Bruce Jennings, "Bioethics and Democracy," *Centennial Review* 34 (1990): 224.

81. Walker, "Keeping Moral Space Open," 38–39.

82. President's Commission for the Study of Ethical Problems in Medicine and Biomedical Research, *Deciding to Forgo Life-Sustaining Treatment: A Report on the Ethical, Medical, and Legal Issues in Treatment Decisions* (Washington, D.C.: Government Printing Office, 1983), 163.

83. See Cate McBurney, "Ethics Committees and Social Change," in *Bioethics and Social Context,* ed. Barry Hoffmaster (Philadelphia: Temple University Press, 2001), 180–98.

Before concluding that a conception of the bioethics consultant role more in keeping with democratic professionalism, though imperfect, is the best attempt thus far at managing the tensions and expectations of the role, a nagging question about public and private spheres of decision must be confronted. While it is clearly appropriate to emphasize the representative or direct public role of the bioethicist on an ethics commission or even an IRB where there are distinct statutory guidelines, it may be less appropriate to emphasize publicity in the context of some clinical decisions. Though much IEC work is bureaucratic, the closer one moves toward the sphere of clinical decision, the more private it seems and the less one wants public deliberation to reach. This reflects once again the liminal and overloaded character of bioethics. Though "bioethics owes its very existence to the argument that medicine, science, and technology raise questions of morality and human value that society must address openly and publicly," this does not remove the need, at times, to keep this public moral discourse "in check." Health care decisions about issues such as genetic screening clearly have public ramifications, affecting as they do the "traditions and institutions that sustain democratic values."[84] But many other decisions may be inappropriate to consider as anything but private decisions where the patient's voice should be privileged above that of all other citizens. Being a guardian of reflective moral spaces may sometimes mean keeping a public gaze away from difficult private dilemmas.

The place and character of reflective, public-spirited discourse in key social practices such as medicine is difficult to specify. Debates over the role of bioethics practitioners point to the promising idea that ethics counselors may be the facilitators and mediators of such discourse. This idea is worth pursuing much further in practice and in theoretical discussion if only because the current institutional status and normative expectations of ethics consultation are untenable.

84. Jennings, "Bioethics and Democracy," 222.

8

CONTEXT AND CONSEQUENCES:
THE DUTIES OF DEMOCRATIC PROFESSIONALS

[I]t was not the fault of the theory if it was of little use in practice, but rather of there being not
enough theory, *theory that a man should have learned from experience.*

—IMMANUEL KANT, *Perpetual Peace* (1795)

Theory Meets Practice: Questions for Democratic Professionalism

Why Isn't It Enough Just to Be Good at What We Do?

Cases of democratic professionalism in practice demonstrate that this is a complex and demanding ideal. Challenges exist in managing resources, especially the time taken up by professionals in facilitating lay participation and genuine, not token, public engagement. Pressures are placed on traditionally trained professionals to adapt to new ways of working that do not fit easily into standard judgments of what good work looks like. There are ongoing issues of how to incorporate task sharing and lay participation into complex organizations and how to understand the status of these new features of professionalism. Most important, perhaps, are the difficulties involved in saddling people and organizations already charged with performing challenging tasks—to bring accurate and relevant information, assure justice, provide humane health care—with yet more tasks related to community engagement and dialogue.

"Why isn't it enough just to be good at what we do?" asks the professional in training. "Why are you asking for this additional feature of a professional role, that by your own account, takes time away from other features?" "Isn't the *democratic* at risk of jeopardizing the *occupational?*" Our three cases all confirmed the validity of the prudential motivations stressed in our theoretical discussion of democratic professionalism: a healthy self-interest, especially in response to economic constraints, in preserving authority and integrity has driven reformers in journalism and criminal justice and has allowed in lay reformers in medicine. Precisely because democratic professional task sharing is a demanding ideal, that reform-minded professionals have prudential reasons for pursuing it is noteworthy. "Being good at what we do" in the minds of these reformers is connected constitutively to lay participation and public involvement.

In all the cases, economic pressures, in one form or another, set the context for democratic professional reforms. Public journalism is a striking example of this, having emerged in one of the most economically challenging sectors of the highly competitive media world. Newspapers, struggling for audiences alongside network and cable television outlets and Internet news sources, felt the pressure of an aging and diminishing readership to reach out and rebuild public interest. The bioethics movement also arose in an economic context in which the patient–doctor relationship had fractured as a result of an increasingly specialized and bureaucratized medical practice. A clear message of public interest in overseeing the norms of medical research and practice was that this relationship had to be tended to and rebuilt on sturdier grounds. Restorative justice reformers similarly faced publics seemingly willing to mete out harsher retributive sentencing with concomitant demands for criminal justice resources while resisting the taxes or drain on other needed state services these public expenditures entail. The cost-effectiveness of deprofessionalizing aspects of criminal justice practice has been central to the practical rhetoric of restorative justice reformers. Though substantive, nontoken community involvement in any democratic professional effort is unlikely to come cheap, such involvement can help legitimate those services and practices that become better understood as a result.

Integrity issues similarly played a central role in motivating democratic professional reformers and their supporters. How to be a guardian of solid and useful civic information at a time of both information saturation and the increasingly porous boundaries between celebrity-centered infotainment and traditional news is a question that motivates many public journalists. Responsibility to victims, offenders, and their communities pressed restorative justice professionals to consider changes to their mainstream, retributive model of bringing justice. The moral meaning of health care under conditions of rapid technological innovation, disciplinary specialization, and organizational change is the core issue for both bioethics reformers and their supporters within the medical domain. In all these cases, too, a cultural skepticism about the intentions and motivations of professionals heightened the importance of integrity issues. Deprofessionalization themes are common to the rhetoric of all three democratic professional movements, as mainstream norms and practices are critiqued for impeding genuine professional goals—bringing information, justice, humane health care—and contributing to public skepticism.

Finally, despite their critical awareness regarding social trustee professionalism, all three cases demonstrated a professional and organizational interest in retaining distinct experience- and training-grounded authority over certain tasks, albeit while remaining committed to sharing experience and authority. Restorative justice professionals, for example, have retained significantly large roles in assuring procedural fairness and other traditional norms. Public journalists keep the authority to write and broadcast the news as they see fit, even as they opened up the process to lay interests and lay voices. Medical professionals diagnose, prescribe, and treat alongside lay consultants who can intervene with patients and staff in cases that raise pressing ethical issues. All the cases supported the idea that in a culture skeptical of authority and distrustful of privilege, professionalism can achieve a deserved democratic deference if it is transparent to the public and open to lay involvement, in addition to being skilled.

The prudential motivations for task sharing and public engagement were strong enough in the three reform efforts examined that they raised questions about how to more precisely define the values and characteristics of democratic professionalism. In addition to public engagement and task sharing, which the earlier theoretical arguments endorsed, the case studies pointed to the additional values and characteristics of fallibility, interorganizational networks of communication, and resistance to formalizing lay roles as correctives and guides.

Each of these correctives and guides challenges, from different directions, an overly heroic notion of democratic professionalism. Heroism is a problem because by definition it is not a routine attitude, and democratic professionalism as we have approached it in this work is something to be expected of some professions and professionals all the time, not just once in a while and by a few super specimens. If we are interested in "civic engagement and the empowerment of citizens," Harry Boyte argues, this has to be seen as "a function of institutional cultures, not simply of individual proclivities."[1] In the way I have described and defended it, the democratic professional ideal is not, to use the philosophical term, *supererogatory*—virtuous and good but above and beyond what could be legitimately expected of an average person. Nor is it *utopian*—beautiful in theory

---

1. Harry Boyte, *Everyday Politics* (Philadelphia: University of Pennsylvania Press, 2004), xi.

but far too idealistic to have practical results. I criticized tendencies toward the heroic in each of the reform movements because routinely falling short of the democratic professional ideal runs the risk of hollowing it out and, worse, turning it into a promotional exercise rather than a genuine attempt at fostering civic engagement and more public deliberation.

Expressions of fallibility correct the mistaken tendency of some democratic professionals to consider public interests in their practices adequately represented by focus groups or even well-attended town hall meetings. Though such public deliberation is a core component of democratic professionalism, to think that any one profession can represent public opinion is overly heroic. Related, inter-organizational networks of communication can help link the task sharing in one professional domain to larger discussions and activities in multiple public spheres. Without such a network, to think that microforums could have much influence in broader public debate and action is utopian. Finally, continually refreshing connections to lay participants, making and renewing linkages to community members who have not been involved or have not participated recently, may serve as antidotes to reprofessionalizing tendencies that emerge even in domains committed to democratic professionalism.

Which Professions Should Democratize?

Consider a second practical question: What are the characteristics of professions that mark them out for these special duties that fall on democratic professionals? Who is so lucky and why them and not others?

One approach would be to say that the more an occupation begins to resemble a traditional profession, with markers of skill and status such as specialized education, characteristic privileges such as work autonomy, and market protections such as licensing procedures, the more one might wish to ask such a profession to serve public interests in return. This inherently social trustee argument runs aground on the "professionalization of everybody" problem.[2] There are professional wrestlers, professional cat burglars, at least in the movies, real estate professionals, and more. Beauticians, for example, are considered by some to be members of a profession and go through specialized training and state licensing procedures in order to practice. They can also be said to promote task-monopolizing activities by claiming to cut hair better than most laypeople armed

2. See the commentary by Harold Wilensky, "The Professionalization of Everyone?" *American Journal of Sociology* 70 (1964): 137–58.

with scissors and bowls. But it is absurd to claim that by virtue of these characteristics they must be obligated to share tasks and engage publics.

The theoretical and case discussions in previous chapters point toward the discernible political effects of professions as primary criteria for concluding that a profession ought to take democratic professionalism seriously. Journalists look less traditionally "professional" than beauticians in a number of respects: they lack licenses and may not need any formal training to practice. However, the profession of journalism has major effects on the political communication, civic knowledge, and modes of accountability in modern democracy. The professionals active in the restorative justice movement include lawyers and judges but also reform-minded criminal justice administrators. Whether the profession shares all the core features stressed by sociologists—knowledge, control over work, self-regulation, and a sense of social purpose—is less important than whether it shares those features that potentially impact the public culture of democracy. Discretionary authority, stemming from workplace autonomy or other sources, a degree of freedom from market pressures, and the ability to influence social values are key factors here. So, for example, issues in criminal justice and health care raise significant moral questions that need to be addressed by the public in whose name the professionals in those domains practice. Short-circuiting public awareness of these issues via task monopoly negatively affects democratic accountability.

I have been sensitive to the fact that professions are occupations that must deliver products and services to survive. Recognizing and acting on democratic obligations makes for complexity and demands trade-offs between conventional and democratic professional norms. Democratic professionalism is a balancing act that requires power sharing with laypeople while demanding a strong commitment to serving core social purposes by developing and applying the best cognitive skills and physical talents possible. Just as we should be wary of utopianism, we should also be careful not to overly politicize these occupations. Nevertheless, democratic professionalism follows the radical critique in recognizing the already political nature of professions and asks some to be more explicit and constructive about their effects on citizenship and public knowledge.

Another set of clues that a profession has democratic obligations is the discourse of ethics related to it found either in academic scholarship or in practitioner dialogue. Where there is a live debate about the ethics of a profession, there is most likely a role for public engagement and lay participation. We see discussions of media ethics, ethics for lawyers, criminal justice ethics, and medical ethics, but also military ethics, engineering ethics, and the like. These discussions persist because all these occupations serve social purposes but are not completely guided by the dominant steering mechanisms of the marketplace and the state. Because they act "for us" yet cannot ever be guided completely by us, critical attention to issues of ethics emerge. At the very least, such ethics discussions suggest that some insight and collaboration with affected publics may be required for professional practices to be acceptable. Where there is an ethicist, there are likely public voices needing to be heard—something illustrated by the case of bioethics.

Avoiding the Nondeliberative

The discussion of what counts as a potential democratic profession draws attention to the reasons the ideal is nonprudential for some. These normative reasons for task sharing, encouraging lay participation, and attempting to engage the larger public in issues related to professions hold good even if the prudential reasons did not obtain. For example, there are normative reasons for lay participation in newsgathering even if it turns out this is not an economically efficient use of resources. Professions having a discernible impact on public deliberation have primary obligations to avoid nondeliberative effects. Task sharing and public engagement may be the best way to satisfy these obligations.

The democratic theory behind democratic professionalism holds that deliberative, participatory, and task-sharing public spheres are important to resolving collective problems. The obligation to encourage lay participation and task sharing is rooted in this theory. The strongest professional obligations are to avoid the nondeliberative in professional practice, but this may well lead to more positive duties to facilitate community engagement. For example, when public journalists realized that the mainstream approach to forming and reporting news stories was, in their view, dampening down public interest in both politics and news, they began to integrate public participation into the news process. Stimulating lay participation and engaging in task sharing is a second-order duty that gets its obligatoriness from its connection to the first-order obligation to avoid the nondeliberative.

This way of conceiving the duties of democratic professionalism puts professionals on the hook without asking them to be heroic or substitute political activism for occupational competence. It is desirable for democratic professionalism to be routine, realistic, and self-endorsed, not a mere moralistic ethic—a pack of "shoulds" and "oughts." Asking professionals to be heroes or political activists is a flawed, short-term solution to the problems faced by both professionals and the publics they affect. Some examples will show, however, that what I am asking is in itself quite demanding.

Reasonable, Respectful, and Honorable Public Debate

The cases of public journalism and restorative justice are contrasting examples of what professions might do to avoid negatively impacting public deliberation. In the first case, I argued that it was a mistake to think that news organizations could take it on themselves to create representative public forums that could deliver the voice of the community. Either more formal institutions—of state and local government, for example—would need to be involved in order to assure representativeness, or claims to have adequately listened to the public would need to be discounted.

Yet, much hard work must be done to help public discourse become more reasonable, respectful, and honorable. Rather than simply play off opposing sides of a story, public journalists have rightly chosen to dig deeper and gather multiple perspectives. Casting off mainstream professional habits that ritualize reporting into adversary, personality-oriented, attention-deficit modes is a duty journalists owe democracy. Involving laypeople is a successful way of performing this duty.

In the case of restorative justice, I argued that not enough had been done to connect the microforums of community review boards to the larger public debate over criminal justice. Criminal justice professionals owe more work on public engagement because more has been professionalized out of the public domain. Now, just because decisions or tasks have become professionalized does not mean they need to become more public under the democratic professionalism ideal. In the case of criminal justice, however, what criminal justice professionals do to offenders in the name of the public is too far out of the reach of public deliberation.

A leading criminologist, Michael Tonry, asserts that current U.S. criminal justice policies "are the harshest in American history and of any Western country."[3] Most Americans currently think that sentences are too lenient and favor

---

3. "Crime and Punishment in America," in *The Handbook of Crime and Punishment*, ed. Michael Tonry (New York: Oxford University Press, 1998), 3.

"get tough" constraints on judicial and probation discretion such as mandatory minimums and three-strikes sentencing.[4] But what Americans currently think may be a product of recent political history and therefore vulnerable to rational debate. In the American political culture of the past three decades, crime has been used as a campaign issue to wedge voters away from lenient liberals and toward "get tough" conservatives. Because of this history and for fear of losing even more voters to the Republican Party over this issue, Democratic campaigns scarcely deviate on the topic of criminal justice from the Republicans' tough-minded stance. In short, commonsense views of crime control policy have not been given much rational challenge in recent times—at least in the electoral forums of normal politics.

In dialogue-oriented restorative justice forums, by contrast, citizens come in contact with real cases, real victims, and real offenders, rather than the abstractions popularized in campaigns and in media treatments. Some evidence shows that punitive attitudes do diminish with such direct experience.[5] Some public opinion researchers believe that American public opinion skews toward the punitive because of misinformation, lack of knowledge, and overly abstract survey questions. When polled about whether they support "get tough" legislation such as three-strikes policies, people are rarely presented with the financial costs and therefore do not face the very real budget trade-offs such policies mandate. Roberts and Stalans write, "When asked directly whether they support such [recidivist statutes such as three-strikes] legislation, three-quarters of Americans respond affirmatively. However, more refined research reveals important limits to the public support."[6] When asked survey questions with robust characterizations of offenders and offenses, less punitive responses emerge. Although American public opinion is undoubtedly consistently punitive, it is also "mushy"—vulnerable to argument. Americans know that punishment is a lose-lose proposition and are open to alternatives, at least for some classes of offenders.[7] Widespread participation, if structured so that people's views are debated respectfully but forcefully, may correct unreasonable—inaccurate, incoherent, or incomplete—

4. See Julian V. Roberts and Loretta J. Stalans, *Public Opinion, Crime, and Criminal Justice* (Boulder, Colo.: Westview Press, 1997).

5. John Braithwaite and Philip Pettit, "Republican Criminology and Victim Advocacy," *Law and Society Review* 28 (1994): 765–77.

6. Julian V. Roberts and Loretta J. Stalans, "Crime, Criminal Justice, and Public Opinion," in *The Handbook of Crime and Punishment*, ed. Tonry, 48.

7. See Francis T. Cullen, Bonnie S. Fisher, and Brandon K. Applegate, "Public Opinion About Punishment and Corrections," *Crime and Justice* 27 (2000): 7, 46–47.

policy preferences created by campaign and media misinformation, popular stereotypes, and lack of knowledge.

The same thing can be said for taking responsibility for what is done in the name of the public. Restorative justice advocates do not want criminal justice administration to work like a normal bureaucracy, "out of sight, out of mind," smoothly providing public goods. Public safety is a good, of course, but punishment is a bad that the public, they think, needs to reflect on more rather than less. It needs to have more discussions rather than fewer about criminal justice policy. But this "into sight, into mind" perspective is on the margins of contemporary American political culture. According to indicators listing issues of importance, most Americans seem to want to think and talk little about crime and crime control unless mobilized by media or politicians.[8] At least in contemporary America there is little sign of an eager, participatory community base that will take up criminal justice responsibilities evacuated by state actors. Such a base will need to be developed at some cost of time and social resources.

Americans do not tend to think that what is done to offenders and victims in the criminal justice process is the responsibility of all citizens since criminal justice is so often seen as a fixed and logical set of rules enforced by legal professionals. More lay participation in the process, however, should reveal the political origins of the rules and the process and therefore the responsibility citizens have in a democracy to make sure criminal justice expresses the values under which they truly wish to live. Taking responsibility, then, means realizing that criminal justice procedures are not set in stone, that they express values a reflective public may or may not endorse, and therefore that such a public has a responsibility to develop policy that does further the values it endorses.

Equality and Accessibility in Hierarchical, Knowledge-Centric Domains

The medical profession is another example of how avoiding the nondeliberative can very well lead to more positive duties of task sharing and public engagement. The bioethics reform movement is in some respects a successful response

8. Roberts and Stalans write, "Until recently, when placed in the context of other major public policy problems, crime has not assumed a very high profile in America. . . . Over the decade 1985–94, crime was never identified as the country's top problem by more than 2 percent of the population." Since 1994, however, even although crime rates were declining, crime increased in importance as a political issue, with one survey putting it at the third most important social problem. The answer is clear: "These statistics seem to attest to the importance of the media and the influence of politicians in setting the nation's agenda" (*Public Opinion, Crime, and Criminal Justice*, 53–54).

to inadequate representation of patient and research subject interests within hospitals, clinics, and research institutions. Ethics committees involving lay participants unlicensed in medicine have been a way of including those interests and diminishing the social distance between the medical domain and the public.

Like restorative justice, I argued that the bioethics movement could do much more to ensure that public interests and a diversity of voices are heard in the medical domain. This is different from representation in its simplest formulation, in which ethics committees or staff attempt to represent the multiple interests and values found in the community at large. Rather, the more important question is whether a committee is continuously open to the concerns of the general public, or whether it was formed, structured, and driven by the interests and values of medical professionals, administrators, or even bioethicists. Representatives, after all, can too quickly speak the language of decision makers rather than the members of groups they purportedly represent.

One indication that a committee is driven by public concerns can be seen in its founding purposes and its organizational structure. Were proponents of the committee articulating community concerns with health care and biomedical research, and are these concerns reflected in the committee's charter? What community groups, if any, have been active in support of a committee? What care, if any, has been taken in the organization of the committee to encourage public participation in meetings and other educational outreach activities? Another indicator can be seen in the budget, time, and staff or devoted to the committee and how independent, organizationally, it is from hospital administrators and management.

Though it is right to be critical, from a democratic professional standpoint, of the limits and exclusionary tendencies of the methods and scholarly norms of academic philosophy, the role of bioethicist is properly independent of public judgments. An ethics committee is a deliberative body and is not merely representative; the bioethicist serving on the committee or on the staff does not have to think the same way as the average community member, who may have very little working knowledge of health care institutions. Instead, their pressing task is to clarify the terms of the debate. One presumption leading to the creation of such entities as ethics committees is that confusion or conflict exists in public debate over biomedical research, medical decisions, and the distribution of health care resources. It does not follow from democratic professionalism that an ethics committee must close the distance between itself and the public by encouraging members to be more representative, to think like the public.

This distance must be traversed by both committee and public; while it is sometimes the case that this distance may keep the committee from dealing with public concerns, sometimes it means that public concerns are incoherent or misplaced.

A sign that a committee is interested in traversing this distance is that it has established some understanding of popular moral reasoning and decision making related to the issues under consideration. Academic moral theory and applied ethics are useful for clarifying abstract bioethical issues in a way that comports well with professional discourse; they may be less useful for resolving problems that emerge in general public debate. Ethnographers point to the need for greater analysis of how average Americans resolve moral issues related to health care decisions. Such a task is no doubt difficult, but discovering how people in different walks of life confront ethical problems is certainly possible. Such information about public moral reasoning is invaluable if committees are to inform general public debate.

Another indication of whether a committee has an impact on general public discourse is the number of newspaper stories and amount of television coverage about it. Nonetheless, public discourse means more than what journalists, essayists, anchors, commentators, and other members of the "chattering classes" are saying to one another. A better measure would include university social science studies of public opinion related to committee activities.

Though inevitable, the distance between the formal small-group discourse of committees and informal widespread public discourse must be traversed energetically and creatively. Ways of bridging that distance must be built into the very methodology of ethics deliberation and other forms of social inquiry performed by ethics committees.

A Public Work Ethic for Professionals: Collaboration and Contestation

Collaboration: Shared Responsibilities and Coproduction of Public Things

Though it seems counterintuitive, the new normative core of professionalism is task sharing and lay involvement. I have argued that in the post-Parsonsian period of considerable cultural skepticism about authority of all sorts, the responsibility to major social values and purposes—justice, information, and health—that professionals have traditionally claimed as distinguishing their work and justifying their rewards and status must now be seen as a shared responsibility. These things that professionals do are properly public things, just as social trustee theorists have always stressed, yet this must mean, as radical critics have insisted, that the public play some role in crafting them, guiding their production and use.

In this spirit, Harry Boyte writes of professions *as* public work and not merely *doing* public work:

> It is in the long-range self-interest of many professionals to become more interactive with citizens in order to accomplish the broader public purposes of their craft. Nevertheless, in their normal training, professionals learn to see ordinary citizens in a particular fashion that greatly limits such interactions—as needy, victimized, and requiring rescue by educated elites. Incorporating the concept and practice of public work into professional cultures, using concepts and practices of everyday politics, unleashes the democratic potential of knowledge power and thus points toward a different sort of professional practice. Public professional work frees the powers not only of ordinary citizens but also of professionals as well. But changing professional practices and cultures is difficult, because the process entails changing identities and practices to make them more public, as well as adding public concepts.[9]

To fully accomplish those values and purposes that have public connotations, professionals must learn how to integrate lay participants into their work lives by learning how to listen to and collaborate with people untrained in the typical skills and knowledge needed in that profession. Professionals must, as Boyte says, "put themselves back into the mix of interests and views that comprise a diverse group of people," attend "to the larger public meanings and purposes of the discipline or profession," and create "settings for interactive civic learning."[10]

Under the public work ethic, the knowledge and service offered by the professional are not seen as commodities but as co-creations of professional and lay participants. Professional knowledge and service are seen, in Deweyan fashion, as social things that gain value precisely because they are shared and not horded. Seemingly utopian at first glance, this is exactly how the professionals in our cases had come to see the products of their domains. Restorative justice professionals,

9. Boyte, *Everyday Politics,* 113.
10. Boyte, *Everyday Politics,* 119.

for example, came to see bringing justice as something that simply could no longer be the responsibility of professionals alone. Bringing justice is a process that has to be shared in order to have efficacy, the buy-in of local communities, and educative effects for both the professional culture of criminal justice and for the larger public, which preferred not to think about crime and criminals.

A public work ethic differs strikingly from both the social trustee model that pervades applied ethics accounts of professional responsibility and the radical critique of technocratic and disabling professionals found in critical theory. Like radical critics, democratic professionals reject the social trustee idea of doing public things for others, but they do not evacuate the public domain. Public journalists, restorative justice professionals, and bioethics consultants in their different ways exemplify how lay members of the public can, in Boyte's words, *co-create* professional knowledge and services.

Worth underscoring in all three cases is that lay participants are doing more than deliberating—they are acting as consultants and advisers to health care workers and administrators, judging offenders, and influencing what is considered relevant news. The civic task sharing so central to the ideal of democratic professionalism is more than a cognitive and intellectual exercise; it is a real-world effort to gain, share, and improve political experience in the realm of middle democracy so often dominated by professionals.

To retain a market for services, democratic professionals still need to be good at what they do as well as good at task sharing. It is a mistake to think, however, that the meaning and importance of those services can ever be fully defined either by professionals themselves or through the mere market demand for those services. Unless people affected, directly and indirectly, by these services are part of a steering or evaluative process, there is something missing from professional judgments and professional authority. What people really want from a newspaper, for example, cannot be determined simply by sales figures or by wise editors' trustee judgments. Greater lay participation in the newsgathering process educates both professional and public in what sort of professional service best serves public interests. Professions *as* public work avoid the risk of transforming common products—information, justice, and humane health care—into mere commodities: infotainment, McJustice, and schmoctoring.[11]

11. On McJustice, see Rekha Mirchandani, "Battered Women's Movement Ideals and Judge-Led Social Change in Domestic Violence Courts," *The Good Society* 13 (2004): 32–37. On schmoctoring, see Arthur Isak Applbaum, "Doctor, Schmoctor: Practice Positivism and Its Complications," in *Ethics for Adversaries* (Princeton: Princeton University Press, 1999), 46–50.

If understood better by academics and practitioners, professional commitments to task sharing and public engagement, though certainly challenging for both the professionals and laypeople involved and sometimes in tension with traditional occupational norms, may be easier to sustain over time than social trustee roles. With collaboration, professional responsibility is shared, labor is divided, and praise and blame distributed more broadly.

Contestation: Challenging and Respecting Public Preferences

Collaboration means being open to the local knowledge, grounded experience, and distinct interests brought into a professional domain by lay participants. A more democratic source of professional authority cannot mean merely adding up preferences, even the preferences of those most closely affected by a professional decision or practice. Challenging opinions to show their basis and be more open to nonconventional perspectives are also facets of democratic professionalism as a public work ethic.

Robert Reich's rejection of two common democratic ways of legitimating professional judgments in public administration is instructive here. Public managers typically rely on utilitarian cost-benefit analysis and interest-group intermediation to guide discretionary decisions. The first model prompts the official to choose the course that benefits the most without disadvantaging others too much. The limits of this model are fairly clear from the discussion of democratic legitimacy in Chapter 1: those who do lose are hardly glad to hear that they are doing so in the service of the greatest good of the majority. Further, weak preferences, if widespread enough, can trump intensely but scantly held preferences.

Interest group intermediation, by contrast, helps justify discretionary decisions by somehow including representatives of major affected interest groups into the decision process. Under this model, the ideal role of the administrator is referee: "[A] skillful practitioner of negotiation and compromise. He was to be accessible to all organized interests while making no independent judgment of the merits of their claims."[12] The difficulty with this model, however, is that it tends to exclude in practice less organized groups and groups with fewer resources or less institutional leverage.

---

12. Robert Reich, "Policy Making in a Democracy," in *The Power of Public Ideas,* ed. Reich (Cambridge, Mass.: Ballinger, 1988), 129.

Reich argues that both models for legitimating discretionary decision making have failed in practice "to respond adequately to affected interests *and*... to yield efficient solutions."[13] Both models rest on mistaken understandings of democracy and deliberation; they "share a view of democracy in which relevant communications all flow in one direction: from individuals' preferences to public officials, whose job it is to accommodate or aggregate them."[14] Public preferences, however, are and should be shaped through public discourse by interacting with others. Resolving conflicts and disagreements is more than the technical problem of finding the right cost-benefit equation or getting the right interest group representatives in a room and letting them pound on one another for a while. What is missing is the idea that disagreements might get resolved if people come together, deliberate, and start to see problems differently. This process of "civic discovery" can help redefine problems and solutions, stimulate voluntary action, open minds to broader social purposes and goods, and produce decisions that have wider and deeper support.[15] Reich knows that with more public engagement there might very well be negative aspects to civic discovery, such as when deeper conflicts are discovered. But deep conflicts left buried can unsettle agreements in the long term; so, even if they are painful and inefficient in the short term, bringing them to the surface may ultimately produce better results.

Democratic sources of expert or professional authority, then, are a different sort of grounding than bare preferences. It means commitment to some space of both collaboration and contestation. Collaboration is necessary for all the prudential and normative reasons stated for lay participation and task sharing. Contestation is necessary to inform one-sided and underdeveloped opinions whether they are held by professionals or lay participants.

Contestation appeared in all the case discussions. Public journalists such as Cole Campbell expressed the commitment to respect but also inform and correct the public opinions of his readers. In Margaret Urban Walker's vision of bioethics consultation as real deliberative process and space, consultants, health care workers, and community members can share experiences and learn from

13. Reich, "Policy Making in a Democracy," 137.
14. Reich, "Policy Making in a Democracy," 138.
15. Frank Fischer is rightly suspicious of Reich's model of "civic discovery," noting that it is ambiguous about just how much public engagement is needed and just how open the public manager is to true, not token, participation ("Citizens and Experts: Democratizing Policy Deliberation," in *Reframing Public Policy: Discursive Politics and Deliberative Practices* [New York: Oxford University Press], 207–8). My point here is that Reich has underscored the weakness of two common ways of how professionals can be more democratic, not that he has the best model of democratic professionalism.

one another. Vermont Reparative Probation was motivated in part by the belief that public opinion about criminal justice goals and values could be improved by more participation and reflection. Part of the crisis of professionalism and the lack of trust or faith in professional authority stems from public ignorance about complex discretionary decisions made by professionals—whether involving sentencing, editorial positions, or health care policies. As Eliot Freidson notes, "[T]he most important problem for the future of professionalism is neither economic nor structural but cultural and ideological." In the face of public distrust about their privileges and authority, writes Freidson, true professionals continue to hold a "devotion to the use of disciplined knowledge and skill for the public good" and "have the duty to appraise what they do in light of that larger good, a duty which licenses them to be more than passive servants of the state, of capital, of the firm, of the client, or even of the immediate general public."[16]

Adding contestation to the value of collaboration that is central to the public work ethic is also necessary to adequately harness professional integrity to a more open and public mode of legitimacy. In all the cases, democratic professionals sought to hold onto a sense of integrity derived both from serving public interests and from upholding professional values and goals as defined, at least in part, by fellow professionals. To be democratic *and* professional, this private commitment to expertise and skill that cannot ever be fully shared with laypeople has to be present. Professionalism is a passion, a life commitment that can demand sacrifice of personal comfort and even safety and that can become, at times, the most pressing facet of a person's life. One feature of social trustee thinking endorsed by democratic professionalism is the point that specialized, expert cultures with some autonomy over their practices and, perhaps, with some special status, privilege, or resources have public value even if they seem odd or unconventional from the outside.

The point of democratic professionalism as an ideal is not to dull commitments to professionalism but to sharpen them and place them in a context where they can be both challenged and respected. In such a collaborative and contestatory context, professional values and goals are given the respect they are due, the legitimacy they need, and whatever status and rewards they deserve on a more solid footing. Democratic professionalism is a critical reconstruction of professionalism in the wake of the collapse of the social trustee model and the

16. Eliot Freidson, *Professionalism: The Third Logic* (Chicago: University of Chicago Press, 2001), 213, 217.

insufficiencies of deprofessionalism as a solution to the antidemocratic tendencies of commercial and technocratic expertise. As an ideal, it emerges from professionals' own self-understanding and nonprofessionals' recognition that there is much to admire and support in professions.

Offering one explanation why philosophers and laypeople untrained in medicine have become so attracted to the study of normative issues in that field, Stanley Hauerwas reflects, along Durkheimian lines, on the exemplary nature of professional work at its best:

> Yet exactly to the extent that medical care has remained committed to those it cannot cure, medicine provides one of the more profound practices on which we can draw in our culture for moral example. I suspect, moreover, that so many of us have been drawn to medicine precisely because by attending to the actual practice of medicine . . . many of us who have been associated with ethics have for the first time discovered what a substantive moral practice actually looks like.[17]

Bioethics as a critical discourse is fueled by the dogged commitment to the well-being of strangers found in the practice of medicine itself. Restorative justice is driven by unceasing concern for fairness, justice, and personal and social transformation. Public journalism is motivated by a devotion to uncovering hard and useful facts that help people make better and more informed decisions. Though this book has stressed how such professionals can and should be guided by concrete public involvement, it is equally important that lay publics be challenged by the knowledge and experience of committed professionals.

Professions, Ethics, and Democracy

Where do the explicitly democratic values of democratic professionalism fit with the other normative constraints and guides commonly discussed as fixtures of professional ethics? The case of bioethics brought such issues to the forefront, but they relate to professions more generally and are particularly pressing if we think about how democratic professionalism can be integrated as a topic in professional

17. Stanley Hauerwas, "Why I Am Neither a Communitarian nor a Medical Ethicist," in "The Birth of Bioethics," special supplement, *Hastings Center Report* 23 (1993): 9.

ethics training whether in organizations and institutions themselves or in college and university courses. What is the status of lay participation and public engagement, exactly, compared with the values commonly treated in professional ethics casebooks and analyses: consent, privacy, autonomy, and truth telling, for example? The latter seem like different kinds of concepts, and the textbooks certainly have treated them as such. This complex question cannot be treated sufficiently here, but I do want to offer some thoughts and indicate directions for a fuller treatment since democratic professionalism is an ideal with rich potential for reconceiving professional and applied ethics.

One way of looking at the normative status of participation in collective decision making is to see it as something separate that must be given its due even if it is in tension with other values. Here, a longstanding dispute in political theory about how well democracy fits with liberal commitments to civil liberties and civil rights is relevant. In a well-known essay on philosophy and democracy, Michael Walzer claims that "it is a feature of democratic government that the people have a right to act wrongly."[18] With this assertion, Walzer defends the distinct value of sovereignty for citizens of a democracy against the value of following the "right" path. Walzer recognizes that popular sovereignty cannot be accepted as a trump value, but he argues that philosophers too easily discount popular sovereignty to privilege values that their own intellectual training and experience lead them to favor. Even Jean Jacques Rousseau, often heralded as the philosopher of popular sovereignty, doubted the public's capacity for reason.[19] Rousseau, according to Walzer, sensibly held that it would be illegitimate for popular assemblies to renounce their own sovereignty or support laws that discriminated against classes of citizens. But Rousseau went too far when he sought ways of limiting popular sovereignty to ensure that the people's will was in accord with his vision of correct values, as in his endorsement of the near-divine legislator who would shape communal institutions so that a general will might emerge.

If democratic legitimacy means collective decisions by the individuals who are the subjects of those decisions, the role of the philosopher or ethics expert in a democracy cannot be to determine which, if any, of those collective decisions

---

18. Michael Walzer, "Philosophy and Democracy," *Political Theory* 9 (1981): 385.

19. See Benjamin Barber, *Strong Democracy: Participatory Politics for a New Age* (Berkeley and Los Angeles: University of California Press, 2004), 200, for a view of Rousseau as a theorist of popular sovereignty.

are "right" by external standards of justice, fairness, autonomy, and the like. Walzer holds that philosophers in a democracy should adopt an attitude of "philosophical restraint"—"simply the respect that outsiders owe to the decisions that citizens make among themselves and for themselves." Walzer's democratic philosopher is not a legislator manqué, but a "sophist, critic, publicist, or intellectual," someone who "can still claim to be right, [but] cannot claim any of the privileges of rightness."[20]

This approach to conceptualizing participation as a value separate from and potentially conflicting with other important public values fails to appreciate how saturated any defensible conception of participation already is with a number of other values that check and guide it. Amy Gutmann, among others, has pointed out how even conceptions of democracy as a power-sharing procedure such as Walzer's contain constraints on popular will. Walzer himself endorses principles of nondiscrimination as fundamental constraints, writing, "The people must will generally. They cannot single out (except in elections for public office) a particular individual or set of individuals from among themselves for special treatment." Gutmann points out that democracy cannot really be said to be valuable without some constraints on repression; democratic power sharing has not really taken place, for example, if those in power refuse to leave, or repress those who challenge their authority.[21]

In Gutmann's view, taking these principles of nondiscrimination and non-repression seriously means setting these and perhaps other related restrictions on the sphere of democratic choice and popular influence. A democracy may do well to constitutionalize such principles and empower high courts to review legislation and executive acts to see if they are repressive or discriminatory. In doing so, Gutmann argues, such a democracy is not becoming less democratic, it is becoming more solidly democratic since part of the meaning of democracy is sharing power and these rights ensure the "real" rather than "symbolic" sharing of power. In Gutmann's words, to ensure the fairness of the democratic process is to "protect democracy from itself."[22]

If Walzer fails to see how saturated democracy is with other public values, so does Gutmann fail to see how values such as nondiscrimination and

20. Walzer, "Philosophy and Democracy," 396.
21. Amy Gutmann, "How Liberal Is Democracy?" in *Liberalism Reconsidered,* ed. Douglas Maclean and Claudia Mills (Totowa, N.J.: Rowman and Allanheld, 1983), 25–50.
22. Gutmann, "How Liberal Is Democracy," 31.

nonrepression are saturated with democracy. Their substance and meaning shift over time and in response to different historical events and experiences. The practice of public values guides and constrains democracy, yet that the practice of democracy guides and constrains the interpretation and use of public values is equally true. This is so in many ways, not least of which are the pressures of public opinion on those officials who sit in judgment and make decisions.

Wider Reflective Equilibrium

The tensions between democracy and other public values could be relaxed if what appear as two sources of legitimacy were actually coordinated. A prominent approach in ethics, stemming from the later work of John Rawls and its practical extension by Norman Daniels, holds that public procedures of ethical deliberation can clarify principles while still allowing moral disagreements. Since reasonable people disagree on what constitutes a good life and the best ends of the various institutions in which they participate, processes must be instituted to assure that decisions respect these differences. Such processes have at least four stages or conditions: a publicity condition that dictates that the reasons behind decisions be made public; a reciprocity condition that limits the majority to making decisions on the basis of reasons that are recognized as valid even by those in the minority; a due process condition that allows the minority some opportunity to challenge and revise the decision; and an accountability condition that holds the prior conditions open to formal oversight and regulation. Writing in the context of managed-care decision making, Daniels and Sabin further elaborate these conditions:

1. Decisions regarding coverage for new technologies (and other limit-setting decisions) and their rationales must be publicly accessible.
2. The rationales for coverage decisions should aim to provide a *reasonable* construal of how the organization should provide "value for money" in meeting the varied health needs of a defined population. Specifically, a construal will be "reasonable" if it appeals to reasons and principles that are accepted as relevant by people who are disposed to finding terms of cooperation that are mutually justifiable.
3. There is a mechanism for challenge and dispute resolution regarding limit-setting decisions, including the opportunity for revising decisions in light of further evidence or arguments.

4. There is either voluntary or public regulation of the process to ensure that conditions 1–3 are met.[23]

On its face, this procedure for reaching ethical collective decisions regarding professional services appears to escape Walzer's choice between public and philosophical legitimacy by being both public and philosophical. Yet, each of these conditions permits remarkably expansive interpretations. Is the publicity condition met by simply declaring a formal decision-making meeting "open to the public" even if the meeting is held at a time and location practically inaccessible to working people? What if it is held only in the nation's capital, in a remote wing of a bureaucracy? Is the reciprocity condition satisfied when nobody complains, or is it necessary to actively search out potential opposition among affected citizens? Is the due-process condition met when only those informed about and active in the public decision-making process know they have such recourse and possess the capabilities to articulate grievances? Is the accountability condition met when those who have a stake in limiting public participation in regulation declare the publicity, reciprocity, and due-process conditions satisfied?

Procedures are only as public as they are concretely open to public participation. Daniels and Sabin's discussion leaves much leeway for a form of public deliberation where deliberative experts decide what counts as satisfying the underlying conditions. Read democratically, however, the model of deliberation they propose points to a different conception of applied and professional ethics expertise similar to Walzer's philosophical constraint. An expert in applied and professional ethics who is interested in a process of ethical deliberation will want to facilitate more rather than less substantive achievements of these conditions. Such a person would likely seek more than minimal compliance with these requirements. Where there is little access, little formal representation of dissent, sparse participation, and a small scope of accountability, there is also little public legitimacy.

This book started by arguing for a conception of democracy in which public deliberation could give voice to ethical issues and press officials and citizens to high standards of respectful and reasonable debate. It is fitting to come full circle to a conception of professional ethics in which public deliberation plays a central role. These reflections on the place of commitments to such deliberation

---

23. Norman Daniels and James Sabin, "Limits to Health Care: Fair Procedures, Democratic Deliberation, and the Legitimacy Problem for Insurers," *Philosophy and Public Affairs* 26 (1997): 323.

within professional ethics point to the nexus between knowledge of the ethical and knowledge of those others we will only ever come to know, work with, appreciate, and question in the fluid, challenging politics of middle democracy. Opening doors to this participation within professional domains and in those parts of public life influenced by them has and will continue to enliven and enlarge professional ethics and citizen politics.

CONCLUSION:

THE UNIVERSITY'S ROLE IN THE

DEMOCRATIZATION OF PROFESSIONAL ETHICS

[T]he nucleus of the cluster of the professions is the profession of learning itself.
—TALCOTT PARSONS, "Remarks on Education and the Professions" (1937)

Neophytes currently undergoing professional training lack instruction in the democratic consequences of the domains they will enter—the hospitals and clinics, newspapers and news studios, courtrooms and corrections facilities. At a time when ethics scandals in accounting, journalism, and other professions have drawn fresh attention to the need to rethink ethics pedagogy in professional schools, opportunities exist to incorporate the teaching of explicitly democratic duties to foster lay participation and task sharing into ethics seminars and workshops and to creatively awaken students' attentiveness to the prudential and normative reasons that support this new vision of professional integrity. This book supports such an effort by reorienting the teaching of professional ethics, focusing attention on the actions of democratic professional reformers, and fueling further discussions of the important roles of professionals in democracy.

Setting a Good Example

Flamboyant ethical failures in the last five years have eroded public trust in some of the country's most prominent firms and, more generally, in the concept of professionalism. Dramatic cases of professional dishonesty, fraud, concealment of public records, and other abuses have exposed chronic problems.

On May 25, 2006, former Enron chief executives Kenneth Lay and Jeffrey Skilling were convicted on multiple counts of fraud and conspiracy by a Texas jury. At its highpoint, Enron was the seventh largest company in the country, but the picture of success executives presented to Wall Street was built on fabricated profit numbers supported by compromised accounting. Caught up in the debacle was Arthur Andersen, a big five accounting firm known for impeccable professional standards. It had violated these standards as pressures grew within the accounting firm to support one of its largest clients, one with which it had closely intermingled business consulting interests. After a criminal indictment and then conviction in 2002, Andersen went bankrupt. Though the conviction was overturned on appeal to the Supreme Court, Andersen is now a nonentity in the accounting world, with only two hundred of the twenty-eight thousand employees once employed in the United States.[1]

On May 1, 2003, Jayson Blair resigned from the *New York Times* after it was discovered that his recent front-page article on a Texas soldier missing in action in Iraq had liberally borrowed from an article published in a Texas newspaper without attributing the source.[2] An internal inquiry by the *Times* later found evidence that he had plagiarized on many other occasions, fabricated interviews, claimed datelines from Maryland, West Virginia, Texas, and other states while he was writing from New York, and falsified expense accounts to cover his tracks. These severe breaches of professional ethics had occurred while he had covered prominent stories, such as the Washington, D.C., sniper case in the fall of 2002 and the story of Private Jessica Lynch's capture and rescue in Iraq. Blair wrote five articles on Lynch, some of which had Palestine, West Virginia, as a dateline. The *Times* now doubts whether he had ever visited West Virginia to interview the Lynch family.[3] Responding to what it called a low point in the 152-year history of the paper, the *Times* replaced executive editor Howell Raines and managing editor Gerald Boyd and conducted a major internal review of fact-checking procedures.[4]

Responses to these dramatic ethical failures have sought greater transparency and accountability to public interests. Reacting to Andersen and Enron, Congress passed the Sarbanes-Oxley legislation, increasing government oversight of corporate accounting practices and prohibiting accounting firms from providing both auditing and business consulting services to the same clients.[5] What had once been seen as a matter best handled within professions, a matter of

1. Jonathan D. Glater, "Enron Trial Stirs Memory of Andersen," *New York Times,* February 21, 2006, C1.

2. Jacques Steinberg, "*Times* Reporter Resigns After Questions on Article," *New York Times,* May 2, 2003, A30.

3. Dan Barry, David Barstow, Jonathan D. Glater, Adam Liptak, and Jacques Steinbert, "Correcting the Record: *Times* Reporter Who Resigned Leaves Long Trail of Deception," *New York Times,* May 11, 2003, A1.

4. Byron Calame, "The Miller Mess: Lingering Issues Among the Answers," *New York Times,* October 23, 2005, D12.

5. Glater, "Enron Trial."

professional autonomy, is now an issue for official public scrutiny. At the *Times,* in addition to leadership changes, the newspaper empowered a public editor and charged him with the tasks of "publicly evaluating, criticizing and otherwise commenting on the paper's integrity." The public editor understood his charge as being a representative of the public, a conduit for lay criticism of reporting and editorial practice who had an "all-access backstage pass" to get answers from *Times* journalists and managers.[6] He was given space in print every other week to pass along readers' comments, address readers' concerns, and assess the newspaper's attempts at rebuilding public trust after the Blair episode. Though the first and present public editors are both seasoned journalists, their role is to inject outsiders' and lay perspectives into the assessment of professional standards at the most respected newspaper in the country.[7]

Many concerned about an ethical crisis in American professions point to the university as a critical part of the solution. University faculty serve as gatekeepers to professions, sources of professional knowledge, standard bearers of technique, and role models of professional ethics. University curricula are normally the first stage of socialization in professional ethics. As William Sullivan writes, "As students experience it, the knowledge and skills that faculty . . . expect *is* the profession, for practical purposes. Therefore, it matters a great deal just what is put forward as significant through the medium of requirements, subject matter, and modes of assessment."[8] In the professional schools where neophytes learn to think like journalists, lawyers, and doctors and begin to take the first steps of professional practice, ethics training is already a fixed part of the curriculum. For those not attending professional school, courses in professional ethics, applied ethics, and critical thinking about values are commonly encouraged if not mandated for undergraduate degrees.

Professional ethics as it is currently taught in most universities, however, tends to be either abstracted from the contemporary professional workplace or embroiled in workaday issues. A survey of ethics textbooks reveals a bipolar landscape, which is also evidenced in course syllabi as well. On the one end are texts that pit Kantian, consequentialist (utilitarian), virtue ethics doctrines against one another, with the goals of sensitizing students to core strengths and weaknesses

6. Daniel Okrent, "The Public Editor: An Advocate for *Times* Readers Introduces Himself," *New York Times,* December 7, 2003, D2.

7. Byron Calame, "The New Public Editor: Toward Greater Transparency," *New York Times,* June 5, 2005, D14.

8. William M. Sullivan, "Markets vs. Professions: Value Added?" *Daedalus* 134 (Summer 2005): 23.

of these traditions, introducing major concepts such as autonomy, justice, and impartiality and, above all else, developing moral reasoning skills. On the other end are texts that present quasi-historical accounts of the development of medical, legal, and journalistic ethics, discuss codes of ethics, and describe common ethical problems faced by organizations, such as the definition and institutional response to workplace sexual harassment, and what counts as a violation of current laws related to professional practice.

The limitations of current ethics training are made clear by two major research projects devoted to professional ethics training and pedagogy that shift focus away from abstract problem-solving techniques and workplace issues and toward the importance of what can be called character building. The decade-long Good-Work project, led by Howard Gardner at Harvard University, has interviewed journalists, scientists, professors, lawyers, and others to seek out ways to support "good work"—high-quality, socially responsible, professional work.[9] Since 1999, the Carnegie Foundation for the Advancement of Teaching has aimed at the same target through its program on Preparing Professionals as Moral Agents, focusing on clergy, legal, nursing, engineering, and teacher education.[10]

Both research teams have pinpointed deficits in professional ethics education. In law schools, for example, in the midst of a training that stresses impartial, realist analysis of legal cases purged of normative assumptions, budding professionals are required to take an ethics for lawyers course. "Most often," write scholars affiliated with both the GoodWork and Carnegie projects, "this course is structured around legal cases that concern alleged violations of the American Bar Association's ethical code. Students apply their analytic skills to these cases, approaching them the same way they deal with challenging legal cases in torts or contracts." By contrast, these scholars recommend what can be called a "moral exemplar" model of training, praising a course at the University of North Carolina law school that asks students to interview widely respected and honored lawyers and judges about their career decisions. Students in such courses "have

---

9. See Howard Gardner, Mihaly Csikszentmihalyi, and William Damon, *Good Work: When Excellence and Ethics Meet* (New York: Basic Books, 2001). The ongoing project Web site is http://www.goodworkproject.org (accessed June 2007).

10. The first book in a series that will cover the professional training of nurses, doctors, engineers, lawyers, and the clergy is *Educating Clergy: Teaching Practices and Pastoral Imagination* by Charles R. Foster, Lisa Dahill, Larry Golemon, and Barbara Wang Tolentino (San Francisco: Jossey-Bass, 2006). Information on the project is available at the foundation Web site: http://www.carnegiefoundation.org (accessed June 2007).

the opportunity to internalize heroic images of professionalism, and to draw on these when confronting difficult moral problems."[11]

Conducting interviews, studying moral exemplars, taking cues from faculty who practice what they preach, and being part of an educational process that is marked by integrity and social responsibility are all significant reinforcements to mainstream professional ethics training at the undergraduate and graduate levels. They reflect the need for professionals who have the dispositions and moral stamina to successfully brace themselves against the pressures of status, money, and power when these menace integrity and core professional values. Cultivation of character, to the extent that this is possible in adulthood, is no doubt a worthy addition to today's professional ethics curriculum.

The democratic professionalism perspective advanced in this book challenges these curricular reforms to go some steps in a different direction. Professional ethics training in law, medical, and journalism schools and in the mid-career workshops for professionals conducted at universities and by professional organizations should include the following goals:

Develop democratic self-reflectiveness: Cultivate an awareness of both the negative and positive impact of a given profession's norms and practices on core aspects of contemporary citizenship, such as knowledge of and trust in social and political institutions.

Encourage public contributions to professional ethics: Recognize that understanding and resolving, if only temporarily, ethical problems facing professionals will necessarily include laypeople affected by professional choices.

Encourage professional contributions to public ethics: Recognize that professional knowledge and experience can respectfully be brought to bear on inconsistent, mistaken, or incomplete public attitudes.

Create spaces and opportunities for meaningful lay participation: Be sensitive to the ways professional knowledge and practice would be strengthened by lay involvement and concrete task sharing.

Academic attunement to reform movements within the professions such as the public journalism, restorative justice, and bioethics movements discussed here is one way to encourage growth of a more democratic professionalism.

11. William Damon, Anne Colby, Kendall Bronk, and Thomas Ehrlich, "Passion and Mastery in Balance: Toward Good Work in the Professions," *Daedalus* 134 (Summer 2005): 32.

These movements are on the front lines of the struggle to rebuild public trust in the everyday practice of journalism, law, and medicine. Attunement means teaching about success stories as well as failed attempts, the overly grandiose projects put forward in the name of a more democratic professionalism and the cases of power sharing in professional domains that hindered rather than facilitated effective problem solving.

Reorienting professional ethics education along the lines suggested here is possible because of current public and academic interest in changes to professional education. Yet, it must be acknowledged that the American university currently finds itself in peculiar straits. At a time when higher education in the United States serves as a global model and a powerful magnet attracting the gifted and able from all over the world, it is under increasing scrutiny from federal and state governments demanding more accountability for university budgets, less discretionary authority for faculty in their classrooms, and more responsiveness in the practice of both teaching and research to the direct economic needs of their region or state.

The Public University

It may seem quixotic to ask universities to embrace a more democratic conception of professionalism at a time when the professionalism of university faculty is under sharp attack by some for being overly influenced by left-wing politics. No mere war of words, the current battle in the ongoing culture wars embroiling campuses involves the "academic bills of rights" proposed but not yet signed into law in fifteen states and the U.S. Congress. These bills borrow their principles and language from mock legislation proposed by the Students for Academic Freedom group organized by conservative activist David Horowitz.[12] The bills demand significant scrutiny of classroom techniques, syllabi, and hiring and promotion decisions to make sure that public universities do not discriminate on the basis of political allegiances. Ohio Senate Bill 24 introduced in 2005, for example, lists as one mandate that "[f]aculty and instructors shall not infringe the academic freedom and quality of education of their students by persistently introducing controversial matter into the classroom or coursework

12. See http://www.studentsforacademicfreedom.org/abor.html (accessed June 2007).

that has no relation to their subject of study and that serves no legitimate ped-agogical purpose."[13]

Reminiscent of the radical critique of professional power, Horowitz claims that the ur-profession of the academy has a subterranean political agenda that should be brought to light and transformed. While the earlier critique urged professionals to become more critical about how their knowledge and skills played a role in supporting—sometimes indirectly—dominant social, political, and economic values, Horowitz urges academics to be more critical about their opposition to such dominant values and sensitive to ways that their own left-liberal views lead them to dismiss the dominant values and mainstream politi-cal opinion of their students. To reclaim their professionalism, Horowitz insists that faculty take care to steer clear of partisan symbolism and commentary while on the job: "We don't go to our doctor's offices expecting to get political lectures. That is because doctors are professionals who have taken an oath to treat all, regardless of political belief. To introduce divisive matters into a med-ical consultation would injure the trust between doctor and patient that is cru-cial to healing. Why is the profession of education any different? It isn't."[14]

Though universities likely will be able to fend off such legislation by tin-kering with their internal professional ethics codes and their student grievance policies, the reservoir of public distrust that some state and national politicians seek to tap through such legislation will be harder to treat. A *Columbus Dispatch* editorial declaring Ohio Senate Bill 24 as "unworkable," for example, also noted that "[i]f Ohioans, more than half of whom voted Republican in the presiden-tial election, think that their views have been banished from higher education, then the public tax support and private donations to those schools could be undermined."[15] Such sensitivity to whether the university is "for us" or rather "above us" and "against us" may be at the root of a more serious and more gen-eral weakening of public commitments to higher education in states like Ohio.

Democratic professionalism goes to the heart of such distrust, advocating a greater role for lay members of the public within university life and a greater role for university-trained professionals in public life. By reducing the social distance between professionals and the public they serve, efforts in democratic

13. See http://www.legislature.state.oh.us/bills.cfm?ID=126_SB_24 (accessed June 2007).
14. David Horowitz, "College Professors Should Be Made to Teach, Not Preach," *USA Today,* March 24, 2005, A13.
15. "Challenge to Colleges: Higher Education Ought to Seek Greater Diversity of Viewpoints on Faculties," *Columbus Dispatch,* February 15, 2005, A8.

professionalism confront the crude us/them thinking behind recent ideological attacks on the university. True inclusion of lay voices entails respect but not automatic deference and certainly not the atrophy of critical discourse advocated by Horowitz. Where mainstream views and values clash with what is accepted wisdom in a given profession, professors and practitioners must feel free to challenge them strongly even if a (decreasing) share of their salaries is subsidized by tax revenues. Collaboration and contention are a powerful combination, bringing different perspectives, specialized knowledge, and deep passions together to confront questions of health and well-being, justice, public information, and others that have no single good commonsense or academic answers: when should someone be called "dead," what is the right sentence for aggravated assault, when is something "news"?

The need for more ethical professions is a need for stronger and more democratic professions to socialize and motivate the next generation of doctors, nurses, reporters, editors, lawyers, judges, and many others to meet new challenges creatively, skillfully, and collaboratively. The theory and practice of modern professionalism shows how the devoted commitment to performing socially necessary tasks must be aligned with a willingness to work with laypeople and to both accept and challenge lay views of proper goals, standards, and practices. What is it to serve the public good without an adequate understanding of the public? This Deweyan problem faces all thoughtful students of the professions, and many are acting to resolve it. Less aloof, democratic professionals are no less worthy of respect than their social trustee forebears. We see this as we begin to notice those already playing a role in our everyday lives.

INDEX

Abbott, Andrew, 71–75, 84
Academic Bill of Rights, 272–73
academic profession, 272–74
Ackerman, Bruce, 32
acquisitive society, 54
Andersen, Arthur, 267–68
apathy, 113, 125. *See also* citizen participation
applied ethics, 8–9
Ashworth, Andrew, 196
authority
    of administrators, 107
    democratic, 101, 259
    of doctors, 59–60
    expert, 119
    functionally specific, 57
    political, 109, 111, 114
    professional, 64, 67, 83, 92, 95–96, 101–2
    skill and training based, 247
    social grounds of, 163
    technocratic, 124
    trust based, 123
autonomy. *See* professions, self-regulation

Baker, Brenda, 189
Barber, Bernard, 47
Bazemore, Gordon, 190
Beecher, Henry, 209–10
Bessette, Joseph, 30
Binghamton *Press and Sun Bulletin*, 150–51
bioethics, 82, 91, 207–9. *See also* bioethics
    consultants
    authority in medical decision making,
        210–12, 217
    courts, 215
    criticisms of, 225–38
    democratic professionalism, 207, 216–17,
        221, 237–43, 246–47, 253–55
    doctor-patient relationship, 211, 216, 217,
        246, 261
    expert commissions, 213–14
    expertise in, 227–29, 231
    human subjects research, 209–10, 213, 217

    institutional constraints on, 212, 218, 231–32,
        241
    lay participation, 217, 242
    methods of, 225–26, 228, 230–31, 233–37,
        240, 254–55
    new technologies, 210–11
    nonmedical training in, 209, 216, 224
    power relations, 236–37, 239, 241
    public deliberation, 238–40, 242, 255
    public interests, 208, 210, 229, 254
    reprofessionalization of, 207, 224
    sites in health care organizations, 214–16,
        227, 236, 243, 254–55
    social critic role, 233–36, 239
    social movement features, 208–9, 217
    social science, 225, 230, 234
    task sharing, 217–18
    trust, 217
bioethics consultants, 207, 218–24
    authority, 218, 220–21, 236
    independence, 241, 254
    liminality, 218–21, 225, 227
    overloaded role, 222–24, 227
    pluralism, 222–23, 230
    public responsibilities, 219–23, 228, 235,
        242–43, 254–55
    relationships with doctors, 219–21, 232, 236
    responsibilities to patents, 219–23, 230, 243
    status, 218, 220
    training, 222, 224
Blair, Jayson, 268–69
body, 59–60, 221
Bohman, James, 14
Bosk, Charles, 212
Boyte, Harry, 39–40, 247, 256–57
Braithwaite, John, 186, 188, 190
Brint, Steven, 81, 82, 84
Broder, David, 140

Callahan, Daniel, 212, 234
Campbell, Cole, 147, 149, 161, 170, 259
capitalism, 47, 117

Carey, James, 142, 155, 160
case study method, 38, 133, 135–36
Centano, Miguel, 85
centralization, 113–14
Charlotte Observer, 146–47
Charon, Rita, 233
Christie, Nils, 80, 92, 96, 103, 175, 179, 183, 191, 193
Churchill, Larry, 230
citizen participation
    and freedom, 115–16
    low levels of, 27, 126
    normative status of, 262–64
    professionals as barriers to, 85–91, 96, 100, 102, 106, 133
    as watchdog on elites, 110
citizenship
    consumer model, 36, 95, 184
    habits of, 108–9, 113
    public work model, 40
civil associations, 108, 113
civil society, 114
Clear, Todd R., 190–91
Clifford, James, 237
collaboration. *See* task sharing
collectivity-orientation, 58, 75. *See also* social responsibility
competition, 71, 73, 84
complacency, 20
complexity, 28, 99, 115–17, 128
Constant, Benjamin, 22–24
contestation, 258–61, 274
cost-benefit analysis, 259
credibility. *See* trust
Crigger, Bette-Jane, 220–21
crime, 189, 251–52
criminal justice. *See also* restorative justice
    politics, 252
    public involvement in, 183–93, 204–5, 251–52
    task monopoly, 92
    values, 183
Croly, Herbert, 4–5, 116
culture, 21, 118

Daly, Kathleen, 177
Daniels, Norman, 264–65
deference, 102, 106, 107, 109, 111, 114
    democratic, 111, 118, 130, 247
deLeon, Peter, 87–88, 90
deliberative norms, 15–18, 165–68, 240, 264
deliberative opinion poll, 30–32

delusions of civic grandeur, 100, 138, 163–70
democracy
    deliberative, 14–15, 17–19, 24
    direct, 108, 110
    middle, 10, 13, 37–38, 99, 104, 266
    role of citizen, 38, 262–64
    social context, 37
    theories of, 24, 84, 262–64
democratic professionalism, 100, 114, 173. *See also* bioethics, public journalism, restorative justice
    authority, 163
    communication networks, 248
    in complex organizations, 245
    contestation, 258–61
    defined, 10, 130, 249
    difficulties of the role, 132, 136, 160, 221, 245
    duties of, 248, 250–51
    as an ethical perspective, 3, 132
    fallibility, 248
    heroism, 247
    integrity, 246, 260
    lay participation, 193, 246, 250, 256–57
    motivations for, 245–47, 250
    participatory democratic values of, 101
    political role, 41, 131, 136, 249–50
    professional self-interest, 41, 130–31, 245–46
    in public administration, 258–59
    public deliberation, 10, 136, 250, 258
    public work, 255–58
    reform movement, 3, 10, 132, 135, 246
    task sharing, 130, 193, 255, 258
    traditional professional services, 257–58
    trust, 273–74
    as utopian, 247
deprofessionalization, 80, 96–97, 99–101, 246, 261
despotism, 108, 112–13
Dewey, John
    associated intelligence, 116–17, 121, 173
    democracy as a way of life, 37, 115, 117
    democratic professionalism, 5, 106, 115–22, 131
    experts, 4–5, 102
    face-to-face democracy, 4
doctors. *See* medicine
Dryzek, John, 14
Durkheim, Emile
    functionalism of, 52
    moral particularism of professions, 6, 134
    moral socialization in professions, 48–49

self-regulation of professions, 50
solidarity in professions, 50–52
Dworkin, Ronald, 8, 166

education, 61–62, 120–21, 132, 261–62
efficiency, 74, 124
elections, 111–13
elites, 106, 112
Engelhardt, H. Tristram, 231
engineering, 61, 62, 81
Enron, 267–68
equality, 107, 112
Esquith, Stephen, 83
ethical deliberation, 264–66
ethics commission, 90
Euben, Peter, 83
experts, 92, 93, 117, 119, 125, 228
  in ethics, 262, 265
  role in government, 4, 28–29, 85

fairness, 98
Fallows, James, 141, 143
Feinberg, Joel, 189
Fischer, Frank, 80, 86–88, 106, 122, 125–29, 131
Fishkin, James, 30, 32
Flynn, Patricia, 232
Foucault, Michel, 6, 80, 94, 96–97, 103
Fouhy, Edward, 139
Fox, Renee, 223
Frader, Joel, 224
Freidson, Eliot, 64–68, 260
Friedland, Lewis, 147
functionalism, 52

Galston, William, 8
Gardner, Howard, 270
grounding, 135–36. See also case study method
guilds, 52, 100
Gutmann, Amy, 16, 37–38, 240–41, 263

Habermas, Jürgen, 6, 16, 33–34
Hauerwas, Stanley, 261
Have, Henk ten, 225–26
health policy, 97
higher education. See university
Hoffmaster, Barry, 230
Horowitz, David, 272–73
Hughes, Everett, 45, 46, 59

ideology, 64, 68–70
Illich, Ivan, 80, 91, 93–94, 96, 103

individualism, 47, 113, 120
industrial development, 47
inequality, 36
informal justice, 98
injustice, 20
interest groups, 259
intermediary institutions, 108, 113

Jefferson, Thomas, 38
Jennings, Bruce, 40 n. 61, 93, 242–43
Jonson, Albert, 210
journalism. See also public journalism
  adversary norms, 26, 143, 168
  conflict emphasis, 144
  democratic professionalism in, 120–21
  democratic values, 167
  infotainment, 140, 150
  legitimacy of, 171
  market-driven, 139–40, 142
  and nondeliberative politics, 26, 140–42
  use of official sources, 144
  professional norms, 142
  public trust, 143
journalists
  authority, 171
  privileges, 142
  public opinion about, 141–42
  social trustee role, 142, 143
  status, 142
  as watchdogs, 143, 149, 168–69
judges, 109, 111, 114, 118
jury, 107–11, 118

Kari, Nancy, 39
Karp, David R., 190–91
Kennedy, Edward, 213
King, Martin Luther, 20
Kleinman, Arthur, 235, 238
knowledge
  conventional, 118
  definitive of professions, 45, 58, 71, 84, 102
  local, 128
  public, 116
  technocratic, 85–91
Krause, Elliott, 100

Larson, Magali Sarfatti, 68–70
law, 49, 61–62, 81, 114
Lay, Kenneth, 267
League of Women Voters, 170
Lee, Richard Henry, 38, 110

legitimacy, 88, 91, 99, 103, 240–41, 262
  cost-benefit analysis, 258
  defined, 18
  interest groups, 258
  jury, 111
  of professions, 62, 74, 122–23, 126, 163, 260
  public deliberation, 18–22, 264–65
  public participation, 128
liberalism, 54
liberty, 22–24, 107
Lichtenberg, Judith, 156
Lippmann, Walter, 4–5, 28–29, 116–17, 120
Luntz, Frank, 26

Maine Sunday Telegram, 153
Majone, Giandomenico, 93
Manin, Bernard, 21
Mansbridge, Jane, 30, 38
market, 47, 48, 82, 100–101
Marx, Karl, 57
medicine, 64–67
  commitment to patients, 261
  cost-control, 67
  legitimacy, 60, 219, 240–41
  moralizing effects, 49
  patient vulnerability, 60–61
  privileges, 60
  public interests, 82
  quality standards, 67
  social distance of, 211, 216, 254–55
  social functions, 58, 62, 81
  social trustee model, 211, 216
  task monopoly, 92
Merritt, Davis, 138, 144, 155–56
Miller, David, 21
mistakes, 61, 89
modernity, 56, 101
monopoly, 68, 70
Montesquieu, 112
Moreno, Jonathan, 216, 219
Moyers, Bill, 171

New York Times, 268–69
newspapers, 139, 169
Noble, Cheryl, 227–29
nursing, 65

occupations
  compared to professions, 48, 76, 249
  competition with professions, 84

  normlessness in, 49
  self-interest in, 54, 56
official communication, 26, 166–68

paraprofession, 65
Parsons, Talcott
  functional exchange, 56, 59, 62
  historical importance of professions, 6, 56
  pattern variables, 56
  knowledge as definitive of professions, 45
  social responsibility of professions, 46, 81
  the university, 56
Patterson, Thomas, 167
Perry, John, 182
policy analysis, 87
policy analysts, 89–91, 93, 126, 129
political ambition, 109
political education, 111, 121. *See also* political socialization
political instability, 108–9
political science, 6, 44
political socialization, 107–11, 127
political theory, 7–9, 13–14, 83, 105
politics, 26
popular sovereignty, 262
power, 131
  central administrative, 113–14
  commercial, 62, 80
  judicial, 111
  of professionals in society, 83, 97
  of professionals over clients, 62–63
  prescriptive, 91–94
power sharing
  in government, 108, 110, 114
  in the workplace, 101
principlism, 82
privacy, 59–60
professional deviance, 46, 59
professional domains, 3, 41
professional ethics
  apolitical character of, 83
  attention to real-world dilemmas, 8–9
  attunement to reform movements, 271–22
  codes, 72, 74, 99, 209
  democratic professionalism, 3, 132, 249–50, 261–66, 271–72
  methods of teaching, 262, 267, 269–72
  public deliberation, 265–66
  scandals, 267–69
  social trustee model, 44
professional honor, 55, 63

professionalism. *See also* democratic
professionalism
connotations of, 6
models of, 43, 63, 102, 130
radical critique model, 79–80, 83–84,
98–99, 102
rhetoric of, 68
social trustee model, 63, 75–77, 80–83,
98–99, 247, 260
of university faculty, 272–74
professionals
apolitical, 44, 62, 75
barriers to public, 85–91
current reform efforts among, 2, 79, 103,
105, 126
identity of, 55, 58
privileges of, 56, 59, 60, 61
technocratic, 85–90, 124
training of, 45, 58, 74, 97, 132, 267
professions
academic study of, 7–9, 44–47, 79–80, 131
citizen dependency on, 96
defined, 44–45, 84–85
functional exchange, 56, 59, 62
integrity, 122–23, 260
jurisdictions of, 72, 84
knowledge as definitive of, 45, 58, 71, 84, 102
legitimacy of, 62, 74, 122–23, 126, 163, 260
licensing in, 45, 92
mediating role, 95
moral particularism, 48
moral socialization, 50, 61
political functions, 51, 77, 106, 123
political relevance, 83, 99, 249
public interests, 46, 67, 82, 250
public opinion about, 4, 72, 141–42, 269
self-regulation, 45, 49–50, 65, 82, 84, 101,
123, 269
social distance, 273
social functions, 53–55, 58–59, 70, 82, 84
social integration, 51
social responsibility, 45–46, 52, 58, 81, 122
standardization, 69
state regulation, 48, 268
technical competence, 58, 62, 73, 86, 90
Progressive Era, 4, 5, 116, 124
psychiatrists, 96–97
public administration, 89, 113, 258–59
public deliberation, 15, 29
conceptions of liberty, 24
effects on public preferences, 20–21, 252–53

ethics, 264–65
expectations for citizens, 25
fostered by professionals, 10, 13, 40–41, 76,
99, 104, 106, 119, 121
impeded by professionals, 93, 251
mass deliberation models, 32–35
motivations for, 36, 119
organizational difficulties, 163
practicality, 22, 25
public interest, 20, 259
representative models, 130–32
social movements, 35
values conflicts expressed in, 19, 259
public editor, 269
public health, 70
public ignorance, 27–28, 117
public journalism
agenda-setting power, 155, 156
alienation, 138–40, 155
authority, 156
citizen oversight boards, 156
civic education, 159–62
complex public issues, 150
costs of, 154–55, 161
criticisms of, 154–55, 160, 164
delusions of civic grandeur, 138, 163–70
democratic professionalism, 135–36, 246–47,
251
division of labor, 162
election coverage, 144–46, 152–53, 164
fallibility, 164, 169–70
focus groups, 147–48, 153–54
investigative journalism, 157
logistical challenges, 162, 163, 165, 167
motivations for, 138–43
objectivity, 154–55, 156
opinion surveys, 145, 146, 150, 153, 164
power sharing, 156
public deliberation, 152–54, 157, 163–70
public forums, 146, 152, 154, 155
public listening, 143–49
purposeful news, 149–51, 154
representations of public interests, 158, 163–64
role of citizens, 146, 148–49, 158–62, 161
role of journalist, 137, 149, 164
social trustee model, 160
state institutions, 167, 169
strategic manipulation, 167–68
task sharing, 144, 148, 150
values of traditional journalism, 137, 143,
154–58

public preferences, 20–21
public sphere, 34, 37
public work, 39–40, 256–57
punishment, 183, 189, 251–53

Rawls, John, 7–8, 264
reflective equilibrium, 264–66
Reich, Robert, 258–59
republican principle, 38
res publica, 8
restorative justice, 174. *See also* Vermont
      Reparative Probation
   authority, 180, 204
   conceptions of community, 183, 185, 191–93
   compared to other models of criminal
      justice, 175, 180, 182
   court professionals, 194, 199
   criticisms of, 188, 196
   deliberative democracy, 188, 205–6
   democratic professionalism, 179–82,
      246–47, 249, 251–53
   deprofessionalization, 201–2
   division of labor, 174, 197–200
   effects on community, 183–91, 203–4
   goals, 175, 186
   informal nature, 177, 185
   lay participation, 173–4, 180, 182–93, 204,
      251
   motivations for reforms, 173, 176, 181
   new roles in, 200–203
   normative theory of, 179–81
   offenders, 177–78, 197
   offenses suitable for, 179, 194, 198, 204
   political support for, 175–76
   power sharing, 180, 182
   public opinion, 181, 190–2, 203, 205, 260
   public responsibility, 182, 188, 203–5
   recruitment, 97, 201
   Salt Lake City program, 178, 179, 186, 199
   stages of the criminal justice process, 178
   task sharing, 182–93
   tensions with traditional criminal justice
      values, 197
   trust, 180
   types of program, 175, 177, 201
   Vermont Department of Corrections, 181,
      182, 194, 200–201
   victims, 176–77
   widespread public participation, 205–6,
      251–52
risk, 61

Rosen, Jay, 139, 158, 163
Rosenberg, Charles, 231
Rothman, David, 211, 217
Rousseau, Jean Jacques, 262

Sabin, James, 264–65
San Francisco Chronicle, 151
San Jose Mercury News, 163, 169–70
schools, 120–1
Schudson, Michael, 139, 142, 160
Schweigert, Francis, 190
scientific method, 118–20
self–interested behavior, 47, 53
Shalit, Ruth, 228
Sirianni, Carmen, 147
Skilling, Jeffrey, 267
Smyth, William, 85
social capital, 35
social control, 94
social functions, 53, 55, 59, 70, 82
social integration, 51
social movements, 35
social norms, 59
social responsibility, 45–46, 52, 58, 81, 122
social science, 118–21, 127
social work, 81
state, 48, 61, 65, 72–74, 100–101
status, 59, 102, 119
students, 120–21
Sullivan, William, 40 n. 61, 46–47, 106, 122–25,
      131, 133, 269

Tallahassee Democrat, 153–54, 156
task monopoly, 80, 92–93, 97, 99, 101, 103, 119
task sharing, 105–15, 118, 125, 129–30, 217,
      255–60, 274
Tawney, R. H., 47, 53–55
technocracy, 85–86, 124, 126
Thompson, Dennis, 16, 37, 240–21
three strikes policy, 192
Tocqueville, Alexis de, 89, 106–15, 130
Tonry, Michael, 251
Toulmin, Stephen, 9, 214
township government, 107–11
Tribe, Lawrence, 93
trust, 107, 126, 128
   democratic, 95
   economy of, 98–99, 123
   levels of, 29, 95, 273
   professions, 60–61, 69, 81, 95, 102, 125, 260
   university, 273–74